D1106174

PSYCHIC WAR
IN
MEN AND WOMEN

PSYCHIC WAR
IN
MEN AND WOMEN

Helen Block Lewis

New York: NEW YORK UNIVERSITY PRESS · 1976

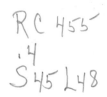
Library of Congress Catalog Card Number: 74-21634
ISBN: 0-8147-4960-7

Library of Congress Cataloging in Publication Data

Lewis, Helen B
 Psychic war in men and women
 Includes bibliographical references and index.
 1. Psychology, Pathological. 2. Sex role.
3. Sex discrimination. 4. Ethnopsychology.
I. Title.
RC455.4.S45L48   155.3'3   74-21634
ISBN 0-8147-4960-7

Manufactured in the United States of America

To the Memory of
Rose Block
John Block
and Sally Feldmesser
with gratitude for their affection.

Preface

Psychic War in Men and Women is about the way an exploitative society injures the two sexes differently. It draws heavily on an intellectual tradition stemming from the Enlightenment—and indeed from classical antiquity—which details the baleful effects of human civilization on human beings. One thread of that tradition holds that civilization itself is intrinsically inimical to humanity: Rousseau, for example, described how civilized beings had lost their compassion (pitié), and Freud described how civilization is built upon the painful repression of human sexuality. Another variant of the same tradition denies any intrinsic opposition between society and the individual, but rather sees exploitative society as destructive of human nature: thus, Marx emphasized the alienation which capitalism engenders, and more recently the Marxist Freudians—notably Reich and Fromm—have traced in detail how a profit-driven society deforms human relatedness. Feminist criticism is still another legacy of the Enlightenment: although feminist thinkers are divided about the noxious role of the profit-system, they are united in directing their criticism against the human deformations which result from the widespread social inferiority of

women. *Psychic War in Men and Women,* gathering evidence
relevant to all three of these social critiques, focuses on how the
two sexes are differently acculturated into exploitative (and nonexploitative) societies.

Twentieth century advances in the disciplines of genetics,
anthropology and psychology, particularly the psychology of
infancy, have brought forward a mass of new evidence which
supports all three social critiques. These relatively recent
findings highlight the profoundly social and affectionate nature
of our species. For example, the principal evolutionary (genetic)
change from primate to human life involves the emergence of
human culture as our species' biological adaptation, with, as a
concomitant, an enormous increase in the impact of nurturant
social forces on human behavior. From studies of infant psychology we know in some detail how infants of both sexes begin their
acculturation in affectionate interaction with adult caretakers,
and how failures of this affectionate interaction have disastrous
consequences for development. From birth onward, the human
infant in intimate interaction with its adult caretakers absorbs
the culture's moral codes; all of a human being's behavior is
profoundly influenced by these early moral imperatives.

The genetically-based sexual differentiation also makes a
difference in the acculturation process. There is evidence from
the study of infancy that the mother-infant interaction is
different for boys and girls, if only because females have a same-
sex and males an opposite-sex caretaker in the person of their
mother. But the sexual differentiation is only one basis for the
cultural assignment of sex roles and anatomy contains no
inherent prescription for women's social inferiority.

To complicate matters still further, human culture is janus-
faced. Not only has it brought with it an enormous increase in
the power and scope of nurturant social activities on the part of
both sexes, but it can encourage and justify human inequality,
exploitation and warfare, all in the name of (affectionately-based)
moral codes; in other words, human culture codifies not only
affectionate bonds between people but the aggression which
arises when these bonds are broken. Both sexes are psychically
injured by growing up in societies which exacerbate the conflict
between aggressive and affectionate values. As Freud showed,
some members of our species go mad trying to reconcile these

contradictory internalized values. This book traces how sex differences in these conflicts mold differing superegos, pushing men and women along alternate routes of madness.

It is a great pleasure to acknowledge the debt I owe to the many friends and colleagues who helped me in writing this book. For several years, I was a member of a small, informal "women's studies" group, consisting of Gertrude Baltimore, Susan Coates, Zenia Fliegel, Evelyn Raskin and myself. Our study group gave me much needed criticism and help in my struggles with the issues in *Psychic War in Men and Women*. Especially since the group by no means agreed with my point of view, I worked hard at meeting their criticisms, always sustained by their friendship and encouragement.

A number of other people have read the manuscript or parts of it. I am particularly grateful for important criticism from Geraldine Barist, Deboral Edel, Hannah Goldman, Irving Goldman, Judith Herman, Helen Walker Puner, Evelyn Witkin and Herman Witkin. Helen Puner was especially generous in the time and care she took in helping me to clarify my ideas. My editor at New York University Press, Nat LaMar, gave me superb help and I am grateful to him for his patience and persistence in getting me to say what I meant. As always, my husband, Naphtali Lewis, has been unfailing in his support, and in the wisdom of his counsel.

Easton, Connecticut
    March, 1976

Contents

Contents

INTRODUCTION

"Expendable" Warriors and "Inferior" Childbearers

It is a fair estimate that 100 million people have been killed by war since 1900. Responsibility for this mass slaughter rests directly upon the male members of the species, Homo sapiens, since it is men, not women, who have started wars and mostly men, not women, who wage wars. This is true in developed civilizations and in primitive cultures. It is a striking universal difference in the behavior of the sexes; no observation about a sex difference in behavior is so indisputable except the equally clear fact that women, not men, are genetically equipped to bear and suckle children. Of course, these two strikingly different behaviors—that men, not women, wage war, and women, not men, bear children— have different roots. That men wage war, while women do not, is a cultural phenomenon. No known genetic program dictates the absence of warfare by females. In contrast, a genetic factor dictates childbearing and nursing in women, not men. Warfare, moreover, unlike childbearing, has no clear, similar forerunners in infra-human species. All infra-human primates and other animals, both males and females, kill other animals. But infra-human species kill either directly for food or in direct defense against death or against invasion of territory.[1,2] The human male, alone among animals, slaughters masses of his own species without the direct motivation of hunger or individual personal danger to his life. Warfare by human males is a culturally developed and sanctioned activity. Men participate in it in order to fulfill the dictates of their conscience or to avoid threats of punishment. In most cultures women are excluded from warfare by law or by custom. In fact, women are not only excluded from warfare, but in some primitive cultures from weapons-making as well.[3]

In modern times the actual slaughter of masses of humanity is lawfully accomplished by a few men and in an impersonal way— by pressing buttons which release bombs or missiles of tremendous destructive power. Nothing like this impersonal destruction, and for such an abstract reason as "honor," can be found as a pattern of killing among infra-human species. In contrast, clear forerunners of the female maternal pattern of hosting life are to be found, genetically based, among infra-human species.

These two enormous differences between the sexes dramatize the interaction between the effects of culture and the effects of genetically based sexual differentiation upon male and female behavior. In creating male rather than female warriors, it might be said that cultures have made rational provision for the preservation of the species. As Lévi-Strauss has taught us, both totemic rituals and primitive myths are rational "codes" by means of which human beings express an understanding of their place and function in the world.[4] The nearly universal, culturally prescribed exclusion of women from warfare can represent a rational encoding of an understanding that it is more adaptive to preserve more females, who are host to the young, than males whose biologic role in reproduction ends with the ejaculation of sperm. In this respect, many species of sexually differentiated lower organisms also behave as if their males were more expendable.[5]

That Homo sapiens is a cultural animal is a relatively new concept in the history of science. The study of the evolution of human culture began with Darwin's discovery that Homo sapiens had evolved from lower animal forms. Evolution effected a transformation of fur-bearing animals into culture-bearing ones. How the emergence of human culture affected women and men differently is a question which has rarely been asked. Only the Marxists, specifically Engels,[6] suggested that the culturally sanctioned subjection of women is a by-product of the development of exploitative social institutions, particularly the socially sanctioned economic exploitation of many human beings by a few. But Engels, who interprets childbearing only as an economic handicap which made women vulnerable to exploitation, does not see that cultures have also protected their "means of reproduction" by excluding women from warfare.

How it happened that with the development of Homo sapiens as a cultural animal, there also developed social systems based on the exploitation of the many by a few is a historical question to which we may never have an answer. Once such an exploitative social system has developed, however, warfare becomes a necessity for the maintenance of power to exploit. And, however it comes about, women are excluded both from warfare and from the possibility of becoming exploiters by that means. As Simone de Beauvoir correctly insists, women have everywhere been accomplices in their own subjugation.[7] This has been paralleled by their acceptance of exclusion from warfare. And this acceptance has occurred even at the price of their own subjugation, as a kind of folk wisdom which has operated to preserve the species.

That both men and women need to be free of exploitative social systems and from warfare is self-evident. It also seems clear that the liberation of women will not come about if they turn the tables on men and they become the culturally sanctioned persons who push bomb buttons in order to maintain exploitative power. Women's exclusion from warfare has entailed exclusion from becoming murderers and exploiters. This exclusion has always functioned as a kind of "liberation" by default. It was not a liberation from male domination but from culturally sanctioned mass murder. And although women's subjugators are men, it is not men's maleness which is the crux of the matter, but their exploitative and warlike activities.

There is a controversy within the feminist movement about whether male domination is the chief evil for women. Some radical feminists argue that it is, while other feminists, like myself, believe that exploitative social institutions push people (of either sex) into dominating others. In this view, women would be no better off if the handful of exploiters in the world were all women: The majority of women as well as men would still be oppressed. The fact that men are more often exploiters than women does not warrant an indictment of maleness instead of an indictment of exploitative social institutions.

The controversy rests on two different assumptions about the original nature of human beings. The view that male domination is an outgrowth of exploitative social institutions rests on the assumption that both males and females are inherently affectionate in their natures. In this view, exploitativeness is not an intrinsic element in human nature, but a cultural distortion of it into which men may be pushed more easily, perhaps because men are not childbearers. This assumption about human nature rests on the evidence that infants of both sexes begin their lives in affectionate relationship with their caretakers. As we shall see in Chapter 6, hard-headed scientists who observe infants have been impressed with the inherently social nature of human beings. Moreover, the affectionate interaction between infants and caretakers which forms the groundwork of human life is hard to destroy. As Anna Freud and a co-worker showed, for example, three-year-old children of both sexes, each of whom was deprived of both parents in a Nazi concentration camp before the child was six months old, astounded their rescuers by exhibiting the most passionately loyal, sensitive, and empathetic caretaking of each other.[8]

The radical feminist view that male domination alone is the chief evil for women rests on the assumption that males have an intrinsic "need for a sense of power" over women.[9] This is a view of men as essentially evil, or more evil than women. It is a tempting view in the light of the endless wars which men have waged and in the light of the fact that they are much more often the exploiters in societies where exploitation exists. But it is a subcategory of the view that human nature is *intrinsically* egotistical and exploitative. Such a view itself reflects the influence of the prevailing exploitative milieu which assumes that domination is the stuff of life.

Even so liberated a thinker as de Beauvoir believes that the original relationship between people is hostile. In her monumental work, *The Second Sex*, de Beauvoir, while partly following Marxist thinking, assumes that each human self differentiates itself out of an intrinsic need ("an original aspiration") to dominate others.[10] In this view, men have more of this intrinsic need than women and so women automatically assume the position of the "other" who is dominated. But recent research on mothers and their infants suggests that the self of both sexes differentiates itself best (in dialectical fashion) not out of experiences of hostility or domination but out of closeness and affection. Since both sexes are affectionate in their natures and both are victims of an exploitative economic and social system in so many parts of the world, it seems more sensible for them to join in a common struggle to turn the world upside down rather than to turn themselves inside out.

The existence of an exploitative power group within a society is an extremely potent force in creating a positive valuation of aggressive personalities as "powerful," and a negative valuation of gentle personalities as "weak." This is illustrated most clearly in the perspective which comes from observing another culture than our own, but one which is similar to it.

The noted anthropologist, Oscar Lewis, made a study of a Canadian Blackfoot tribe, the North Piegan Indians.[11] Although the North Piegans are a male-dominated society, they nevertheless contain a small group of so-called "manly-hearted" women, who were the particular focus of Lewis's investigation. The North Piegans, although not an industrialized, capitalist society, are like ourselves in having a sharp contrast between rich and poor members of the tribe. The few rich exploit the many poor. They are like us also in the high value which they place on private property and individual prestige. Among the North Piegans, horses, medicine pipes, painted tepees, war charms, war bonnets, war songs, and ritual knowledge are all private property and all status-enhancing. There is even what Lewis describes as a "striking commercialism" in the North Piegan religion. The North Piegans are also like ourselves in being a male-dominated society. Among the many evidences of male domination are a double standard of morality, wife-beating, and exclusively male participation in tribal government.

The ideal of women's behavior among the North Piegans is submissiveness, reserve or shyness, faithfulness, and kindness. But Oscar Lewis observes that poor North Piegan men also exhibit more humility and submissiveness than rich ones, in keeping with their low social and economic position.

A small group of "manly-hearted" women (an English translation of a Blackfoot term) is characterized by aggressiveness, social boldness, competitiveness with others, and sexual promiscuity. Lewis observed that they tended to be either older women who had been hard-working and efficient people, or else they had been the favored daughters of their fathers. They were surely *richer* women. Fourteen "manly-hearted" women out of a total of 109 women owned more property than the rest of the women combined.

"Manly-hearted" Piegan women are rebels against male domination, but their rebellion takes the form of accepting male values. As Oscar Lewis points out, this small group of women are "deviants" in their society. And they are products particularly of a deep contradiction between the affectionateness of North Piegan child rearing and the brutalities of later male domination. North Piegan women are routinely beaten by their husbands, but they are beaten for the first time in their lives *after* marriage. North Piegan parents do not beat their children. The rebellion of North Piegan "manly-hearted" women against male domination has us cheering for them. But, in imitating the values of aggressive and dominating men, they are still caught in a framework of power values, and a framework in which power and masculinity are confused. Staying submissive is, of course, no solution. But *we* can see that North Piegans, both men and women, should unite against the forces which keep them poor and submissive, and that this would be easier if masculinity and femininity were not confounded with power and submission. We can see, in short, that the North Piegans, like ourselves, need a revolutionary change in power relationships not only between men and women but between rich and poor.

For centuries of human civilized existence, patricians and plebians, slaveowners and slaves, landowners and serfs, haves and have-nots, capitalists and laborers, rich and poor have stood in opposition to each other as exploiters and exploited. Within this framework, women have stood in inferior power to men of their own class, and the family has been a transmission belt for power-based authoritarian values, personified by the father. But, as we shall see, the evidence from anthropology suggests that things are different in non-exploitative societies. In these societies the position of women is more likely to be one of equality, and the family is not a transmission belt for dehumanized values but for the good things in human culture: nurturant social institutions, and accumulated wisdom.

Even in exploitative societies, however, childhood experiences of gentleness, warmth, and affection are hard to submerge in the "icy waters of egotistical calculation." [12] It is not easy to mold men into expendable warriors or women into inferior childbearers. The contradictions which develop between the affectionate experiences of childhood and the dehumanized relationships of adulthood create insoluble conflicts for both sexes. These conflicts take different forms in women and men. This book will document the ways in which our society creates psychic war within the two sexes and so perpetuates the war between them.

References

1. N. Tinbergen, *The Study of Instinct* (New York: Oxford University Press, 1951).

2. K. Lorenz, *On Aggression* (New York: Harcourt, Brace World, 1966).

3. R. D'Andrade, "Sex Differences and Cultural Institutions," E. Maccoby, ed., *The Development of Sex Differences* (Stanford, California: Stanford University Press, 1966).

4. C. Lévi-Strauss, *Structural Anthropology* (New York: Doubleday, 1967).

5. N. Berrill, *Sex and the Nature of Things* (New York: Dodd, Mead, 1953).

6. F. Engels, *The Origin of the Family, Private Property and the State* (New York: International Publishers).

7. S. de Beauvoir, *The Second Sex* (New York: Knopf, 1957).

8. A. Freud and S. Dann, "An Experiment in Group Upbringing," *Psychoanalytic Study of the Child* 6 (1951), 127-168.

9. "New York Radical Feminist Manifesto," cited by Juliet Mitchell, *Woman's Estate* (New York: Pantheon Books, 1971), p. 64.

10. S. de Beauvoir, op. cit.

11. O. Lewis, "Manly-hearted Women among the North Piegan," *American Anthropologist* 43 (1941), 173-187.

12. Karl Marx, *The Class Struggle*.

PART I

*Affectionateness: The Nature of Human
Nature*

CHAPTER 1

Human Nature: Male and Female

Are human beings, of both sexes, affectionate by nature? If we put aside, for the moment, the large numbers of human societies in which the adults behave exploitatively, and look only at human culture as compared to primates' social life, the answer is yes. Human beings are acculturated, which means that they are the most thoroughly domesticated creatures on earth. As one anthropologist puts it, culture is human beings' ecology.[1] Acculturation means that every aspect of human life is infused with the morality which is explicit or implicit in the culture. And morality, whatever is superstructure, is most profoundly rooted in the affectionate attachment between parents and child.

Human beings are profoundly governed by their affectionate, moral natures. And, in dialectical fashion, this also means that the failure or frustration of their affectionate natures leads them, especially the men among them, into the most bloodthirsty, sadistic aggression known on earth. Human beings, especially men, are the only creatures who kill other members of their own species for social reasons—lost affection, lost "honor" or other highly "moral" reasons. Women, whose affectionateness has an outlet in childrearing, are not so prone to become aggressive. As we shall see, in Chapter 6 and in Chapter 14, men and women develop different patterns of self and superego in becoming acculturated. In this chapter, let's look at what the sexes have in common: their cultural nature. As we shall see, human culture is unique in the scope that it allows to affectionateness as a force governing human behavior.

It is particularly when we look at human infants in interaction with their caretakers in comparison with the mother-infant interaction among primates that we get some sense of the scope of human affectionateness. And since women are infants' principal caretakers, they are primary agents governing the affectionate social interactions which, beginning in infancy, so thoroughly infuse human life. So we might expect that girl infants might be programmed to respond more smoothly to their mothers and to develop even more profound affectionate attachments than boy infants who will later on play a lesser role in infant caretaking. We shall come back later in this chapter, and more fully in succeeding chapters, to the implications of women's child rearing as being responsible for a difference between the sexes in affectionateness. But before we tackle that question, let's compare our social nature with that of our nearest relative, the primates, and see the evolutionary changes which have occurred.

Before we look at the evolutionary picture, let's look briefly at the way in which male-centered thinking has slanted the picture of human evolution. In her delightful book, *The Descent of Woman*,[2] Elaine Morgan tells us how the image of Tarzan, the Mighty Hunter, coming down out of the trees, has dominated scientific speculation about the course of human evolution from primate forms. Morgan suggests, instead, that human evolution was determined by the survival needs of a hypothetical female primate Miocene ancestor, carrying her clinging infant. Specifically, Morgan proposes that the female of the species, pressed by the millions of years of terrible drought which characterized the Pliocene epoch (following the Miocene epoch) discovered a semi-aquatic existence in which she and her offspring were better off than anywhere else. In the course of the millions of years she spent at the seashore—in and out of the water—her needs dictated the human characteristics of both sexes. Amusingly enough, the male characteristics can be seen to follow in necessary congruence with the changes which Morgan assumes were first made by the females trying to nurture their young. So, for example, human upright posture—walking on two feet—was an invention not of the Mighty Hunter come down out of the trees but of the female carrying the young who found walking in water most comfortable on two feet (just the way semi-aquatic beavers do when they go into the water carrying something). So, also, the hairless skin which characterizes human beings is a result of the fact that the females didn't need a hairy coat in water—in fact, a watery fur coat is no good at all. On the other hand, long hair on the head is very useful in providing something for the clinging infant to grasp. As a result, men are hairier than women, except for men's bald heads.

Most instructive is Morgan's account of how androcentric evolutionary theory has dealt with the evolution of women's bodies. Morgan tells us that in a prime tenet of "all androcentric thinking everything about the female was designed primarily for the benefit and convenience of the male, to make her (a) more attractive to him and (b) more accessible to him. . . ." [3] Male-centered theorizing thus supposes that women's breasts evolved as a sexual stimulus for men. Morgan suggests, instead, that the survival benefits of a modification in lactation ought to be connected with the needs of the baby rather than with the sexual preference of the child's father. The change from a chimp's tiny flat nipples to a woman's breasts was required by the needs of suckling an infant while sitting on the shore. A nipple brought down lower on the body is needed and a lump of something less bony and more convenient for small hands to grasp. "And since you [the infant] is what evolution is all about, what you need you ultimately get. You get two lovely pendulous dollopy breasts, as easy to hold on to as a bottle, and you're laughing." [4] The alternative explanation of the "Raquel Welch phenomenon" is thus the theory of a baby needing a handhold. Similarly, women's rounded buttocks, more rounded than men's (and both more rounded than primates') are attributable to the need for an extra padding to suit women's convenience sitting on the shore, rather than as a sexual stimulus to men.

When it comes to still another important evolutionary change from female primates into human beings, the fact that the vagina has moved forward from the rear and deeper into the body cavity, male-centered theorizing has again concentrated on the effects of these changes on male sexual arousal rather than the convenience of females. A vagina further forward to the front of the body and deeper into the body cavity is adaptive for a sitting, semi-aquatic animal. So is the hymen which covers the vagina and keeps sand out. Male-centered theorizing could only suppose that the hymen was invented to keep men out.

In response to the forward-placed vagina, the human penis is longer than any other primate's, and the human male has switched from rear mounting to a frontal approach in intercourse. Androcentric thinking suggests that this happened to meet the needs of the Mighty Hunter. Tarzan, out foraging, had to keep the females back home happily waiting for him, and so he developed a long penis with which to cement the pair-bond. Front-mounting also gave him signals from his beloved's lips and eyes and so made sexual experience more meaningful for him, thus inducing monogamy! Morgan suggests that he just couldn't get into the forward-placed, hidden vagina, except with a long penis and from the front.

Whether or not the aquatic theory of human evolution is ultimately accepted, the idea that the course of human evolution is determined by the survival needs of females carrying their young is most enlightening. Instead of pegging evolution to the needs of Tarzan coming down out of the trees, we can peg it also to the needs of the mother-infant interaction. This gives us a model in terms of which to think about human culture, which is an enormous evolutionary advance over primate society, not only because the Mighty Hunter has grown mightier, but because human culture allows so much greater scope for affectionateness as a force in behavior.

Let's consider, as an example, the extra amount of affectionateness in the sexual behavior of human beings as compared with primates. Human sexual behavior is very different from primate sex life which is governed by a biological clock functioning in the females of the species. Note, again, that the significant evolutionary change has occurred in the female. Human women do not have the estrus cycle. In this they are alone among mammals. With estrus absent, human beings have lost the prepotent hormonal stimulus to copulation which all other mammals have. As if in compensation for the loss of this hormonal stimulus, however, sexual feeling between human beings can renew itself through profound feelings of mutual, loving commitment. Human sexuality is not estrus-controlled. It is, instead, a more affectionate kind of sexuality, especially compared with primate sex.

Before we proceed, some explanation is needed of the functions of the estrus and the menstrual cycles, so let's pause briefly to get them straight. The menstrual cycle is found in other primates as well as ourselves. It appears along with puberty and is a monthly affair coinciding with the discharge of the unfertilized egg from the uterus. The estrus cycle, in contrast, appears in all mammalian species, *except* ourselves. Its effects on sexual behavior are dramatic—much greater than the effects of the menstrual cycle on sexual behavior. For example, a female primate in heat—that is, at the peak of her estrus cycle, develops a "pink swelling" in her genitals and this is a potent stimulus to males. During estrus peak, the female primate also is sexually aroused. She shows increased sexual appetite, seeking the company of males and soliciting them to mount her. Only when she is in estrus can she copulate and so conceive an infant. Among primates, then, and other mammals as well, an internal biological clock in the female governs the sexual behavior of both sexes and the resulting conception of the young. The female's biological clock indirectly governs the sexual arousal of the males.

Among human beings, in contrast, sexual behavior is no longer governed by an internal biological clock in the female. The major evolutionary change is that human sexual behavior is governed by personal feelings and cultural laws as well as by hormones. Among primates, whose sexual activity is governed by estrus and pink swellings, it matters little to whose pink swelling the male is responding. Intercourse is an affair of the moment, not of particular individuals. Among human beings, in contrast, sexual behavior is personalized. At least, it has the capacity for being personalized. (Of course, when people have been drained of their affectionateness by the stress of being exploitative and exploited, sex can become depersonalized and mechanical, in need of sex manuals for its "improvements.")

This is not to imply that our primate cousins are not also highly social and affectionate animals. In fact, among primates there are important, friendly associations between mother and infant, between juveniles, between females, and there are even those "bonds" between males which have so impressed Lionel Tiger.[5]

(Incidentally, the greatest amount of grooming occurs between females.) But among primates, these affectionate social behaviors have little, if anything, to do with copulation, which is a quite different business. It is only among human beings that such primate-type affectionate social behaviors as kissing, grooming, and high-spirited playfulness have been incorporated into the sex act, when two people are making love (not just copulating).

Compared with primate sex, human sex is replete with revivals of the affectionate intimacies which children shared with their parents. As the biologist, Desmond Morris, puts it (and Morris is no sentimentalist about animal behavior, including our own): ". . . the human animal 'makes love' to a complete and special individual . . . we now perform the mating act not so much to fertilize the egg as to fertilize a relationship." [6] (Let's note, in passing, Morris's ginger use, in quotation marks, of the four-letter word "love." Scientists are always unhappy about using the word "love" because it's so "unscientific." We'll come back to "science" and words like "love" and "affectionateness" in Chapter 6.)

As Freud discovered, this personal relationship which is fertilized in human sexual behavior is the end-product of the vicissitudes of the affectionate, loving interactions between each of the partners and the particular persons important in his or her past. Among primates, also, affectionate interaction between mother and infant is important in adult sex. A failure of affectionate interactions between mothers and their infants can impede adult sexual behavior. The Harlows' experiments,[7] which were undertaken under the influence of the Freudian idea of importance of early childhood experience, showed unequivocally that adult male monkeys which had been deprived of their mothers were duds when it came to sex. When maternally deprived adult male monkeys were confronted with a pink swelling in the female, they "just didn't know what to do." Female monkeys deprived of their mothers allowed themselves to be mounted and bore infants, but turned out to be very poor mothers. Among human beings, distortion of the affectionate bonds in infancy leads not just to a failure of adult sexuality. It sometimes leads to Don Juan behavior. It also results in a wide variety of neurotic symptoms and character deformations in which distorted sexuality plays a hidden part. We'll come back to this fundamental discovery of Freud's again, especially in Chapter 12.

The loss of estrus and with it the lost biological regulation of sexual behavior has different implications for the sexuality of men and women. With pink swellings gone as a no-fail stimulus, adult men are no longer as certain of their erections and ejaculations as their primate cousins. Alex Comfort puts it this way: "Perhaps the oddest biological feature of human psychosexual development is its surprising and un-Darwinian vagueness of aim." [8] This is another way of saying that all sorts of non-biological stimuli evoke human sexual arousal—people of the same as well as opposite sex, fetishes, whippings, and the like. It is also the case that men are much more prone to sexual perversions than women (as we shall see in Chapter 18). This fact may be rooted in the absence of estrus and pink swellings among women as well as in the greater strain put on men's affectionateness because they are so often expected to become exploiters.

Women for their part lost a built-in decision-maker about whether to have intercourse when they lost the estrus cycle. The loss of a built-in decision-maker about intercourse gave woman a conscious choice about whether to have sex or not. And this conscious choice is now made vis-à-vis man who is also able to make a conscious choice but uncertain of his erection. The noted zoologist, Nathaniel Berrill, points out that human males, alone among primates, are able to perform rape.[9] They are clearly the only primates who need it. (Berreill further suggests that women's inferior social position in so many societies on earth is a reflection of their loss of control over the frequency of intercourse.) Human sex life is thus uniquely affectionate; in dialectical fashion, it can also involve rape. And the silent ingredient operating behind both affectionate and brutal behavior is the existence of human culture.

An evolutionary change from hormonal to social control of human sexual behavior which carries with it such dangers as uncertain erections and rape would involve the threat of species extinction if it were not for the emergence of human culture as a regulator not only of sex, but of all human life. The trick seems to have been to get the animals to internalize the social forces. Indeed, when we look at human life as compared with primate life, we find that human culture, its profound, all-encompassing influence absorbed within the individual, has become the species' adaptive survival mechanism. Parents in a family are the purveyors of human culture to their offspring; of the two parents, mothers play a special role in people's childhoods, and so a special role in cultural transmission. And the transmission takes place mainly through the affectionate feelings which arise between parents and their children. This is another of Freud's important discoveries, as we shall see in Chapter 12.

The family can be a transmission belt for patriarchal and exploitative values. It is also always a transmission belt for affectionate and egalitarian values. How else would human beings be able to identify, abhor, and resist injustice and oppression, even in the midst of brutal tyranny? And it is the internalized conflict between exploitative and affectionate values which drives men and women crazy, as Freud also showed.

What is this cultural nature of human beings? Uniquely, human beings, unlike any other animals, are found living together in family-reckoned, that is, kinship groups according to a common tradition about life and death. These are "voluntary" organizations for the adults, in the sense that adult members of the society may elect to leave it or the society may elect to ostracize a member. Human society is very different in this respect from insect societies in which the organization results from the interdependence of structurally different, specialized members whose role is fixed by heredity. Among human groups, the only significant structural differences between members are those between the sexes.

It is likely that the human family as a cultural institution developed in response to the enormously increased length of human infancy compared to primates. Chimpanzees, for example, reach puberty by five or six years of age and are adults at age eight or nine. Human beings take much longer to grow into adulthood. At the same time, paradoxically, since reproduction is no longer regulated by the female estrus cycle, human beings can reproduce themselves faster than primates. J.V. Lawick-Goodall [10] tells us that chimpanzees in the wild have offspring every three or four years. This is much less often than the yearly human baby who regularly appears in so many parts of the world. Some help would seem to have been needed for mothers without estrus, and the provision was the family. This, in turn, made the socialization of the human infant dependent on the father as well as the mother. As the anthropologist Weston LaBarre, puts it: "human infants . . . unlike the other mammals, depend on the father in a new familial and socializing sense to an extraordinary degree." [11] The much-maligned nuclear family, whatever its disadvantages as a trans-mission belt for patriarchal and exploitative power, is an advance over primate society in that it greatly increases the role of the father in socializing the young. Although fathers still have less to do with infant rearing than mothers, they can also experience the "amplification of tenderness" [12] which results from rearing babies. And the babies have an extra source of affectionateness from their fathers.

It's not just that human infants have a longer infancy than their primate cousins. Human infancy is totally social, while primate infants have some nonsocial experiences of a direct encounter with the physical environment. All infra-human primates, al-though completely dependent on their mothers for nutrition and although they cling to her much of the time, are nevertheless capable of locomoting on their own when they are only a few days old. The human infant is very different in this respect. He or she is physically helpless, but at the same time equipped to sense and respond to people emotionally from the earliest moment after birth.[13]

This is a relatively new discovery in psychology. We now know that the human infant is not in a "big, buzzing, blooming con-fusion" [14] as we used to believe, but socially responsive and socially powerful. One recent study showed that the newborn's body movements are synchronized with adult speech.[15] As any mother or father knows, infants make their caretakers hop to it to assuage their crying and produce their smiling. By the time the infant vouchsafes its first smile—at three months—parents, as well as infant, are pretty thoroughly hooked into an affectionate bond.

This affectionate bond in turn guarantees that what transpires between parent and child is experienced as a moral atmosphere: what Melanie Klein [16] calls "good me," and "bad me," "good world," "bad world." This moral atmosphere into which the human infant is directly plunged, and without the relief of being able to walk away from it for at least a year, is the culture's means of domestication. None of a human being's functioning escapes nurturant social influence. Being the providers of this nurturant social influence makes the parents most potent molders of the human self, and mothers the most potent of all.

Primates, in contrast, can explore the physical environment

directly from very early on, and so, in infancy, are much better adapted to it than human infants. A human infant exposed to the environment is dead within days; a primate infant with luck can find his or her way back to mother. Moreover, an adult human being, transported to the "wild," without the tools and clever devices which are the products of culture, has a much harder time adapting than a chimpanzee. Human beings thus have the structural and functional capacity to be cleverer than primates in adapting to conditions of existence, but only as socialized adults.

This does not mean that primates have no social life. Primates also live in groups, sometimes, as in the case of gibbons, in units resembling the nuclear family, that is, mated male, female, and juveniles. It is interesting in this connection that gibbon males have been observed to be very affectionate and playful with the juveniles in the group.[17] In the case of chimpanzees, the group consists of a female and her young, in loose, temporary association with several males. Primate groups are ordered with respect to "dominance-submission." Adult males fight each other for dominant positions within the group, both with respect to food and access to females in estrus. Males, however, are dominant over females. Primate social existence is thus ordered on the basis of physical strength and power.

Primates also order their existence in a habitual way. Hediger, for many years the curator of the Berlin Zoo and a distinguished naturalist, tells us that primates both in the wild and in captivity, divide their physical environment into the equivalent of house sites, roads, and meeting places.[18]

Primates are also able to use rudimentary tools. Köhler's Sultan put together two sticks to make a long pole needed to rake in a banana.[19] Recently, J.V. Lawick-Goodall described how chimpanzees in the wild created an instrument for digging ants—by stripping the branch of a tree.[20] Primates, however, have not institutionalized work; they do not work for hire or for prestige. They do not take slaves. Again, in contrast, only human beings (the lucky few) work for the love of what they are doing. But human beings can also become alienated from their work. They are forced to work by compulsions having nothing to do with the content of their tasks.

There is nothing in primate life corresponding to the cultural institutions which invest every aspect of human life. Nor is there anything resembling an abstract concept of a family with its kinship system and an incest taboo. Human life is inescapably governed by the morality which is intrinsic in human culture. A very long infancy—not just the longest but the most thoroughly social infancy known on earth—in which they are tended by familial caretakers, not just mothers, assures that human adults emerge as superego-bearing animals, each guided by deeply-felt moral precepts. The culture, as we have seen, relies on these internalized moral precepts for its perpetuation, and thus the perpetuation of the species. The superego-bearing human animal, who has imbibed morality with mother's milk, emerges with a sense of personal identity which only madness or death can destroy. Nothing like it exists among primates.

Human beings have names. As Lévi-Strauss puts it: "Everything takes place as if . . . every individual's own personality were his totem: it is the signifier of his signified being." [21]

Only human beings have elaborate, personalized ways of going crazy; only human beings voluntarily plan to commit suicide for lost love or lost honor. And, as we shall see, this inalienable sense of self is the product of growing up in a completely socialized world in which affectionateness has an enormous role, not just in sexual life, but in the morality which is so distinctively human.

The incest taboo is an example of morality which illuminates the uniqueness of the human self, and its development out of affectionate experiences with its parents. The incest taboo, a cultural universal, is such that the idea of having sexual intercourse with someone who is of one's family or kinship group evokes horror. (Let's put aside the fact that different cultures reckon kinship differently.) In many societies incest is considered so dangerous that it is punishable by death. Now, as we have seen, among primates, whose sexual behavior is governed by a biological clock, sexual intercourse and affectionate behavior are quite separate and distinct activities. The particular individual does not matter; estrus is the stimulus. Among human beings, whose sexual behavior is commingled with all manner of affectionate remnants of infancy, an incest taboo keeps the personal record straight. In sex, human beings not only reproduce themselves, they symbolically express their personal autonomy in a physical union. The human self, which is formed in affectionate interaction with its caretakers, develops its autonomy partly by internalizing images of beloved caretakers—by identifying with them. No wonder the human self abhors reliving its infant experiences, however affectionate, in a physical union with the *actual* person with whom it has identified. Autonomy becomes a nightmare or a farce if the symbolic figure within the self is also the actual person with whom one enters into sexual union. And, in keeping with the difference in formation of the male and female self, mother-son incest is everywhere a graver crime and much less frequent than father-daughter incest,[22] as we shall see in Chapter 4.

Human nature, in summary, is human cultural nature, which means that it is the most highly socialized and most affectionate on earth. It is also uniquely moral. This morality, which can be so life-giving and so destructive, is the distillation of each individual's experiences with beloved and loving parents. And, as we shall see, these loving experiences, equally necessary for both sexes, create different patterns of self and superego in men and women.

References

1. Weston LaBarre, *The Human Animal* (Chicago: University of Chicago Press, 1954).

2. Elaine Morgan, *The Descent of Woman* (New York: Bantam Books, 1972).

3. Ibid., p. 52.

4. Ibid., p. 32.

5. Lionel Tiger, *Men in Groups* (New York: Random House, 1969).

6. Desmond Morris, *Intimate Behaviour* (New York: Random House, 1971), p. 101.

7. H. F. Harlow, M. K. Harlow and W. W. Hansen, "The Maternal Affectional System of Rhesus Monkeys Behaviour," 10 (1968), 1-14.

8. Alex Comfort, *The Nature of Human Nature* (New York: Harper & Row, 1967).

9. N. Berrill, *Sex and the Nature of Things* (New York: Dodd, Mead, 1953).

10. J. V. Lawick-Goodall, *In the Shadow of Man* (Boston: Houghton Mifflin, 1971).

11. Weston LaBarre, op. cit., p. 305.

12. Harriet Rheingold, *The Social and Socializing Infant*, D. Goslin, ed., *Handbook of Socialization Theory and Research* (Chicago: Rand McNally, 1969), p. 782.

13. Ibid.

14. William James, *Principles of Psychology* (New York: Holt, 1890).

15. W. Condon and L. Sander, "Neonate Movement is Synchronized with Adult Speech," *Science*, 183 (1974), 99-101.

16. Melanie Klein, *Envy and Gratitude* (London: Tavistock Publications, 1957).

17. C. R. Carpenter, "A Field Study of the Behavior and Social Relations of the Gibbon," *Comparative Psychology Monographs*, 16 (1940).

18. H. Hediger, *The Psychology and Behaviour of Animals in Zoos and Circuses* (New York: Dover Publications, 1968).

19. W. Köhler, *The Mentality of Apes* (New York: Vintage Books, 1959).

20. J. V. Lawick-Goodall, op. cit.

21. C. Lévi-Strauss, *The Savage Mind* (Chicago: University of Chicago Press, 1966), p. 214.

22. F. Beach and C. Ford, *Patterns of Sexual Behavior* (New York: Harper and Bro., 1951).

CHAPTER 2

Mothers and Their Infants
(Mice, Rats, and Monkeys)

   If the psychological implications of the most salient difference
between the sexes, the difference in reproductive function, were
stated in the most simple-minded way, it would be that, as a group,
females have a personality congruent with their host function:
They are more maternal than males. Maternal behavior is one
variety of affectonate behavior; on this reckoning, women might
be expected to have more affectionateness than men as a result of
their maternal function. In a culture whose economy is based on
the exploitation of people, and which therefore fosters
exploitative attitudes, this characteristic of women is hard to think
about objectively. It is readily woven into culture myths about
women. Affectionate behavior is also a particular blessing in an
exploitative world, as Christ and Buddha both demonstrated.
Women's affectionateness is either scorned because it makes them
easier to exploit, or else women are worshipped, like gods, for their
moral superiority. Leaving aside both scorn and worship of
women, let us look at maternal behavior among other mammals,
such as mice, rats, and monkeys. Even there, as we shall see, it is
hard for scientists to speak of affectionateness. They call it
"behavioral synchrony" or "affectional system."

One of the difficulties in connecting women's reproductive function with their affectionate capacities is that the process by which the first characteristic determines the second is not at all clear. That reproductive function is inherited is certain; therefore, it is assumed that affectionate behavior which plays an integral part in the care of infants must also be inherited. But it is only the physical structures and glandular processes which have so far been linked to inheritance, while studies of the behavior patterns, at least at the human level, have only just begun. Recent so-called ethological studies of human mothers and their infants have been undertaken by Bowlby, a psychoanalyst and his students, who respect the importance of affectionate behavior in human development.[1] We'll look at the work on human mothers and their infants in Chapter 6.

Another difficulty in connecting women's reproductive function with their affectionate capacities is that the psychology of human emotions has been so little studied, especially the psychology of the positive emotions, like affection. Affectionate behavior is so sacred to us that tampering with it arouses our strongest protests. Ethical considerations also limit experiments about affection in human beings. No wonder affectionateness is so little studied experimentally, even though there are any number of man-made and natural catastrophes which offer ready-made "experimental" opportunities for studying the strength of human affectionate capacities. (An example is Anna Freud's [2] study of infants who had been early orphaned by the Nazis, but who subsequently became profoundly attached to each other.)

Culture myths also tend to deprecate the importance of affection as a subject for scientific study. Even though anger usually interferes with rational thinking, we can find many reasons for it as a necessary defense. Aggression is a very serious subject of scientific study. Affection, on the other hand, is treated more like a luxury, in conformity with its realistic place in the operation of the world's "important" business. It is interesting that Darwin [3] tried to understand maternal love as adaptive for species survival. We shall return to Darwin's observations shortly.

At the level of animal behavior, however, it has been possible to study the affectionateness inherent in maternity. Work on mice, rats, and monkey mothers and their infants could be undertaken because it is more tolerable to experiment with the reproductive and affectionate behavior of infra-human species than it is to interfere with these fundamentals of human life. Maternal behavior among rodents has been divided, for example, into its component parts, such as licking, retrieving, and crouching over the young. Studies have been made of the sequence of development of these specific behaviors, which comprise the mother-infant interaction. Consequences of the quality of the mother-infant interaction have been traced. Even in the case of rodents, a concept of "behavioral synchrony" between mothers and infants seems best to describe what happens. "Synchrony" refers to the fact that mother's behavior is exquisitely adapted to the needs of the young and that it changes as the needs of the young change. One review of the evidence summarizes as follows: The "motivational condition of the mother, and the developing socialization of the young . . . are established and maintained by the reciprocal exchange of stimulation. . . ." [4]

Maternal behavior in rats cannot be the model for the maternal behavior of women, since women are acculturated beings while rats are not. "Behavioral synchrony" between mothers and infants is, however, a conscious goal for human beings. That this synchrony exists so far down the evolutionary scale suggests that its manifestations can operate, and in more elaborated forms, at the human level, if only human maternity were not deformed by exploitative forces within society.

A third difficulty in studying affectionate behavior is intrinsic in studying any behavior which has an instinctive or inherited component. This is the difficulty in conceptualizing instinctive behavior. Darwin's emphasis on natural or instinctive behavior was designed to show how similar human beings are to animals, and how, therefore, evolutionary forces (as opposed to divine forces) could govern human beings. In this context, the concepts of natural instinct which Darwin employed had a progressive or enlightened meaning. But at the time Darwin wrote "instinct theory" was little more than a way of stating a materialist basis for the unknown, since neither the genetic mechanism of inheritance, nor an adequate psychological description of the behavior termed "instinctive" was available. The concept of "instinct" was thus a substitute for knowledge and usually led into some form of circular reasoning about human nature. One response to Darwinian theory was, paradoxically, a movement in psychology away from the use of instinct theory in explaining both animal and human behavior and in the direction of developing an adaptive learning theory as a way of explaining phenomena previously called "instinctive."

In most theories of learning, animal behavior is conceptualized as a system developing out of individual experiences in the satisfaction and frustration of body-tissue needs, such as food, water, and sex. In this concept, both human and animal organisms are conceived to be operating out of individualistic needs which are reduced to one principal need: survival. The social nature of both animals and human beings is derived by a process of learning from their transactions with others and with the environment—in the pursuit of individual survival.

It should be noted, at this point, that individualistic learning theories often confuse Darwin's concept of adaptations which insured species survival with *individual* survival mechanisms that are then assumed to be the dominant motives for existence. Learning theories thus imply an individualistic (if not exploitative) view of human and animal nature. (An example is the "cupboard love" theory of the development of human affection, as we shall see in Chapter 6.) Learning theories are also likely to be mechanistic. Although not all learning theories are by any means the same, they tend to come down on the side of reducing behavior to its mechanics, leaving out the feelings which infuse the mechanical system. Studies of maternal behavior in animals have been able to illuminate the issues which are involved in the traditional opposition between instinct theory and learning theory. The solution seems to lie in the fact that instinctual behavior requires "holistic" and social concepts of how animals function.

As suggested earlier, studies of maternal behavior in infra-human species have had to make use of concepts such as "behavioral synchrony" and "affectional system." These concepts are needed to describe a biologically given system in which females behave affectionately toward their young. Neither individualistic nor mechanistic views of this affectionate behavior on the part of infra-human females quite do justice to the phenomena being described. Synchrony, for example, describes the relationship between suckling and lactation: As the infant suckles, lactation increases. The synchronous character of the mother-young relationship during lactation also insures that optimal ecological and social conditions will prevail insofar as these are under the control of the mother.[5]

Before we look more closely at the evidence on animal affectional systems, let's look first at some observations made by Darwin [6] about emotions in general, including maternal feeling. Darwin understood emotions both on the animal and the human level to be biologically adaptive, that is, to insure species survival. Darwin's view was that emotions, even such personally disruptive ones as shame, made species-survival sense. (Darwin was, incidentally, one of the first scientists ever to mention the phenomenon of shame.) He had no difficulty with a view that women are more affectionate in their natures than men, since this has a clear species-survival value.

Darwin reviewed expressions of a wide variety of emotions in both animals and human beings: distress, terror, sexual arousal, fighting, grief, laughter, contempt, disgust, astonishment, helplessness, and blushing. He theorized that these emotions are (or were at one time) adaptive, and in this sense understandable phenomena rather than irrational events. Three principles of adaptation were derived from his observations. Some emotional expressions were originally "serviceable" to the organism, became habitual, and persisted through inheritance in the organism's repertory, even though no longer necessarily useful. Other emotional expressions were understandable as attempts to control useless inherited "habits"; and still other emotional expressions were products of the direct action of the nervous system. This last principle clearly anticipates Cannon's *The Wisdom of the Body* in its treatment of the adaptive value of emotions.[7]

Darwin observed, for example, that emotional expressions varied in "outward signs," depending upon how much direct action of the nervous system was required for discharge of the evoked emotion. Pain, for example, is shown by writhing; rage by violent fighting gestures. Maternal love is shown by only "slight caressing movements, with a gentle smile and tender eye" because although "no emotion is stronger than maternal love," it does not habitually lead to action. In contrast, love between the sexes leads to increased heart rate, rapid breathing, and flushed face because sexual love is "not inactive like that of a mother for her infant." [8] Darwin thus clearly assumes a biologically adaptive "maternal love," expressing itself in the form of an underlying tender or affectionate attitude in women.

Maternal behavior in infra-human animals was one of the earliest experimental problems undertaken as comparative psychology began to flourish under the impetus of checking Darwin's hypotheses. The search for the processes by which maternal behavior functions led not only to an analysis of the component parts of maternal behavior, but to experimental manipulations designed to study the relation of maternal behavior to hormones; to prior learning experiences in caring for pups; and to characteristics of the litter.

Essential components of maternal behavior at the infra-human are present without prior experience. A review of the evidence [9] tells us that the "primiparous [bearing her first litter] rat is able to act in adequate maternal fashion and . . . without specific prac- tise to engage in those activities which are necessary for the survival and growth of a litter." Although breeding experience is not essential to maternal behavior, previous experience with parturition, however, does have an effect on maternal behavior. Specifically, for example, it increases maternal efficiency in dealing with abnormal conditions of parturition.

Rat mothers are discriminating with respect to their own young. They will retrieve their own young in preference to alien young of the same age. Among mice, female pups will be retrieved by mice mothers in preference to male pups! [10] Even this far down the evolutionary scale mothers distinguish between the sex of their infants.

There is also evidence that mothers differ in the degree of maternal care which they can give. These differences are often a function of the various kinds of treatment to which mothers themselves have been subjected. Mothers who were "stressed" when they were infants transmit "fearfulness" to their young. A similar finding exists at the monkey level, as we shall see in a moment.

An exquisite interplay of hormonal, perceptual, and experiental factors governs "instinctual" maternal behavior in rats.[11] For example, rats, when pregnant, will retrieve a food pellet in preference to a pup; shortly after parturition, however, they will retrieve a pup in preference to a food pellet. Parturition, in other words, does something to make the female rat prefer retrieving pups to retrieving food. All of the many physiological and experi- ental changes set in motion by parturition which are responsible for maternal behaviors have not yet been exactly identified, but it has been proposed that an increase in circulating estrogen and a decrease in progesterone trigger the onset of maternal behavior. Prolactin is also a possible trigger.

The pups themselves create another important set of factors. One rather unexpected finding is that some concept of "pup attraction" is required to account for the extent to which rat babies are approached by all the adults around them. "Pup attraction" is not completely under hormonal control but is an intrinsic stimulus to adults, if the adults are repeatedly exposed to pups for fifteen days. Thus, normal and castrated *male* rats, virgin female rats, and female rats which have had their ovaries removed or have had the part of the brain removed which governs hormonal secretions—all will retrieve pups who have been around them for fifteen days.[12] In other words, basic maternal responsivity to pups is not dependent on hormones, or even on gender for its arousal. "Pup stimulation" or "pup attraction" will keep mothers maternal, and it will even evoke "maternal" behavior in males!

If pup attraction exists on the rodent level and, moreover, is apparent in male rats as well as in females who have just become mothers, how much more likely does it seem that ingredients for an affectionate interaction between human beings and their infants should exist as a biological given and capable of an enormous elaboration as a result of the cultural nature of human beings. Unless, of course, cultural forces suppress affectionate behavior in spite of the threat which this carries of ultimate species extinction.

Mother-infant interaction has also been extensively studied in monkeys.[13] The Harlows' work has considerably advanced the notion that affectionate behavior toward the young is part of a species-survival system which insures an optimal ecology for the young. The Harlows conceptualize an "affectional system" to describe the relation between mother and infant. They have demonstrated that maternal deprivation of infant monkeys has the outcome of emotional disturbance when the monkeys grow up. Adult monkeys who have been maternally deprived are damaged in their sexual functioning, as well as in their maternal effectiveness, and male monkeys are more profoundly injured by maternal deprivation than females. [14]

The Harlows' work has been important evidence of a link between early affectional experiences and later sexual and maternal behavior in monkeys. These experimental findings tend to confirm clinical observations on human beings. Bowlby summarizes it best when he writes that in human beings "overlaps between attachment behavior, parental behavior and sexual behavior are commonplace." [15]

When it comes to the two sexes, there is evidence that mother monkeys punish their male infants more than they do their females.[16, 17] The mothers not only punish male infants more, but they hold them less, pay less attention to them, and carry them around less than they do their female infants. Why this is so is not clear. Male infants may be more aggressive than females and so induce more aggression in their mothers in return. Or the mothers' extra aggression toward their male infants may be species-adaptive in the sense that it trains males to be dominant when they are adults. In primate groups, as we saw in Chapter 1, order is established on the basis of physical strength. As we have already seen, however, this basis for the social order among primates need not be a model for human society.

Among monkeys it has been possible to trace a chain of connection between aggressive or peaceful social conditions prevailing among the group, the quality of the mother-infant affectional system, and the resulting adult "personality" which perpetuates the prevailing social conditions. An important study has been made by Rosenblum of two groups of monkeys, bonnets and pigtails, who differ markedly in their social behavior, their affectionateness of temperament, and in the quality of the mother-infant interaction.[18] Bonnet and pigtail monkeys have been studied in the laboratory and observed in the wild to be strikingly different in their natural degree of aggressivity. (The ecological conditions or genetic factors which produce this difference are unknown.) Pigtail monkeys brought into the laboratory are noted for their "destructive, aggressive encounters." Adult females, juveniles, and infants are severely wounded or killed; violent aggressive encounters develop even after tranquility has apparently descended upon the laboratory. On the other hand, in bonnet monkeys, hostile encounters are exceedingly rare. Pigtail adults do not make close contact with each other, nor do they spend much time in close physical proximity, except when grooming. On the other hand, virtually all bonnets, including adult males, spend long periods of the day in closely formed "group or sub-group contact huddles." Pigtails and bonnets are also different in the way they greet the arrival of a new baby. It is characteristic of all primates to be interested in the arrival of a baby. Bonnet mothers, within moments of delivering their young and even often prior to the expulsion of the placenta, resume membership in their group. Other group members are allowed, moreover, to explore and handle the new infant. Pigtail mothers, in contrast, remain separated from the group after delivery and will often vigorously attack group members who approach them and their babies.

These initial differences in maternal behavior follow a consistent trend of difference as the infant develops. Pigtail monkeys are more restrictive of their infants' beginning movements away from them; they retrieve their infants oftener and are in general more restrictive during the first six months of the infant's life. Bonnet infants, in contrast, engage in consistently higher levels of positive interaction with other adult members of the group. Bonnet infants seem to belong to what can be called an extended family. Bonnet monkeys, consistent with this trend, play more with each other as peers than do pigtails. Moreover, pigtail monkeys are more likely to form an enduring relationship with their mothers and their brothers and sisters; but while pigtail monkeys are clannish, bonnets are friendlier to strangers. It is of interest that the two species do not differ in the total amount of play. But bonnet monkeys' play is "social"; pigtails' play is more of the nonsocial "exercise" kind.

The weaning of a bonnet infant from its mother follows a very different course from that of a pigtail infant. Pigtail infants are much more frequently and forcibly rejected by their mothers; in reaction, pigtail monkeys seem more attached to their mothers. Moreover, they react to the arrival of a sibling and to separation from the mother with more overt depression. The following table summarizes the differences which have been established between bonnet and pigtail monkeys.

Thus, evidence about the relationship between close attachment between mother and infant and infant's proneness to depression has obvious parallels with human behavior. The comparison of bonnet and pigtail social structure also makes clear that, as among ourselves, the social structure is of great importance as background to the mother-infant interaction. No

Table 1
COMPARISON OF BONNET AND PIGTAIL MONKEYS IN
SOCIAL BEHAVIOR, MOTHER-INFANT INTERACTION
AND INFANT ATTACHMENT°
°(Adapted from L. Rosenblum, in R. Schaffer, ed. *The Origins of Human Social Behavior.*)

Behavior	Bonnets	Pigtails
Gregariousness	High	Low
Cohesiveness of Family Unit	Low	High
Maternal Protection	Low	High
Maternal Rejection	Low	High
Peer Play	High	Low
Infant Interaction with Adults	High	Low
Response to Birth of Sibling	Minimal	Disturbance
Response to Maternal Loss	Brief Agitation	Depression

one knows just why pigtail monkeys live at a greater distance from each other than bonnets and why they are so aggressive and destructive toward each other any more than we know why bonnet monkeys are more gregarious and friendly to "strangers." Rosenblum doubts that ecological differences in the wild account for the differences observed in the laboratory. He guesses that in the wild pigtail monkeys would be found sitting with brothers and cousins, while bonnet monkeys would be found sitting with friends and neighbors.

But whatever the source of the difference in aggression between the two species of monkeys, the mother-infant interaction which occurs in the context of an aggressive environment is different from the interaction in a friendlier environment. Specifically, within the context of aggressiveness, infants develop a more intense attachment to their mothers and suffer from depression on separation; their mothers also protect *and* reject them more. Within the context of a friendly environment, infants develop a "cooler" relationship to their mothers and suffer less from depression; their mothers protect *and* reject them less.

Pigtail monkeys' aggressivity reminds us of ourselves with our close-knit nuclear family and a mother who both protects and rejects her infants—and her male infants even more than females. This kind of mother-infant interaction is clearly the product of raising infants in a hostile and destructive world, and one in which men are expected to play a more aggressive part.

Here, of course, the analogy with human beings ends. It does not follow that the less intense attachment among bonnet monkeys is necessarily a model for human beings to emulate. Intense, particular attachment, and its corollary, depression upon loss, is the price that human infants pay for growing up in a cultural order, each individual with a precious self which is a distillation of experiences with parents to whom each child is precious. Intense, particular attachment is not itself pathological; human beings living in a friendly society develop it and also suffer its loss. Human beings have, however, sought to protect themselves against a hostile society also by developing intense, particular attachments to each other. And, in particular, women in a hostile and devaluing world have had to use their affectionateness as a defense as well as a "given" mode of response.

The comparison between bonnet and pigtail monkeys suggests that the level of aggressivity in the group is a factor determining the quality of the mother-infant interaction. A close-knit family is more adaptive to a hostile world than is a "cooler" family life. The enemy, however, is not the close-knit family, but the exploitative world to which it is adaptive. The critical issue for human beings is not the shape or size of the family, but the extent of exploitativeness to which the family must adapt. A close-knit human nuclear family has been adaptive to exploitativeness by forming a haven from the world, and then pushing men very hard to get out of the haven. A close-knit human family could also be adaptive to a cooperative society by forming a base from which human beings of both sexes could grow, without either renouncing or devaluing their affectionateness.

References

1. John Bowlby, *Attachment and Loss*, vol. 1 (New York: Basic Books, 1969).

2. A. Freud and S. Dann, "An Experiment in Group-upbringing," *Psychoanalytic Study of the Child* 6 (1951), 127-168.

3. Charles Darwin, *The Expression of the Emotions in Man and Animals* (London: John Murray, 1872).

4. Jay Rosenblatt, "View on the Onset and Maintenance of Maternal

Behavior in the Rat," L. Aronson, E. Tobach, D. Lehrman and J. Rosenblatt, eds. *Development and Evolution of Behavior* (San Francisco: W. H. Freeman and Co., 1970), p. 504.

5. Ibid.

6. Charles Darwin, op. cit.

7. W. Cannon, *The Wisdom of the Body* (New York: Norton, 1932).

8. Charles Darwin, op. cit., p. 79.

9. Howard Moltz, "Some Effects of Previous Breeding Experience on the Maternal Behavior of the Laboratory Rat," eds. Aronson et al., op. cit., p. 481.

10. Meier and Schutzman, cited by Rosenblatt, op. cit.

11. Jay Rosenblatt, op. cit.

12. Campbell and Nisanin, "Basic Drives," *Annual Review of Psychology*, 1969.

13. H. F. Harlow, M. K. Harlow and E. W. Hansen, "The Maternal Affectional System of Rhesus Monkeys," ed. H. L. Rheingold, *Maternal Behavior in Mammals* (New York: John Wiley, 1963), 254-281.

14. G. Sackett, "Sex Differences in Rhesus Monkeys Following Varied Rearing Experiences," ed. R. C. Friedman, R. M. Richart and R. L. Vande Wiele, *Sex Differences in Behavior* (New York: John Wiley, 1974), pp. 99-122.

15. John Bowlby, op. cit., p. 233.

16. G. D. Jensen, R. A. Bobbitt and B. N. Gordon, "Sex Difference in the Development of Independence in Infant Monkeys," *Behaviour* 30 (1968), 1-14.

17. G. Mitchell and E. M. Brandt, "Behavioral Differences Related to Experience of Mother and Sex of Infant in Rhesus Monkeys," *Developmental Psychology* 3 (1970), 149.

18. L. Rosenblum, "Infant Attachment in Monkeys," ed. H. R. Schaffer, *The Origins of Human Social Relations* (New York: Academic Press, 1971), pp. 85-114.

CHAPTER 3

Does "Genetics" Equal "Sexism"?

It is sometimes said that it is useless to consider the influence of genetic constitution on psychological differences between the sexes, because genetic effects cannot be sorted out from the effects of women's oppressive social environment. An analogy has been made between the problem of differences in intelligence between black and whites and the problem of sex differences not only in intelligence but in temperamental qualities as well. In one respect this analogy is apt, since genetic differences were readily assumed to be the reason for observed differences in black and white I.Q., just as genetic factors are readily assumed to be somehow the reason for the inferior social position of women. And just as, in the absence of equivalent environments for blacks and whites, the operation of genetic differences in intelligence cannot be assessed, so in the absence of political and social equality of men and women, the operation of genetic sex differences in personality or capacities cannot be assessed.

In other respects this analogy, although appealing on the surface, is actually misleading. In the case of black and white groups, as in the case of most so-called "racial" (really ethnic) groups, the extent of a common gene pool in any particular group is doubtful to begin with. In the case of males and females, however, the genetic basis for sexual differentiation is clearly known: Females have an XX and males an XY as one of their twenty-three chromosomal pairs. This is not to imply that all the genetic factors responsible for sexual differentiation have been located or that the operation of located genes in determining development is well understood. Also, it does not imply that the environment is "unimportant" in the development of sexual differentiation—it is a truism that the interaction between genetic and environmental factors is responsible for all living functions. Nevertheless, it does remind us that males and females are each genetically homogeneous groups, and different from each other in a way no racial groups can ever be. Furthermore, the anatomical and physiological end products of having an XX rather than an XY are incomparably different. Having a body which can be host to a developing fetus and then suckle an infant is uniquely female. It can only be contrasted with *not* having such a body so constructed. This is a different order of comparison from a variable number of points on the same scale of intellectual functioning.

In a recent exchange of remarks at a symposium on the origin of human social relations, a noted behavior geneticist expressed himself as "almost surprised" if he were told that the behavior of the two sexes in infancy is not different.[1] The geneticist was replying to a psychologist, who had expressed himself as surprised at finding the two sexes not alike. Early in life, said the psychologist, they "have so many tasks in common—eating, drinking, shelter and warmth"—they should be alike.[2] The geneticist was basing his expectation on the fact that the chromosome content of every cell of their bodies is different from the moment of conception.

This is not to suggest that we can infer what psychological characteristics are inherent in maleness and femaleness just because we know that the sexual differentiation is genetically determined. On the contrary, where human beings are concerned, it is an inordinately difficult task to trace the interaction between biological determinants and cultural forces. Moreover, the genetic information contained in the chromosomes interacts with the environment on many different levels. As one investigator put it, summarizing recent experimental work on sexual behavior, it is necessary to conceptualize chromosomal sex, hormonal sex, gonadal sex, morphological sex, gender role in sex, and behavioral sex.[3] Behavior genetics, which specializes in trying to trace genetic factors through the maze of other determinants which govern behavior, is a relatively new branch of science. It has had success, so far, in tracing the genes for such human characteristics as color blindness and some blood diseases, but so far no complicated psychological characteristics of human beings have been definitively traced to specific genes. As we shall see in a moment, this is in part because the measurement of psychological characteristics is itself so difficult. One cannot be sure of exactly what one is tracing when one uses an I.Q. test, whereas in color blindness the method and object of assessment are relatively clear-cut.

Nevertheless, there have been beginnings of tracing important human psychological characteristics. Three of these characteristics are particularly important for our purpose because they involve ways in which the sexes are observably different. These three characteristics are: "sociability," (alternatively called "person-orientation"); "spatial ability," that is, the capacity to visualize oneself accurately and manage things in space; and aggression. Let me emphasize that there is so far no evidence of a genetically determined *sex* difference in these three characteristics of human beings. But there is some evidence that these characteristics are under *genetic* control.

Let's look more closely at the evidence. Let's take the "person-orientation" evidence first. The studies of this characteristic made use of one method of behavior genetics, the method involving comparison between identical and fraternal twins of equivalent socioeconomic status. Identical twins have the same chromosomes; fraternal twins are no more alike than any two children in the same family. If the chromosomes are contributing something substantial to the characteristic being studied, identical twins should be more alike in it than fraternal twins. One recent, carefully controlled study of identical and fraternal twins showed that the appearance of the infant's first smile occurs closer to the same age for identical twins than for fraternal twins.[4] This study also suggested that "stranger anxiety," an indicator that the infant is attached to its mother, occurs closer to the same age for identical than for fraternal twins. A genetic component is thus apparent in this earliest indicator of human sociability or affectionateness.

Other studies of older children, using the same method of comparison between identical and fraternal female twins, showed that a trait called sociability or person orientation is also under genetic control.[5] The trait is measured by a battery of relatively reliable standardized tests. The two sexes are observably different in sociability—women being more sociable than men. And they are pushed by our culture (see Chapter 14) to be so. But the cultural push may be joining some genetic factor which pushes in the same direction, and so is obscured by the cultural factor.

The evidence on spatial ability is also illuminating. The study of this human characteristic used another method of behavior genetics. This method is the study of resemblances between opposite-sex parents and their children. More resemblance is expected between fathers and daughters than between fathers and sons. This is because the Y chromosome, which fathers pass to their sons but not to their daughters, does not carry any genes. Genes are carried *only* on the X chromosome. The Y chromosome, as far as can be determined, is just the material which determines sex.

Since fathers pass Y to their sons and an X to their daughters, and since X contains genetic material and Y does not, fathers and daughters should resemble each other more than fathers and sons. Similarly, since a son's X comes from his mother, the resemblance between mothers and sons should be at much the same level as the resemblance between fathers and daughters. In fact, such a pattern of family resemblances has been obtained in tests of spatial ability.[6,7] This suggests that spatial ability may be governed by a gene on the X chromosome.

As we shall see in Chapter 7, spatial ability and the perceptual style called field dependence or field independence are similar to each other. Men, in our society and in many others, are better at spatial ability and field independence than women. This is because men are pushed in the direction of field independence since they are pushed more into the world, and they are also pushed into activities involving spatial visualization. Hunting is a prime example. But does this mean that field dependence or spatial ability cannot also be governed by a gene? No, not at all. It means only that where the environmental pressures strongly foster the development of a characteristic, genetic variations in that characteristic will be muted or submerged.

An example from cross-cultural studies of field dependence will

help to clarify the point.[8] Agricultural societies provide an environment in which the children grow up with many clear-cut
demarcations in the world, for example, fields laid out in plots,
rows of planting, by which they can readily learn to orient
themselves. Agricultural societies, depending on accumulation of
resources also, as we shall see in Chapter 5, train their children
more to obedience than nomadic (that is, low-accumulation
hunting and fishing) societies. Eskimos are not only a nomadic,
hunting society, but they live in an environment which,
perceptually, is largely snow and horizon. Children of both sexes
are not only trained to self-reliance, but they have to be more field-
independent than in an agricultural society. Everybody has to do
more work to organize the environment into workable space
concepts, that is, to impose organization on to undifferentiated
space.

So one would expect that the Eskimo people of both sexes
should be somewhat more field-independent than an agricultural
people. This has actually been shown to be the case. Moreover,
among the Eskimo people, there are *no* sex differences in field
dependence. But this does not mean that field dependence is
altogether determined by social pressures. Personality characteristics can be genetically determined *and* responsive to social
pressures.

The two sexes are also observably different in their level of
aggression. Men are observably more aggressive than women.
Men also have a Y chromosome, while women do not. A linkage
between the Y chromosome and aggression in males is thus
suggested. Furthermore, both prisons and mental institutions for
the criminally insane (where more men than women are
committed in the first place) also have an extra complement of
men with an XYY pattern in their midst.[9] Having an extra Y
chromosome is, of course, a genetic anomaly, only very rarely
observed. In order to pursue the question of whether the linkage
between the extra Y chromosome and criminality is real or some
artifact of uncontrolled social factors, one line of investigation
began studying infants with the XYY chromosome pattern with
the intention of tracing their development compared to matched
controls. It was the ethical implications of this type of investigation, as exemplified by Walzer's study at Harvard, which
recently generated great controversy in Boston. Some critics, who

were opposed to this whole line of inquiry, feared that infants might be stigmatized in their parents' eyes and perhaps grow up to be criminals in a self-fulfilling prophecy. Others supported the right of scientists to pursue their idea of an important problem, provided both scientists and their subjects were aware of and prepared for the risks.

The controversy over studying the XYY genotype illustrates that strong passions are evoked because aggression itself is so charged a concept, with different implications, depending upon what aspect of sex differences one is talking about. When people refer to men's supremacy over women in many societies and derive it from ancient men's hypothetical role as defenders of women and children, then aggression is a "good" (or at least necessary) and the Y chromosome can become the supposedly natural basis for men's superior social position. When, however, people refer to men's greater participation in warfare and violent crime, then aggression in men is an "evil." The Y chromosome line of explanation provides a basis for the view that men are inherently more aggressive than women, more warlike, and more inclined to violent crimes. It has even been proposed that elimination at least of violent sex crimes could be most directly accomplished, if not by changing men's genetic endowment,° then at least through hormonal treatments.[11]

As almost everyone will agree, warfare and violent crimes are actually social problems, rather than an expression of the XY chromosome pair. Investigators who pursue the genetic factor in men's aggression can perhaps be criticized for pursuing a needle in a haystack. But their research ought not to be stopped unless serious review indicates insoluble ethical problems. For one thing, the needle may even be there. One encroachment on freedom of inquiry can lead to other encroachments. If it should turn out that there is a genetic basis for greater aggressivity in men than in women, then the genes are pushing in the same direction as exploitative cultural forces.

As a postscript to the XYY question, the evidence is not yet

° It is amusing to note that while a woman, Shulamith Firestone, has suggested an alteration in women's childbearing genetics as a solution to the inequality of the sexes,[10] no one, of either sex, has so far come forward with the corresponding suggestion to alter men's genetics. There are, however, as we shall see in Chapter 18, those who treat male sex criminals by giving them female hormones.

conclusive, but it does look as if there is some link between having an extra Y chromosome and being a criminal.[12]

In their monumental *Psychology of Sex Differences*, Maccoby and Jacklin [13] accept the genetic basis for aggression in males (via the established fact that there is genetic control of differing sex hormones). This line of reasoning also directly suggests a genetic basis for maternal behavior (via the same route of genetic control of hormones). Although Maccoby and Jacklin have "no doubt that women throughout the world are perceived to be the nurturant sex," they do not accord the notion that nurturant behavior in women is genetically based the status of an equal hypothesis with the genetic control of male aggression. This is partly because nurturance has been much less studied than aggression.

But the neglect of the possible genetic basis for women's affectionateness or nurturance also reflects an androcentric bias. The scientific respectability of a genetic basis for male aggression reflects a greater respect for aggression than for nurturance as a powerful psychological and historical force. Thus, many more scientific studies of human aggression than of human affectionateness have been made. The dearth of evidence about human affectionateness keeps hypotheses about its genetic basis in a secondary position.

In the same survey of the literature of sex differences, Maccoby and Jacklin also conclude that the greater sociability of women as compared to men is a myth.[14] This conclusion is, in my opinion, premature, as I shall try to document in the chapters which deal directly with this issue. Instead, Maccoby and Jacklin emphasize that the picture which emerges from their survey is of "high sociability in both sexes." This is a finding which gives comfort to those, like myself, who believe in the affectionateness of both sexes. Maccoby and Jacklin, however, also tell us that the evidence for men's greater aggressivity than women's is overwhelming and of their belief that male aggression is genetically based.

Disputes over the interpretation of evidence usually reflect a difference in underlying assumptions and attitudes. It has already been evident that this book stresses the role of social and political forces in interaction with genetic differences as determinants of sex differences. Maccoby and Jacklin's point of view with respect to the role of social and political forces is not explicit, although they are explicit in their feminism. They mention war, depression, and technological progress in parentheses as factors which might affect the differing self-satisfaction of men and women.

Maccoby and Jacklin believe that "males have occupied the high-status positions in the large majority of human social groupings." They "do not think this is a historical accident." Although they "leave it to the reader's judgment . . . how often . . . the 'killer instinct' is involved in achieving success in the business and political world . . . clearly sometimes it is and in these cases a smaller number of women . . . will have the temperament for it" (p. 368). By implication, Maccoby and Jacklin thus regard male superiority as an inevitability.

This gloomy picture of women's inevitable inferiority is quickly glossed over, however, by Maccoby and Jacklin's perception that aggression is on the wane. "The day of the iron-fisted tycoon appears to be waning. Business leadership is now exercised (especially at the highest levels in the management of conglomerates) by negotiation and attempts to reach agreement. . . ." It is as if Maccoby and Jacklin had never heard of ITT and Chile, to say nothing of fascism still in existence in so many parts of the world. Their perception of aggression as on the wane reflects a kindly if inaccurate view of the world (in keeping with the stereotype of women's softheartedness). It is, I think, the same kindly view which made Maccoby and Jacklin lean over backward *not* to find women more sociable than men. In any case, as I have already suggested, the evidence in their own pages is more supportive of women's sociability than they allow.

Let's look now at what is known about the way the sex chromosomes determine the differences in body structure between the sexes. This will involve us briefly in some additional fundamentals of genetics. As indicated earlier, at conception the one-celled organism (called a zygote) is already differently endowed in the sense that the male zygote has an XY pair, while the female has an XX pair of chromosomes. At about sixteen days, however, one of the X chromosomes in the female embryo is inactivated; thereafter the female develops with only one X in operation. At this point in its development, it is like the male embryo in having only one functional X. Moreover, which of the original two XX's will be inactivated differs in different tissues of the body. So that the female embryo is what geneticists call a "mosaic": It has different functional X chromosomes in different parts of the body. (It is for this reason that students of heredity expect female identical twins to be less like each other than male identical twins.)

What being an XX or an XY zygote most immediately determines, within the first sixteen days, is the production and circulation within the embryo of different hormones. These, in turn, govern the sexual differentiation which is a first step in embryonic development, apparent long before birth.

At birth, the penis-vagina differentiation is only one obvious difference between the sexes. By adulthood, other genetically based differences in body-size and body-build have become apparent. Women have developed breasts; men do not. If we look at other genetically-based body differences between the sexes, we see that such characteristic differences as height, strength, muscle development are all small differences between "averages." Some secondary sex characteristics, while clearly related to XX and XY chromosomes, are varyingly distributed within the two sexes, so that some groups of males in one area may have less of a masculine trait than some groups of females in another. Thus, males are taller than females by about six inches on the average—but only as a group within the same population. The shortest males in an African population are about the same height as the tallest females in Japan.

Some years ago, two psychologists undertook a study of the sexual differentiation in body-build of middle-class American boys and girls.[15] They studied a variety of body build differences, all valid sex differentiators. These were the differences in measurements which go to make up the traditional difference between the male and female adult figure: the broad-shoulder-narrow hips versus the hourglass shape. As supplementary criteria of male and female body-build they measured penis size, breast size, body hair density, and strength of hand-grip. They found that the sexual differentiation in body-build is a "mosaic." A particular man may have broad shoulders and broad buttocks; a particular woman can have broad shoulders and narrow hips. Sex differences in shoulder girth, hip flair, thigh form, and so forth, are on the average only. Penis size, for example, is not at all related to the "masculinity" of the other body dimensions. Genetic traits are thus varyingly distributed within sex groups, and can overlap between sex groups.

Even more important, genetic traits are responsive to cultural pressures. Responsiveness to cultural pressures on the part of a genetic trait is not evidence that the genetic trait does not exist. Margaret Mead's observation [16] that "feminine" traits are found among men in one culture, while "masculine" traits are found in women in another culture is not incompatible with the notion that the two sexes do also have some different personality traits genetically.

Let's suppose for a moment that girl infants do have the makings of a self which is organized to become attuned to others. The assignment of "self-other" organization of the self to women has a clear adaptive advantage for their host function. A genetic advantage in language skills may be one indication of this kind of organization of the self. A very early advantage in auditory acuity may be another sign. But because child rearing does not have a high priority in our exploitative society the characteristics which go to make up sociability are likely to be devalued. Sociability can also become the basis for women's easy subjugation—and one factor in their too patient acceptance of their subjugation by men. As Maccoby and Jacklin write: "To put it bluntly, they [women] are easier to exploit".[17] Women who are protesting their subjugation may well fear that speculations about the existence of a genetic component in their sociability can be used to help keep them "in their place." But only if there is agreement that the "superior" qualities are aggression and egotism. That invidious use may be made of differences between people or between the sexes is something neither psychologists nor geneticists can control. And neither the psychological nor the genetic study of sex differences is inherently "sexist."

On the whole, psychologists have tended to ignore sex differences, rather than study them directly. Some years ago two psychologists reviewed the way in which the question of sex differences was studied by making a census of the articles on that subject appearing in the most important journal publishing research on abnormal and on social behavior.[18] Of nearly 300 articles in the total census for a two-year period, 38 percent of the studies were on men only, 5 percent on women only, and 22 percent even failed to report the sex composition of the subjects in the experiments! The two psychologists who conducted their survey ended it by exhorting their colleagues to stop thinking that general laws of human behavior could be derived from studying one sex alone. But, as another pair of investigators demonstrated about ten years later, the exhortation was not heeded.[19] A similar review of the principal journal in the field of personality and social psychology demonstrated little improvement in this regard. Yet, interestingly enough, while only eight studies had made sex differences the point of their investigation, forty other studies found sex differences they had not expected to find.

As has happened before in history, egalitarian views of human nature have tended to endorse theories which describe the powerful influence of the environment on human development. This is in part because so many environmental influences in an exploitative society are noxious and need to be stopped. Aristocratic views of human nature have tended to endorse theories of the innateness of human behavior since such theories tend to justify the social inferiority of some people. Many observed differences between men and women can in fact readily be related to social expectations of them and to women's inferior status. Since the hereditary psychological differences that come with the sexual differentiation are, in fact, as yet almost completely un-known, speculation about them has seemed pointless and easily put to the use of justifying women's inferior social position. But information about hereditary differences between men and women need not be put to such use. And while the tendency to ignore sex differences has the advantage of stresssing the common humanity of both sexes, it has the disadvantage of leaving us in the dark. Women cannot afford to blind themselves to genetic components in their own functioning from the fear that the knowledge will be used against them.

The shameful episode which occurred in the Soviet Union during the 1930s in connection with genetic studies ought not to be forgotten in this context. In the early 1930s a Soviet geneticist named Lysenko, operating under strong pressure to assist in Soviet agrarian development, offered evidence, now suspected of being just plain faked, that tomatoes and wheat were not under genetic control. Lysenko went further: He denounced Mendelian genetics as a bourgeois-capitalist fraud. Lysenko gained control of the Soviet scientific apparatus and succeeded in persecuting and silencing workers in the field of genetics, most notably Vavilov, who was Lysenko's chief intellectual opponent. Lysenko has now been unmasked and work in the Soviet Union on genetics has been resumed but not without terrible consequences to a whole generation of scientists. (The same atmosphere still seems to prevail in the Soviet Union.)

A noted behavior geneticist, writing in the context of genetic studies of black-white differences, writes:

> If there are alternative ways of being successful within the society, then differences can be valued variations on the human theme . . . regardless of their environmental or genetic origins. . . . Socially invidious comparisons can, however, destroy the usefulness of such differences. . . . If all children had optimal environments for development, then genetic differences would account for most of the variance in behavior.[20]

What the behavior geneticist is saying, by implication, is that equality of opportunity for men and women would lead to a flowering of their differences rather than a lessening of them. We may add that it should also lead to a gentler relationship between the sexes.

References

1. J. Hirsch, ed. H. R. Schaffer, *The Origins of Human Social Relations* (New York: Academic Press, 1971), p. 67.

2. L. Rosenblum, "Infant Attachment in Monkeys," ed. H. R. Schaffer, *The Origins of Human Social Relations* (New York: Academic Press, 1971), p. 67.

3. V. Nowlis, "Critique and Discussion," ed. J. Money, *Sex Research* (New York: Holt, Rinehart, and Winston, 1965).

4. D. Freedman, "Hereditary Control of Early Social Behavior," ed. B. M. Foss, *Determinants of Infant Behavior* vol. 3 (New York: J. Wiley, 1965), pp. 149-159.

5. G. Lindzey, J. Loehlin, M. Manosevitz and D. Thiessen, "Behavior Genetics," *Annual Review of Psychology*, 22 (1971), 39-54.

6. R. E. Stafford, "Sex Differences in Spatial Visualization as Evidence of Sex-Linked Inheritance," *Perceptual and Motor Skills*, 13 (1961), 428.

7. D. R. Goodenough, E. Gandini, I. Olkin, L. Pizzamiglio, D. Thayer and H. A. Witkin, *A Study of X-Chromosome Linkage with Field Dependence and Spatial Visualization*. In press.

8. H. A. Witkin, "A Cognitive-Style Approach to Cross-Cultural Research," *International Journal of Psychology* 2 (1967), 233-250.

9. E. B. Hook, "Behavioral Implications of the Human XYY Genotype," *Science* 179 (1973), 139-150.

10. S. Firestone, *The Dialectic of Sex: The Case for Feminist Revolution* (New York: Morrow, 1970).

11. U. Laschet, "The Use of Antiandrogens in the Treatment of Sex Offenders," eds. J. Money and J. Zubin, *Contemporary Sexual Behavior: Critical Issues in the 1970s* (Baltimore, Md.: The Johns Hopkins Press, 1973), 311-319.

12. E. B. Hook, op. cit.

13. E. Maccoby and C. Jacklin, *The Psychology of Sex Differences* (Stanford, Calif.: Stanford University Press, 1974), p. 215.

14. E. Maccoby and C. Jacklin, op. cit., pp. 154, 275, 368.

15. N. Bayley and L. M. Bayer, "The Assessment of Somatic Androgeny," *American Journal of Physical Anthropology* 4 (1946), 433-461.

16. M. Mead, *Male and Female* (New York: Morrow, 1949).

17. E. Maccoby and C. Jacklin, op. cit., p. 371.

18. E. R. Carlson and R. Carlson, "Male and Female Subjects in Personality Research," *Journal of Abnormal and Social Psychology* 61 (1960), 482-483.

19. J. Garai and A. Scheinfeld, "Sex Differences in Mental and Behavioral Traits," *Genetic Psychology Monographs* 77 (1968), 169-299.

20. Scarr-Salapatek, S. "Race, Social Class and IQ," *Science* 174 (1971), 1294.

PART II

The Self: Becoming Acculturated as a Male or Female

CHAPTER 4

The Self: Male or Female Sex

The impact of human culture upon sexually differentiated human beings comes first through the formation of the self which develops within the matrix of the mother-infant interaction. This interaction is, in turn, part of a genetically based and culturally influenced reproductive system. Affection, or "attachment" (to use Bowlby's term), is evoked and exchanged between mother and infant; within this matrix, the infant's interest is also evoked in things and their exploration. Out of this first social relationship, the self of men and women is formed.

The human self is a uniquely cultural phenomenon. It is the psychological resultant of what Piaget calls the organism's "assimilation" of its environment.[1] The self is a reference point or organizational system for feedback from the organism's environmental transactions. The self is, however, not only an organizational reference point, but it is modified by the process of feedback. It is transformed by its experiences with others and with things. Instead of being the center of experience, it "decenters," silently adapting itself to the "nature of things," and assimilating the viewpoint of others.

The self's defense, in its own and others' eyes, can, however,

43

become a central motive of the person's activities. As Freud taught us, a very "noisy" self can become the center of experience, and it usually does so when it is torn between conflicting demands from viewpoints it has silently internalized. Human beings have such a culturally elaborated self that they not only perceive things with references to the self (which other animals must also do), but they perceive themselves in the *act* of perceiving themselves, and they evaluate themselves in their own and other's eyes. Because they have a self human beings are also unique in having a superego which, in turn, modifies the self.

It seems reasonable to suppose that the attitude of a mother toward her infant son will be different from her attitude toward her infant daughter, if only in the recognition of her infant's being the opposite sex or the same sex as herself. Where there is strong devaluation of women, the maternal attitude might be expected to be grossly different toward boys than toward girls. But even if there were no devaluation of femaleness, mothers might be expected to regard their little boys as different from themselves.

As we saw in Chapter 2 mother monkeys are more aggressive and less tender toward their male infants than toward their females. Even without been acculturated, monkey mothers rear their males differently from their females. One would expect an even greater difference in infant rearing at the human level, and the most pronounced difference to occur in cultures where women are devalued.

It also seems reasonable to suppose that male infants perceive that they are different from their mothers, if only because they perceive her reaction to the difference. Margaret Mead suggested some years ago that the boy's "earliest experience of self is one in which he is forced, in the relationship to his mother, to realize himself as different, as a creature unlike his mother. . . ." [2] The evidence concerning infant perception which has been gathered since 1949, the year of Margaret Mead's book, makes it clear that infants are able to perceive a great deal more than had previously been supposed. This perception could include the registration of the mother's response to the boy's sex as different from her own. From a difference in maternal attitude we can deduce that the substratum self of girls assimilates "sameness" to mother; that of boys, "difference" from mother.

This is by no means an original idea, but is an outgrowth of

Freudian emphasis on the importance of infant experience. As we shall see in Chapter 5, cross-cultural studies have been made by anthropologists to trace the different effects of cross-sex or same-sex caretaker on boys and girls. For example, in societies where women and children live segregated from the adult males, there are more likely to be severe initiation rites for boys at puberty. Societies without such distance between the adult males and the women and children, are less likely to "brainwash" their boys into equating masculinity with toughness.[3]

One of the most important ways in which the self of a person is organized is around gender identity. The concept of oneself as male or female seems as much of an unalterable given as the self itself. The knowledge that one is male or female is also a major route through which cultural expectations are channeled. That boy infants assimilate difference from their mothers in infancy, while little girls assimilate sameness, suggests that gender identity has a different foundation in boys than it does in girls. This does not imply that gender identity is less clear cognitively in boys than in girls. But it does imply that the substratum self-feeling underlying gender indentity is different for the two sexes. One psychologist[4] has suggested that gender identity involves a different learning task for men than for women. Women, since their first caretaker is of the same sex, have only to learn a "lesson" in mother-person emulation. Boys, in contrast, have to solve a "problem" in mother-person differentiation. On this line of reasoning, the assumption of gender identity is easier for women than for men.

It was Freud who first called attention to the difference in the self of men and women because of having a same-sex or opposite-sex caretaker. Freud was caught by the fact that men have an opposite-sex earliest caretaker, but the same "love object" all their lives. Girls, he said, have a same-sex earliest caretaker, but they have to shift from loving their mothers to loving their fathers. With his customary androcentric bias, Freud saw that as a harder task for women than for men, making it harder for women to develop sexual feeling and making them prone to homosexuality.[5] As is the case with many of Freud's insights, he was surely on the right track in supposing that having a same-sex or an opposite-sex early caretaker mattered. But the difference can be seen as favoring girls in the formation of their gender identity.

Thus it is no surprise that in adulthood men are more prone to symptoms involving gender identity than women. Women are subject less often than men to adult sexual deviations. Women less often than men use fetishism, cross-dressing, voyeurism, or genital exhibitionism as sources of genital excitement.[6] They suffer less frequently from symptoms involving distortions of gender identity: "Who-am-I" symptoms such as are dynamically involved in the perversions. This is more than a clinical observation. In a recent study of 1037 cases at a New York mental health center, men applied significantly more often than women for problems of "sexual deviation." [7]

As we shall see in Chapter 13, the rearing of men by an opposite-sex caretaker has figured heavily in psychoanalytic thinking about the relations between the sexes. Dread of women, and envy of them, have been suggested as unconscious reasons why men find it necessary to keep women in subjection. Although their gender identity is deeply grounded in experiences with their first caretakers, however, women's gender identity which is (like men's) established by the time they are two years old, brings them into an early recognition that their sex is devalued in the culture.

When the time comes for adult sexuality, there is, as Desmond Morris [8] puts it (neatly paraphrasing Freud), a revival of the intimacies which characterized infancy. By the time they reach adulthood, however, grown men and women have selves which are very differently organized. The substratum self of women which contains the information "same sex as mother," as well as the cultural expectations that she will be a mother, create a different framework—a different gestalt of feelings and attitudes for women's sexual experiences than exists for those of men. Women's attitudes toward sex are embedded in the framework of maternity. There are bound to be more references in her sexual experience both to the satisfactions of making a baby and to fears for her own body in the process. Woman's sexual experience has a frequent intruder: the image of herself as mother.

A man's part in reproduction begins and ends with the ejaculation of sperm in intercourse. This experience is ordinarily highly pleasurable, being coincident with orgasm. Orgasm in women, in contrast, is not necessary for her fertilization. (In fact, some observations made by Mary Jane Sherfey [9] from Masters and Johnson's findings suggest that in women who have borne children, the absence of orgasm creates a situation within the vagina which helps to retain sperm, that is, to increase the chances of fertilization.)

For men, however, ejaculation and orgasm in intercourse cannot occur unless there has been a prior event—the erection of his penis. Intercourse for men involves a three-stage process: arousal-erection; intromission; and ejaculation of sperm-orgasm. A man's failure to have an erection or to maintain it prevents intercourse; no such burden of responsibility for intercourse is carried by women. A woman has only to be there and willing to permit penetration. A man must be aroused—a state which is not necessarily under his conscious control. The act of intercourse is thus "easier" for women, and her orgasm plays no role in her fertilization. As Karen Horney writes:

> The man is actually obliged to go on proving his manhood to the woman. There is analogous necessity for her. Even if she is frigid she can engage in sexual intercourse and conceive and bear a child. She performs her part by merely *being*, without any *doing*. . . . The man on the other hand has to do something in order to fulfill himself.[10]

The gestalt of feelings and attitudes governing the experience of the man in sexual intercourse is thus organized around his orgasm: It is "phallocentric." The intruder in a man's sexual experience is the fear of his own failure to have and maintain an erection, and thus to have an orgasm. Fromm has described how the fear of impotence in males increases his need for "mastery." [11] In this connection, there is also cross-cultural evidence that "love charms are much more often employed by men than by women." [12] Cross-cultural studies also tell us that the majority of primitive cultures surveyed believe that men should take the sexual initiative. This belief represents an acknowledgment of necessity. It is based on the fact that arousal and erection are not under a man's conscious control and are best produced spontaneously. Margaret Mead suggests that the "male who has learned various mechanical ways to stimulate his sexual specificity in order to copulate with a woman he does not at the moment desire is doing far more violence to his nature than a female who needs only receive a male. . . ." [13]

It has been suggested that orgasm has the function of emotionally reaffirming the reality of the self.[14] That orgasm in the male affirms the reality of his erection against uncertainty of his penis's arousal and ejaculation seems likely. Orgasm is a more central feature in the framework of attitudes governing a man's sexual experience than a woman's. Women, whose gender identity is more firmly grounded in same sex than men's, do not need orgasm for an affirmation of the *self*, although they may enjoy orgasm as much as men. Woman's framework in intercourse is more organized around her impregnation, which she may or may not desire. Anxiety about impregnation reduces her chances for orgasm.

It is interesting to observe, in passing, how easy it is to be irrational on the subject of orgasm in women, especially in reaction to social attitudes which deny the existence or importance of women's orgasm. An example is the idea, now current, that women are even more potent than men because they have multiple orgasms. This idea is based on a misunderstanding of Masters and Johnson's findings. Once orgasm is initiated in women, there can be multiple repetitions of it, *provided stimulation continues*. Evidence suggests that a refractory period is characteristic of the male ejaculation system.[15] Women, who do not ejaculate, thus also may have no refractory period afterward. But orgasm in the woman having intercourse is more dependent on the activity of the penis than orgasm in the man having intercourse is dependent on the activity of the clitoris or vagina. It is thus more certain as a self-propelled outcome of arousal in men than it is in women. Men are uncertain about the prior step of becoming aroused; women about having orgasm. Both uncertainties can become obsessive.

Not only is the framework for sexual experience different in men than in women, but the childhood residuals with which the two sexes enter pubescent and adult sexual experiences are different. The sexual partner of the man is the same-sex as that of his mother; that of the woman is the opposite-sex from her mother, and almost completely unfamiliar to her. As Simone de Beauvoir writes: "... What she, like her brothers, first caressed and cherished, was her mother's flesh." [16] No wonder that men ordinarily show more initiative in sexual approach to women; they are going toward a person whose sex is familiar to them and who for that reason alone is not to be feared. A woman, in contrast, makes love to a person whose sex was unfamiliar to her during her infancy.

No wonder also that the incest taboo is most stringent and most widespread against copulation between mother and son, while in many parts of the world (including our own Kentucky hills) it is tolerated, albeit disapproved, between father and daughter. An adult act of copulation between father and daughter revives little of infant intimacies between them—there being ordinarily very little intimacy of infancy to revive. The self of the woman can tolerate the reality of copulation with father without breakdown even if she abhors it. For the man, copulation with his mother involves the revival of infant intimacies with the same actual caretaker. It puts a tremendous strain on the reality distinction powers of the man who is not symbolically but actually reviving the experiences of his infancy.

When we consider, further, that men have intercourse with a representative of their opposite-sex parent, from whom they assimilated a difference, it does not seem surprising that empathy for their partner's feelings does not come easily. Nor is it surprising that a man's sexual behavior, occurring as it does in a phallocentric framework, should be characterized by insistence and assertiveness, and an easy use of the other as an object or thing.

Women also have intercourse with a representative of the opposite-sex parent. But this representative does not remind her of her earliest experiences. A girl's important experiences with her father come much later in childhood when her self is already quite developed. Disappointments with her father can be better borne by a self whose gender identity is already formed and grounded in sameness with mother. A woman's heterosexual experience with her adult partner thus carries fewer scars of ancient battles fought mindless and alone.

The differences between the sexes in the organization of the self which have just been sketched are glimpses of universal resultants of the cultural nature of humanity in sexually differentiated human beings. They are differences in the acculturation of the self of men and women which make sex life relatively predictable in any kind of society. These glimpses of universals about the self, male or female, are clouded, however, by the widespread social inferiority of women. In egalitarian societies, where questions of power and submission are relatively unimportant, the anxieties which arise in both sexes from having a same-sex or opposite-sex caretaker might be expected to dissolve in adulthood. Exploitative societies, in contrast, would be expected to magnify the anxieties in the self of both sexes. As anthropologists have suggested, following Freud, the widespread cultural devaluation of women may itself be understood as a "primary-process" transformation of men's unconscious envy of women's maternal role. This mechanism should be more pronounced in exploitative than in egalitarian societies. These are questions which we shall pursue in Chapter 5 and again in Chapter 8.

References

1. J. Piaget, *The Moral Judgment of the Child* (Glencoe, Ill.: The Free Press, n. d.)

2. Margaret Mead, *Male and Female* (New York: Morrow, 1949), p. 167.

3. Nancy Chodorow, "Being and Doing: A Cross-cultural Examination of the Socialization of Males and Females," eds., V. Gornick and B. Moran, *Women in Sexist Society. Studies in Power and Powerlessness* (New York: New American Library, 1972), pp. 259-291.

4. D. B. Lynn, "Sex Role and Parental Identification," *Child Development* 33 (1961), 555-564.

5. S. Freud, *Female Sexuality*, Standard Edition, Vol. 21.

6. R. Stoller, *Sex and Gender* (New York: *Science House*, 1968).

7. Personal communication from Jeanne Safer, Postgraduate Center for Mental Health, New York.

8. Desmond Morris, *Intimate Behavior* (New York: Random House, 1971).

9. Mary Jane Sherfey, *The Nature and Evolution of Female Sexuality.* (New York: Random House, 1972).

10. K. Horney, "The Dread of Women." *International Journal of Psychoanalysis* 13 (1932), 348-361.

11. Erich Fromm, "Sex and Character." *Psychiatry* 6 (1943), 21-31.

12. C. Ford and F. Beach, *Patterns of Sexual Behavior* (New York: Harper, 1951), pp. 108-109.

13. M. Mead, op. cit., p. 210.

14. H. Lichtenstein, "Changing Implications of the Concept of Psychosexual Development," *Journal of the American Psychoanalytic Association* 18 (1970), 300-317.

15. Frank Beach, "Prospect and Retrospect," ed. F. Beach, *Sex and Behavior* (New York: Wiley, 1965, reprinted New York: Krieger, 1974).

16. S. de Beauvoir, *The Second Sex* (New York: Alfred A. Knopf, 1957), p. 377.

CHAPTER 5

How Do Other Cultures Train the Sexes?

All cultures might be expected to recognize women's maternal function and to organize some of the society's basic institutions around this cardinal fact of existence. This would involve cultural provision for keeping mothers close to their infants in order to be able to nurse them. (Bottle-feedings as a viable alternative to nursing has been available even in our own society only since the beginning of this century.) Cross-cultural studies of sex differences in people's occupations do reflect the fact that cultures have made provision for the nurturant function of women. So, for example, in cross-cultural studies of food production, men are *always* the hunters (of large animals), while women are nearly always the stay-at-home cooks and grinders of the grain.[1]

When it comes to molding the children's personalities to be nurturant or self-sufficient, however, cross-cultural studies tell us that the sexual differentiation alone is not sufficient to account for sex differences in personality training. The nature of the economy is also an important factor underlying the culture's provisions for training both sexes. Differences in the training of the sexes are more pronounced where the economy actually rests on skills requiring superior physical strength and where the economy is nomadic rather than sedentary.

Let's look more closely at the evidence. In the first place, it has been shown that in societies in which the economy involves a high accumulation of resources, *all* the children are trained more to obedience than to self-reliance. (The "high accumulation" societies are pastoral or agricultural societies with animal husbandry.) Where, in contrast, the society is a "low accumulator" of resources—as in hunting or fishing societies—*all* the children are trained more in self-reliance than in obedience.[2] This makes a certain amount of sense. In a society where failure to tend the crops or the animals might result in economic disaster, training all the children to be obedient is necessary, while in a nomadic or hunting and fishing economy, training in self-reliance is necessary, especially for the males since they are likely to be the hunters.

It is when we look cross-culturally at how societies do specifically train their boys and girls differently that we get the sense of how economic necessity interacts with women's maternal role to govern cultural differences in child rearing. One of the most widely quoted studies is a cross-cultural study by Barry, Bacon, and Child.[3] They set out to survey ethnographic reports for information about socialization practices, and included 110 cultures in their initial group. Two independent judges rated each culture on sex differences in socialization. Five specific categories were used: responsibility or dutifulness training; nurturance training; obedience training; self-reliance training; and achievement training. It should be noted that both positive and negative methods of training were included in the reckoning, which covered the ages between four or five until shortly after puberty. (It is interesting that 92 percent of the cultures studied showed no sex difference in socialization procedures during infancy. These are subtle enough to be lost without careful observation.)

As one would expect on the basis of maternal role alone, cultures trained girls overwhelmingly more often to be nurturant and responsible, while boys were trained more often to be self-reliant and achieving.

Here is a table showing Barry, Bacon, and Child's results on sex differences in socialization practices.

Table 1
SEX DIFFERENCES IN SOCIALIZATION PRACTICES°
°(Adapted from Barry Bacon and Child.)

Variable	No. of Cultures with Ratable Information	Percent of Cultures with Evidence of Sex Difference in Direction of		
		Boys	Girls	Neither
Nurturance	33	0	82	18
Responsibility	84	11	61	28
Obedience	69	3	35	62
Achievement	31	87	3	10
Self-reliance	82	85	0	15

One amusing footnote about stereotypes: The results on girls' obedience training are clearly the least impressive findings in this table. The percent of cultures which favored "neither" sex nor obedience is 62. Yet, these results are widely quoted as suggesting that girls are more often trained to obedience than boys. (The authors bear some responsibility for this emphasis.)

When, however, the *extent* of sex difference in personality training was separately studied, it became clear that the nature of the economy and of the family structure had a great deal to do with the extent of sex difference in child rearing. A large sex difference in socialization practices was connected to an economy that placed a premium on superior strength such as hunting and the keeping of large animals. Large sex differences were also connected to the extended rather than the nuclear family. The authors explain this second correlation in the following way: They reason that in the small, socially isolated nuclear family, which operates alone as a unit, men's and women's roles need to be more interchangeable than in a more extended family where there are more substitutes for a lost member. The sexual differentiation cannot afford to be too high in the nuclear family, where a lost member cannot so easily be replaced. The researchers argue, further, that the failure of the Israeli kibbutz to effect a lessening of differentiation in sex roles may have been the result of the fact that the kibbutz was an agricultural community organized for hard labor, so that it required males' superior strength for its existence.

Nancy Chodorow has suggested an additional explanation for the fact that the largest sex differences in socialization were found in hunting, herding, and animal husbandry societies.[4] She suggests that these societies not only rest on men's superior strength but on the kind of work that takes men away from the women and children. Chodorow suggests that as a result boys lack a continuous and regular training for their later occupations, which girls more routinely get. In societies where the men are absent, boys do not have a chance to see what the males are doing, while girls, close to their mothers, have a clearer, more regular notion of the relevance of their tasks. Cultures which take the men away from the women and children thus develop more stress on the differences between the sexes.

Cultures which go to great lengths to separate women and children from the adult men also need more elaborate gender-emphasizing ceremonies both at initiation into puberty and at the time of childbirth. One cross-cultural study of primitive societies showed, for example, that those societies which have mother-infant sleeping arrangements which exclude the father either from the hut or from the mother-child bed are likely to have either male initiation rites at puberty or the couvade (male vicarious participation in childbirth) significantly more often than societies without such arrangements for excluding fathers.[5] Male initiation rites at puberty are associated, moreover, with patrilocal societies, while couvade is more likely to occur in matrilocal societies.[6] This suggests that where there are mother-child sleeping arrangements which exclude father, there is a different cultural impact on gender identity in boys and girls. The boys, originally close to their mothers, must later renounce them for participation in a male-run world and their initiation rites at puberty serve as a symbolic expression of their renunciation of their mothers and a painful assertion of masculinity. In matrilocal societies, where femaleness is more valued, male empathy with childbearing can be symbolically expressed in more directly imitative, vicarious participation. Moreover, male initiation rites at puberty are symbolic expressions which contain culturally sanctioned cruelty; the couvade is an expression of sympathy or empathy which hurts no one.

How widespread among cultures is the social inferiority of women? It is generally agreed that in many, if not the majority of human societies which have been studied by anthropologists, women have a position of social inferiority. Margaret Mead once observed that whatever work it is that women are culturally assigned to do, that work is less valued in the culture than the work assigned to men.[7]

One anthropologist, after reviewing the evidence, summarized the sex distinctions which occur in societies around the globe as follows:

> The majority of societies organize their social institutions around males rather than females. For example, out of 565 societies in Murdock's World Ethnographic Sample, 376 societies are labeled as predominantly patrilocal (i.e., sons reside after marriage with the paternal family), while only 84 are matrilocal. With respect to the calculation of descent groups, the ratio is four to one in favor of patrilineal rather than matrilineal descent. For forms of multiple marriage, of 431 polygamous societies surveyed, 427 permit men to have more than one wife (they are polygynous societies), while only *four* [italics mine] permit women to have more than one husband [so-called polyandrous societies].[8]

These sex distinctions in social structure do not, of course, necessarily imply inferiority or superiority of power or social position. As we shall see in Chapter 9, among the Arapesh, descent is reckoned patrilineally, and residence is patrilocal, but both sexes are relatively equal in social power. But when the cross-cultural picture is assembled, it is overwhelming in its male-centered form, if not in its content.

Many attempts have been made to explain the widespread social inferiority of women. Two important categories of explanation may be discerned: the psychological (mainly psychoanalytical), and the economic power explanations. Both explanations have great gaps in them; taken together, however, they tell more of the story. As we shall see in Chapter 8, there is cross-cultural evidence from anthropology as well as from our own history that a significant relationship exists between autocratic power in the culture and the subjection of women. Men are also subjugated in autocracies. The unanswered question is why women are even more subjugated than men, and why it is men rather than women who are in the seats of power. The psychoanalytic explanation illuminates a facet of child rearing which explains one reason why men have a need to dominate women. It does not explain how men translate their need into power.

Let's look more closely at psychoanalytic theories of women's social inferiority. Karen Horney was one of the first to develop a psychoanalytic theory of women's social inferiority. She based it on a psychic defense: reversal by men of their dread of women. Mother's power to withhold nurturance is the power of life and death. It creates sadistic responses in the very young boy and tremendous anxiety because the sadistic experience occurs so early.[9] (Dread of the father, since it occurs later, is more tangible and less uncanny.) As a result of their early, sadistic dread of women, men have a need to reverse things: to impose their power upon women, keeping women in subjection and in positions of social inferiority.

That men should dread their mother's early power is itself an idea rooted in the exploitative atmosphere of our own society, which cannot take women's nurturant attitudes for granted. Why it should be men who dread their mothers more than women do is also unclear. Perhaps it has to do with men having a cross-sex first-caretaker. But even more important is the question of how it comes about that men have the power to impose their infant fantasy-reversal on the culture. How men turn their fantasy into reality is unexplained. The unanswered question, in other words, is the origin of exploitative power to begin with.

Yet, the psychoanalytic explanation does address itself to an important universal in human development: that boy infants have an opposite-sex caretaker, while girl infants have a same-sex care-taker. As we saw in Chapter 4, women have a gender identity rooted in a same-sex caretaker, while men's gender identity is less secure than women's. This creates a psychological force which pushes men into worrying more about their masculinity than women do about their femininity. (It's a far cry from worrying about masculinity to imposing power: only the need is there, not the weapons.)

The way some anthropologists theorize about cross-sex rearing for men goes something like this: For children of either sex, the earliest identity is feminine, since they are reared by women who are the providers of food. The "primary-optative" identity ("good me") is feminine for both sexes. But as little boys grow up, especially in father-absent, patrilocal cultures, boys become aware of the adult males' power, and therefore aware that a "secondary identity" is needed. This helps to account for the cross-cultural finding that male initiation rites tend to occur in patrilocal societies. The function of these rites is to "brainwash the primary feminine identity and to establish firmly the secondary male identity." [10]

Bruno Bettelheim [11] has suggested, from a study of schizophrenic adolescents, that initiation rites, such as cutting the penis, are symbolic wounds inflicted (in schizophrenics, self-inflicted) to assert that men, too, can bear children. These rites are also symbolic expressions of endurance, and masculinity is equated with the ability to bear pain.

One anthropological, cross-cultural study showed that male violence is greatest in cultures (as in the Indian caste system) where the husband and wife may not sleep together, nor eat together, and seldom play or work together.[12] Another cross-cultural study also showed that male narcissism is prevalent in societies where there is greater emotional distance between husband and wife than between mother and child.[13] Emotional distance implies a lack of affectionateness, in fact, in these cultures it is rooted in the subjection of women.

Men do not grow up unsure of their gender identity just because they are reared by women, but because the society in which they grow up also offers them a contradiction between their early affectionateness and the later exploitativeness which is expected of them. The subjection of women is a given of the culture which they absorb. If this were not so, the sex difference in the foundation of gender identity would still be an important determinant of men's or women's personalities, but nowhere near a determinant of such great magnitude.

The subjection of women is a corollary of the development of the exploitative relations between classes. Cross-cultural studies have also shown that autocratic power entails the greater subjection of women.[14] There is, for example, a correlation between autocracy and polygyny, that is, the right of a man to have more than one wife. Polygyny occurs more often in autocracies than in nonautocratic societies. There is also a connection between polygyny and greater sexual restrictiveness, especially against women. The anthropologist, Roy D'Andrade, comments that "both polygyny and autocratic states create or rely on unequal distributions of authority and deference. . . ." [15] They therefore tend to discourage intimacy and equality between the sexes, and to foster sexual restrictiveness.

The connection between autocratic power and the subjection of women is sometimes indirect. One recent study of twenty-seven primitive societies predicted and found a relationship between the extent of wealth transfer accompanying marriage and the severity of sexual restrictiveness after betrothal as compared to before betrothal. [16] Where wealth transfer accompanying marriage is minimal, sexual restrictiveness on the betrothed is minimal. Wealth tends to be associated with autocratic power. Women's value to primitive cultures is reflected in wealth exchanges in marriage, just as it is among our own bourgeoisie, and with equal sexual restrictiveness imposed on the young, especially women.

In short, the inferiority of women is a result of a (male-dominated) exploitative power structure. This is shakily built on a foundation of human affectionateness. The emotional contradictions which are internalized, particularly by men, taken together with their less certain gender identity, create a greater *need* in men to be powerful and to depreciate women. But it is men's real power which somehow turns their culture-myth into reality.

How did exploitativeness arise, and why is it that where it exists, men are the exploiters? These are the questions we will pursue in Chapter 8, after looking more closely at sex differences in both sociability and intellectual functioning in our own civilized society.

References

1. R. D'Andrade, "Sex Differences and Cultural Institutions," ed. E. Maccoby, *The Development of Sex Differences* (Stanford, Calif.: Stanford University Press, 1966).

2. H. Barry, I. Child and M. Bacon, "Relation of Child Training to Subsistence Economy," *American Anthropologist* 61 (1959), 51-63.

3. H. Barry, M. Bacon and I. Child, "A Cross-cultural Study of Some Differences in Socialization," *Journal of Abnormal and Social Psychology* 55 (1957), 327-333.

4. Nancy Chodorow, "Being and Doing: A Cross-cultural Examination of the Socialization of Males and Females," eds. V. Gornick and B. Moran, *Women in Sexist Society* (New York: New American Library, 1972), pp. 259-291.

5. R. D'Andrade, op. cit.

6. R. D'Andrade, op. cit.

7. Margaret Mead, *Male and Female* (New York: Morrow, 1949).

8. R. D'Andrade, op. cit., p. 181.

9. K. Horney, "The Dread of Women," *International Journal of Psychoanalysis* 13 (1932).

10. R. Burton and J. Whiting, "The Absent Father and Cross-sex Identity," *Merrill-Palmer Quarterly* 7 (1961), 85-95, 90.

11. B. Bettelheim, *Symbolic Wounds: Puberty Rites and the Envious Male* (Glencoe, Ill.: The Free Press, 1954).

12. B. Whiting, cited by Nancy Chodorow, op. cit., p. 280.

13. P. Slater and D. Slater, "Maternal Ambivalence and Narcissism: A Cross-cultural Study," *Merrill-Palmer Quarterly* 11 (1965), 241-259.

14. W. Stephens, *The Family in Cross-cultural Perspective* (New York: Holt, Rinehart, and Winston, 1963).

15. R. D'Andrade, op. cit., p. 188.

16. P. Rosenblatt, S. Fugite and K. McDowell, "Wealth Transfer and Restrictions on Sexual Relations During Betrothal," *Ethnology* 8 (1969), 319-328.

CHAPTER 6

What Are Little Girls Made Of?

Have women become exploiters less often than men because it is harder to harden their hearts? Are men *inherently* more aggressive than women? It is worth noticing that there is a subtle difference in these two ways of asking the question. The second way actually reflects male-dominated thinking. Asking the question the first way assumes that women have more of something than men—something like affectionateness. The idea makes us a bit uncomfortable not only because it suggests that women have something more of a good thing than men, but because affectionateness or love have not figured in scientific hardheaded thinking. As the editors of *The Competent Infant,* a recent compendium of research on infants, write, "love" has finally become "an acceptable variable in the experimental laboratory." [1] Love has to be taken into account in dealing with infants, but even there it goes by other names, such as "sociability," or "person-orientation." In some quarters, the idea that human beings of both sexes are social and loving creatures is still considered a somewhat sentimental thought.

When the question is put the second way, men have something more than women, and that something—aggression—is, if not admirable, supposedly indispensable to human survival. This second way of putting the question is also more familiar because it assumes that the whole human species has innate aggressiveness, and that society's function is to curb it. That the history of human civilization is a dismal story of failure to curb men's aggressiveness becomes a tribute to the strength of the aggressive component in the whole species' makeup.

But what about aggression? Is it not also a genetically based characteristic of the species, inherited along with so much else from our primate ancestors? Is it not inherited along with affectionateness? The answer is in much dispute. Aggressiveness has less of an adaptive function in the *cultural* nature of humanity than affectionateness. There may be vestigial remnants of our primate ancestry, especially in men, but the notion that the human species is a "naked ape" insults both people and primates.[2]

It is, in fact, precisely the careful study of primates in the wild which brings evidence that they are not nearly such aggressive creatures as has been described from our knowledge of them in captivity. Even baboons, models for the "naked ape" idea, are much less aggressive in the wild than in zoos.[3] In fact, among chimpanzees, the context which accounts for most aggression is actually just rough-and-tumble play with peers.[4]

As for the development of human aggressiveness, although much has been written about it, very little is actually known. Almost as little, in fact, as is known about human affectionateness. According to a recent review, we are ignorant about some of the most fundamental questions of the course of aggression in human beings.[5]

What is known supports the view that the earliest instigator of aggression in very young infants is physical discomfort and the need for attention. Human aggression starts with the need to restore mother's lost ministrations. During the second and third year of life, infants grow angry over "habit training." They struggle with their mothers over the need for her approval versus their own need to enjoy the workings of their bodies. They also fight over possessions—a relatively advanced symbolic substitute for affection.[6] Most important of all, as children grow up, their reasons for aggressive behavior change. Older children grow angry at insults; their aggression is more often person-oriented and retaliatory. It is "hostile," rather than "instrumental." This is another way of saying that children of both sexes stop getting angry over losing a toy and become hostile when they need to retrieve the dignity of the self—by the mysterious means of humiliating someone else.

A very recent careful study of aggression among American school children, boys and girls from four to seven years of age, showed that older children (both sexes) have fewer episodes of aggressive behavior than younger ones. And this decline in aggression is accounted for mostly by the decline in "instrumental" aggression, that is, aggression aimed at getting back some lost possession. Hostile aggression increases, however.[7] Self-esteem becomes the major reason for older children growing hostile, and self-esteem, as we shall see in Chapter 13, is a "transformation" of affectionate experience.

As all other studies have shown (as as we shall see in Chapter 14), in this study boys were much more aggressive overall than girls. And this difference was mainly due to the boys being more hostile. Even more important, analyses of the nature of the aggressive outbursts showed no significant difference between the sexes in most of the antecedents, that is, the immediate stimuli for aggressions. There is thus no evidence from this study that boys are "wired" differently from girls with respect to hostile and instrumental aggressions. Boys are more hostile than girls because there are more cultural pressures operating against their affectionateness. Boys' greater hostility than girls' is a harbinger of their participation in an exploitative world, which treats people as if they were things.

In this chapter, I am going to begin with the assumption that affectionateness rather than aggression is primary in human nature, and with the related assumption that women may have something of an advantage over men in this primary human characteristic. I am making this choice because human cultural nature as it forms in infancy is grounded in affectionateness. Aggression, in contrast, occurs as a result of lapses in the infant-caretaker relationship. The assumption that aggression is secondary is not incompatible with the hypothesis that it is under genetic control. There could be a built-in system by which the failure of the affectional system activates aggression. For example, infants' crying is a given, activated in protest against discomfort.

If cultural forces are such that the affectionateness on which culture rests is permitted to flower, aggression loses its usefulness and declines as the individual grows older. For example, seven-year-old schoolchildren of both sexes in America have fewer periods of aggression than four-year-olds. If cultural forces, however, suppress affectionateness, then aggression develops in both sexes, but in men more than women, because men are not childbearers.

Foraging, fighting, and dominating are undoubtedly *primate male* activities more often than *primate female* activities. If it should turn out that human males still have genes which fit them for primate life, these genes fit them the less for living in a cultural order. If women still have genes inherited from primate ancestors which fit them for affectionateness, these genes are still appropriate to a cultural order, even to an exploitative society. At least one-half of the species is constructed so that the species should survive. It thus seems reasonable to suppose that affectionateness is primary and aggression secondary in human life, although both may be under genetic control.

But perhaps the best reason to assume that both sexes are primarily affectionate creatures is to watch the developing behavior of infants. During the past two decades there has been a tremendous burgeoning of research on infancy and on the mother-infant interaction. Investigators have inquired into the process by which affectionate bonds are formed. They have carefully plotted, for example, the factors behind the development of the infant's first smile. The evidence goes under several different rubrics: Sometimes affectionate attachment is called "sociability"; sometimes "person-orientation"; sometimes just attachment or social behavior. And within this fast-growing body of evidence there are indications not only that boy and girl infants are different, but that girls have some kind of slight edge over boys in the development of affectionate attachments.

Before turning to affectionate behavior, however, let us briefly review some evidence about genetically determined physical differences between boy and girl infants. Some of these differences in physical development have implications for sex differences in social behavior.

At birth, girl infants are shorter and lighter than boy infants.[8] While these differences in size and weight disappear during the growing-up years, by adulthood they are back. In our area of the world, adult men are five to six inches taller, and they are heavier and stronger than women.[9]

Differences in size and weight between boy and girl infants do not nearly foreshadow the differences in body shape and contour which will characterize men and women after puberty. Nevertheless, the secondary sex characteristics, such as broad shoulders and narrow hips in men versus narrow shoulders and broad hips for women, are under genetic control, as are the sex differences in height, weight, and muscular strength.[10]

These differences between the sexes in height, weight, strength, and body contours are always comparative, not absolute differences. Average differences vary between populations in different parts of the world. Thus, according to one review, the average difference in height between males and females is less than two inches for the Klamath, but six inches for the Nootka North American Indians, while it is eight inches for the Shilluk, an African Negro group in Eastern Sudan.[11] So, also, the secondary sex characteristics are different only comparatively, in groups of males and females, and not in any single comparison between men and women. Thus, for example, the narrowest-shouldered woman in California might have wider shoulders than the average Balinese male. Nevertheless, height, weight, strength and secondary sex characteristics are under genetic control, even though experiential and environmental factors also affect them.

The greater size and strength of the male body obviously fits it better than females' bodies for physical activities requiring muscular strength and size. This may be one reason why in most all known cultures which have warfare, males rather than females are the warriors. The relation between the wide-hipped body shape of woman and her reproductive function is self-evident.

As measured by the rate of ossification of their bones, girl infants at birth are developmentally more advanced than boys, and their rate of physical maturation also seems to be faster. Thus, according to a careful survey,[12] girls begin to walk and talk earlier than boys. Girls' developmental advantage may be a cause *or* an effect of their earlier attachment to their mothers. We'll come back to this point in a little while.

Girls also reach puberty earlier and reach their adult height sooner. It is possible to speculate that the faster pace of women's development has something to do with their finite reproductive period, as compared with men's fertility lasting their lifetime.[13]

Male infants from the moment of conception are more vulnerable to stress, diseases, and unfavorable environmental influences than female infants.[14] Twice as many men die of suicide and accidents.[15] Males are also more prone to sex-linked defects,[16] such as color-blindness and hemophilia.

Many more males are lost between conception and birth than females. Although the birth rate shows little difference between the sexes, the prenatal death rate for male infants is greater than that of female infants.[17] During the first year of life, 32.7 percent more boy infants than girl infants in the United States die of all causes.[18] Throughout life as well, all major diseases hit more males than females. Women are prone more often only to diabetes and stroke.[19] In connection with the greater frequency of stroke in women, it may be noted, in passing, that an index of autonomic stability has been found to be under genetic control.[20] This finding, taken together with the finding that the functioning of women's autonomic nervous system is more labile than men's, suggests that women's apparently readier access to their feelings may have some genetic base. Women's greater proneness to blushing, which we'll talk about in Chapter 13 may also have a genetic component.

Geneticists speculate that the female's biological advantage in surviving from conception onward may be a result of her having two X chromosomes instead of one, so that a bad gene on one X chromosome may have a chance of being suppressed by the second X.[21] The greater vulnerability of males to disease and genetic defect does make it seem as if the males of the species were more expendable, as the zoologist, Berrill, has suggested. Men's direct participation in an exploitative society also surely places them at higher risk during adulthood than women.[22]

There are also clearly established sex differences in sensory capacities at birth. Girls have greater sensitivity to touch, taste, and pain.[23] This greater sensitivity may extend to sound and light as well, although the evidence here is still controversial. The most recent findings have been that when refined electroencephalograph recordings are compared, newborn girls' brain waves occur sooner to light and sound than do boys. The sex difference in photic sensitivity, as measured by shorter latency on the EEG, was observed in Caucasian, Oriental, and black infants.[24]

It has been suggested that newborn girls are more sensitive than boys because they are developmentally more advanced. But this explanation grows less impressive when we realize that females retain their greater sensitivity into adulthood, particularly in the touch, auditory, and pain modalities.[25] So a given seems to be at work in the newborn girl which could permit women to become more sensitive than men, as befits their bio-cultural role as caretaker-persons.

There are two main kinds of studies of infant affectionate behavior. One group of researchers, inspired by John Bowlby, the English psychoanalyst, have studied the affectionate relationship between mothers and their infants in very great detail.[26] Another kind of study observes infants' reactions to a great variety of situations which the investigators assume reflect the state of the infant's psyche.

Many ingenious methods have been developed for "catching" the infant's psychic state. Smiling and crying are, of course, very direct indicators of happiness or its opposite. One investigator[27] has used babbling as an indicator of the infant's positive response and has found that girl infants babble more than boys in response to the human face. Anticipating our story a bit, girls' babbling to the human face more than boys' has also been related to girls' earlier development of language skills.

The length of time an infant spends looking at an object has been used as an indicator of the infant's positive interest or attention.[28] The idea is that the longer the time spent, the more the infant is interested.

The infant's heartbeat has also been used as an indicator of interest on the assumption that this indicator works the same way among infants as among adults.[29] (When an adult at first confronts novelty, heartbeat increases in rate. When an adult is really absorbed in something, his or her heartbeat slows down.)

The question has been asked, for example, whether infants are more interested in faces than in geometric forms, with the implication that greater interest in faces reflects more interest in people, while greater interest in visual forms reflects greater interest in things. There is evidence, in fact, that girl infants show greater attentiveness to and more rapid habituation to human faces than do boy infants. In one study, three-month-old girl infants looked at photographs of faces longer than at schemata or line drawings of normal or distorted faces.[30] Boys of the same age failed to discriminate between the photos of face and line drawings. This finding, of a difference in perceptual discrimination in favor of girls, was held at twenty-four, thirty-six, and fifty-seven weeks of age. Thus, this study suggests that girl infants are more interested in human faces, while boy infants are more interested in things.

There is also other evidence that six-month-old girls are more interested in faces than in geometrical forms, while six-month-old boys are more interested in geometrical forms than faces.[31] As we just saw, six-month-old girls also babble more in response to the human face than do boys. As we shall see in Chapter 7, men are pushed by cultural expectation into an interest in things, and into attitudes which value things above people. Women are restricted to their interest in people.

The results of the two kinds of studies—of mothers interacting with their infants and of infants' responses to a variety of stimuli—all suggest that, as one investigator puts it, infants, of both sexes, are "social by biological origin." [32] The results also suggest that girl infants have something more of sociability than do boys. Thus, I am translating freely from scientific jargon to say that human beings of both sexes are affectionate by nature, with women having a slight edge over men in this respect.

Let's look first at the studies of mother-infant interaction. These studies have not only demonstrated that affectionateness is a force inherent in human development, but they have also shown important differences between infant boys and girls. Infant girls are attached earlier to their mothers than are boys [33]; they also take separation harder than boys.[34] Make no mistake about it, both sexes are affectionate creatures and suffer from the loss of people to whom they are attached. It's just that the affectional system is a bit stronger for girls.

Some feminist thinkers deprecate the results of the mother-infant interaction studies as tending to keep women in subjection by emphasizing their biological role as mothers. Dismissing the information contained in these studies is a mistake something like the mistake of equating genetics and sexism. Of course, the relationship between a mother and infant is embedded in a cultural order and subject to cultural influences. But this does not mean that the affectionate relationship between mothers and their infants has no biological use. Nor does it mean that women should deny their biological heritage because it has been perverted by an exploitative society.

Bowlby postulates a biologically given "system of attachment" between mother and infant, paralleling the "affectional system" which the Harlows demonstrated for primates.[35] It should be emphasized that a biologically given system is not an automatic unfolding of a preordained series of events, but one which involves an interaction between genetic factors and life experiences. Infant-mother attachment behavior follows a similar and predictable pattern. Attachment is not a single response to a single stimulus but a sequence of behaviors—a system which runs a particular course. And it is a system which contributes to the preservation of the species.

Bowlby originally suggested that there are five infant behaviors which are "releasers" of maternal caretaking responses. (Clearly these infant behaviors can also release maternal caretaking behavior in men as well.) Crying, smiling, following, clinging, and sucking are five things infants do which make their mothers tend them. Added to these five "releasers" another researcher has proposed a sixth: eye-to-eye contact.[36]

Bowlby also suggests that infants' exploratory behavior is another biologically given system of interaction between the infant and the environment. But this system comes into operation later than attachment, after the infant has some mobility at his or her command. Novelty in the environment starts the infant's exploratory system going. Another factor stimulating the infant's interest in its environment is its mother's interest in other things besides her baby and her encouragement of the infant's exploratory behavior. There is a relationship between mother's affection for her infant and her encouragement of infant exploration away from her. When mother is a "secure base," the infant is freer to explore around himself or herself. As one researcher, Mary Ainsworth, puts it, infants develop attachment and exploration best when they and their mothers have experienced "mutual delight" in each other's company.[37]

It is amusing and instructive to consider how difficult it is for scientists to try to conceptualize the attachment between infants and their mothers. Bowlby summarized four outstanding theories before his own of how babies become attached.[38] Reviewing these four theories shows us how easily concepts from an exploitative society invade explanations of human affection.

The most widespread theory, which Freud shared with many other thinkers, is that infants learn to love their mothers because their mothers feed them. This is the "cupboard love" theory of human nature, and it is just the kind of view one would expect people (including scientists) to have in a world dominated by the marketplace. Of course, if mothers did not feed their babies and no one else did, the babies would die. But it is also clear to any observer of infants and their mothers that babies do not love a mechanical feeder and baby-tender—that something else is involved besides a quid pro quo. A second theory, which Bowlby calls the "primary object-sucking" theory, is that infants have a built-in propensity to seek the breast. The infant learns that there is a mother behind the breast and becomes attached to her along with it. A third theory, called the "primary object-clinging theory," is that there is a built-in tendency in infants to touch and cling to a human being. Infants learn to love the human being whom they have become accustomed to touching. As we can see, these latter two theories are quite mechanical explanations of infants' affectionate behavior. Furthermore, studies have shown that thalidomide babies, born blind and deaf and without arms with which to touch their mothers, still smile at their mothers, like normal infants.[39] Still a fourth view, which some neo-Freudians, most notably Rank, espoused, is that infants resent being ejected from the womb—the "birth trauma"—and therefore they have a built-in tendency to try to get back into it. This is the kind of depressed view of infants' natures and attitudes toward the world which might be expected from people living in times of continuous warfare. One of the most interesting aspects of these theories of how infants come to love their mothers is that they imply that babies are naturally aggressive—out to *get* something—and they picture mothers as mechanical sources of supply.

Bowlby's own theory of infant-mother attachment is that mother and infant are in something like an "ecological affection system" which involves mutual advantage and serves to nurture the young. The idea that the attachment is mutual and both parties are involved in a cooperative system is the kind of thinking which does not come readily into marketplace calculations. Mutually affectionate feelings of joy and security accompany the attachment between mother and child. Sorrowful and angry feelings accompany separation and detachment. These feelings are biologically given. There are plenty of cultural forces which become entwined in the system; some foster affectionateness, while others destroy it and foster aggression. Affectionateness, however, is intrinsic in human nature of both sexes, although mothers have something more of it than is "given" to fathers. This does not mean that fathers do not get involved in an attachment system with their infants. But they may have to work a bit harder at it, on the average, in order to overcome mother's natural advantages.

On the infant's side, researchers have come to realize that infants, although physically helpless, are socially powerful. As one researcher puts it, infants are made to sense people.[40] Long before they can approach people, even within the first month, they look at people and pay them interested attention. Their faces brighten when people appear. In fact, they pay more attention to people than they do to things.[41] In the second month of their lives, infants follow people with their eyes and in the third month, infants stop crying when people appear and they smile. By that time they have their caretakers thoroughly hooked!

Smiling, as Darwin observed, is a uniquely human response; primates do not have it.[42] Darwin, correctly anticipating Bowlby's findings, considered smiling an innate social response, whose adaptive function is to bring joy to the caretaker, thus insuring the infant's care and species survival. In his own observations of infants, Darwin observed that the first smile at forty-five days, again anticipating present-day findings. Let's pause, for a moment, for a brief digression into the history of research on infants' smiling. It illustrates how much neglect there has been of the scientific study of affectionate behavior.

In 1932, Kaila, a Gestalt psychologist, explored the properties of the human face in order to determine more particularly how it elicits smiling in infants.[43] He used two-dimensional cardboard models, one resembling a human face and one with a bottom half; one with two large light eyes and one with two distinct dark eyes. He also used his own face at various angles. Kaila established that the eyes are the critical part of the human face in eliciting the infant's smile. A visual gestalt consisting of two eyes and a forehead *"en face"* is a key stimulus for the infant's smile. A face in profile, or with one eye covered, does not elicit smiling—in fact such a "face" could make an already existing smile disappear. Kaila assumed that the human face is the first differentiated object in an infant's life space and that its properties are apprehended as a gestalt to which the nervous system is organized to respond. Investigators who followed Kaila were able to construct a six-dotted model which was even better than an actual face in eliciting the infant's smiles: what ethologists would call a "supernormal sign stimulus."

The infant's smile occurs, moreover, even when the infant is born blind.[44] And, as we have just seen recent evidence from thalidomide babies, blind, deaf, and without arms to touch their mothers shows that they, too, smile—at about three months of age.[45] Evidence exists, also, from studies of identical and fraternal twins that the infant's smile at three months of age is under genetic control.[46]

Although there is no evidence that girl infants smile earlier in response to the human face, there is some evidence ° that newborn girls spend more time in reflex "smiles" than boys.[47] We'll come back to the newborn smile in a moment. As for the "social smile," the one that occurs at three months of age, there have been no systematic studies aimed at answering the question whether there are sex differences in its occurrence. This is an instance of the general neglect of studies of infant affectionateness. In fact, between 1932 when Kaila made his first observations and the later research on the stimuli which elicit smiling, twenty years went by. The social behavior of infants and differences between the sexes in infant social behavior have not been topics to which psychologists in great numbers have attended.

There is, however, some unexpected recent evidence that at two or three days of age, girl infants have more periodic bursts of smiling than boy infants. Now, after this digression about smiling, let's go back to a more detailed examination of the work on mother-infant interaction.

Let's consider, first, the problems which arise about how to

___

° This study was cited in Maccoby and Jacklin as finding no sex differences.[48]

measure or at least assess in an objective way the attachment of mothers and their infants to each other. On the mothers' side, the problems are not so severe. Mothers can talk about their feelings, and they can express them in ways another adult can understand. Mothers' behavior can also be studied for feelings that are not spoken but are inferred. Movies can be made of the mothers talking to, patting, cuddling, feeding, and holding their infants. One ingenious researcher measures the frequency with which mothers and infants look at each other, eye-to-eye.[49] The idea is that eye-to-eye contact is a nonverbal form of expressing closeness.

On the infants' side, attachment is both easier and harder to assess because infants cannot talk. Except when they are crying or smiling, their feelings and attitudes have to be inferred. When they are very tiny, the problem of assessment seems straightforward. Smiling when mother appears and crying when she is absent are indicators of infants' attachment. When infants are older, however, after they can walk, their crying on separation from their mothers may be an indication, not of attachment so much as, paradoxically, of the lack of it. Two-year-olds who are well-attached to their mothers have a way of using her as a secure base from which they are pleased to go exploring.[50] Older children's attachment can be assessed by observing not only gladness at mothers' presence, but also by their capacity to tolerate separation from her calmly and their relative freedom to explore the world. Ambivalence is, of course, also expected.

The researchers who have worked with infants and their mothers have labored hard and successfully to develop satisfactory ways of measuring not only gross emotional reactions, but subtler variations in mothers' and infants' interaction. They have been able to develop techniques of observation which capture the ongoing emotional relationship in units of measurement which can be checked and rechecked by others.

The following is an example of the series of episodes which constitute a laboratory test of mother-infant attachment and separation behavior.

During each of these episodes, trained observers record mothers' and babies' behavior. In Episode 1, there is recorded how mother, baby, and exprimenter functioned when the experiment began. In Episode 2, baby roams about with mother present. In

Table 1
SUMMARY OF STRANGE-SITUATION PROCEDURE°
°(Adapted from Ainsworth and Wittig.)

Episodes	Participants	Duration	Behavior Highlighted by Episode
1	Mother, baby, experimenter	30 sec. approx.	(Introductory)
2	Mother, baby	3 min.	Exploration of strange environment with mother present
3	Stranger, mother, baby	3 min.	Response to stranger with mother present
4	Stranger, baby	3 min.°	Response to separation with stranger present
5	Mother, baby	Variable	Response to reunion with the mother
6	Baby	3 min.°	Response to separation when left alone
7	Stranger, baby	3 min.°	Response to continuing separation, and to stranger after being left alone
8	Mother, baby	Variable	Response to second reunion with mother

°Episode was curtailed if the baby was highly distressed.

Episode 3, a stranger is introduced, while mother is still present. In Episode 4, there is a critical episode, the stranger remains and the mother leaves. Episode 5 records the response of the mother and baby to their reunion. Episodes 6, 7, and 8 provide additional observations on infants' reactions to separation and the introduction of strangers.

It is worth noting, in passing, that babies growing up in an extended family and where the extension results in an increase in the possibilities of affectionate exchange, are not at all damaged in their attachments. One of the reasons why the work on mothers and their infants has been greeted with suspicion by feminists is the notion that it suggests mothers should be tied to their infants, as their *only* caretakers. The real message in this work is that it recommends affectionate infant care. Just as this can be provided in an extended village family, so it can also be provided in good child-care centers, as well as by mothers and fathers.

Do girl infants show signs of greater affectionate attachment to their mothers than boy infants? The answer to this question is, in my opinion, yes, but with some reservations arising from the difficulties in interpreting the meaning of infant behavior. In particular, there is considerable difficulty in interpreting an infant's distress upon separation from its mother. As indicated earlier, distress on separation may not only mean attachment, but also the lack of it, or more accurately, ambivalent feelings. The other difficulty in interpretation of the evidence about sex differences in infant attachment arises from the fact that there are two signs of it which have been used. One is "stranger anxiety," which occurs earlier in the infant's life; the other is "separation anxiety," which occurs after the infant is about one year old.

To state the findings crudely for the moment, there is good evidence that girl infants show "stranger anxiety" considerably earlier than boy infants.[51] Girls show the first signs of "stranger anxiety" when they are an average of 6.7 months old. Boys from a comparable group of middle-class families show it at 9.1 months of age. When it comes to separation anxiety, however, one study showed that boys had more of it than girls,[52] while another study showed that girl infants had more separation anxiety than boys.[53] (The reader will have noticed that we are talking about more, that is, more intense separation anxiety, while we have been talking so far only about *earlier* stranger anxiety in girls than in boys.)

There are two main reasons for my concluding that, although the evidence about separation anxiety is equivocal, the earlier appearance of "stranger anxiety" in girls does mean that they become more deeply attached to their mothers than boys. Among the most compelling reasons is the evidence that the attachment between mothers and their girl infants develops more smoothly than the attachment between mothers and their boys. The other set of reasons is evidence that even at two to three days of age, girl infants show more signs of the precursors of affectionate attachment than do boys.

But before coming to this evidence about how mothers interact differently with their boys than with their girls, and to the evidence about what tiny infants of both sexes bring with them to the interaction, let's look at the difficulties in assessing the signs of infant attachment as well as the difficulties in interpreting both stranger anxiety and separation anxiety.

"Stranger anxiety" occurs earlier than separation anxiety. "Stranger anxiety" is at its peak in infants of both sexes between seven and nine months of age. Its indications are a "sobering, turning away, visual avoidance, freezing fussing and crying." [54] Separation anxiety, in contrast, appears later in life in both sexes. It is characterized by "reduced activity in mother's absence, extremes of affect, e.g., overwhelming sadness or furious anger, as well as the range from mild, fussy protests to extremely hard crying." Separation anxiety peaks at thirteen to eighteen months.[55]

The evidence that girl infants showed "stranger anxiety" earlier than boy infants can be interpreted to mean that they are afraid of novelty rather than more attached to their mothers. By the same token, it can be said that boy infants are only expressing their greater attraction to novelty when they show no stranger anxiety at a time when girls already have it. In other words, it is possible to suppose that fear of strangers has a cognitive component as well as an emotional one. For example, in one study, in which four-month-old infants were shown normal or distorted faces (a follow-up of Kaila's early work), the infants looked longest at those clay masks which were most like a normal face.[56] The broken-up face, while actually containing all the elements of a face, presented these elements in disorder. (The disorder is disagreeable even to adults.) Infants' fear of strangers might be a reaction to some intrinsically disagreeable properties of the strange face rather than an emotional reaction signifying attachment to mother.

The reader will observe that the line between the cognitive and the emotional component in fear of strangers is very thin. Infants turn away from distorted faces and look longer at "normal" ones because, as indicated earlier, they are made to sense people as part of an emotional attachment to them. There is some evidence (although slight) that boy infants respond more favorably to novelty than girl infants,[57] but it hardly seems likely that this proclivity on the part of boys is sufficient to explain a two-month difference in the first appearance of "stranger anxiety."

When it comes to separation anxiety, the contradictory evidence from the two different studies cannot at the moment be reconciled. The study, which showed that girls had more separation anxiety, was better controlled.[58] It involved setting up a "barrier" between the infant and its mother. Little girls cried more and motioned for help to their mothers more often. Little boys cried less and made more active attempts to get around the barrier without mother's help. It should be noted, in passing, that the mothers of these infants, observed in relation to them at six months of age, also had talked more to their girl infants (and had breast-fed them more). One other detail of this study is of interest. The girls' toy preference, although not overall different from boys', showed one difference which was significant: Girls chose the toys which had cat and dog faces on them more often than boys.

Separation anxiety is an indicator of attachment which occurs so much later than stranger anxiety that it cannot be taken as an indicator of attachment only. By the time an infant is a year old, distress on separation from mother must be considered an indicator of ambivalence as well as attachment. Lack of distress on separation can similarly have the same ambivalent meaning. It is hard for scientists, like other people, to grow accustomed to the fact that human affectionateness involves itself in very contradictory indicators.

When we look at mothers and their infants in our own society, we find that being a boy infant or a girl infant makes a very considerable difference in the mother-infant interaction. Whether the important factor is having a same-sex or opposite-sex caretaker, or in something mothers do differently to their girls and boys, or in something about being a boy infant or a girl, or some combination of all of these, the picture of mothers and their infants is very different for the two sexes.

One group of studies concerned itself particularly with eye-to-eye contact as an indicator of the mother-infant interaction. In one study,[59] fifty-four mothers and their first babies were studied, beginning with the mother's attitude toward the coming baby during the last trimester of her pregnancy. Restricting the study to mothers having their first babies was a precaution against mixing the behavior of experienced mothers with that of inexperienced mothers. Mother's prior enthusiasm for her coming baby was assessed, as well as the frequency of eye-to-eye contact between mother and infant after the baby arrived. The baby's preference for faces was also assessed. At 3.3 months of age, and for girl infants *only*, there was an interrelationship between mother's previous enthusiasm for the baby, the extent to which she and the baby made eye-to-eye contact, and the infant's preference for faces. Those mothers who had been looking forward more to having their babies were those who had more dyadic gazing (mother and baby looked at each other more), and their infants had more preference for faces. But this package of relationships held only for girl infants, not for boys. That there should have been an early pattern of interaction between maternal attitude and infant preference for faces among girls, not boys, suggests that person orientation is a stronger (not necessarily innate) factor for girls than it is for boys. After three months of age, mother's previous enthusiasm for the baby was no longer predictive of her relationship with the baby for either girls or boys.

In this same study, ratings were also made of the extent of maternal concern for the baby's well-being when the infant was three months old. These ratings were significantly related to dyadic gazing between mothers and their sons, but not at all predictive for daughters. Mothers who were concerned about their sons looked at them more; there was no such relationship between maternal concern and dyadic gazing for girls. This finding suggests that the early relationship between mothers and daughters is quite different from their relationship with their sons, and in a subtle way. By three months of age, mother's looking at her son was connected with "concern," that is, with ambivalence toward boys, while it has no such connection for girls. This finding fits the finding to which we shall return, that mother's relationship to her daughters is smoother than to her sons, if only because mother and daughter are the same sex. Another reason for this smoothness might be that little girls are by this time more organized to respond to people than are little boys.

In another study by the same group of investigators twenty male and twenty-five female infants, all first-born, were studied with respect to their approach-avoidance toward strangers.[60] Mother's attitude toward the baby during the last part of pregnancy was assessed, eye-to-eye contact at three months of age, and approach-avoidance toward stranger at eight and 9.6 months of age. For male infants, there was a positive relationship between extent to which mother and infant had looked at each other at three months of age and extent to which he tolerated a stranger (a male). For girls, in contrast, no such correlations were found. These results suggest that mother's attitude toward her little boy is a more powerful determinant of his social behavior than it is for little girls—whose social behavior is more firmly grounded to begin with, either genetically, or as a result of smoother interaction with mothers, or both.

It was this study which yielded the finding that girls show stranger anxiety significantly earlier than boys. The fact that middle-class American girl infants and Uganda infants of both sexes show earlier fear of strangers suggests that infants who are close to their mothers become earlier attached to her than infants who are kept distant. It will be remembered that Uganda infants (of both sexes) are kept literally very close to their mothers (or to a ubiquitous substitute). They show stranger anxiety earlier than Scottish or American infants. And among American infants, those who are closer to their mothers—the girls—also show earlier stranger anxiety than boys.

Are boy infants kept more distant from their mothers than girl infants in the United States? In fact, one very careful observation [61] of middle-class American mothers and their first babies showed significant differences in the handling of the two sexes at three weeks and again at three months of age. Mothers held their three-week-old boy infants farther away from their own bodies. They more often held a boy baby in a sitting or standing posture, so that the baby was required to support more of his own weight. The observer labels this "stressing the baby's musculature." Mothers stimulated and aroused their boy infants more, and they attended to them more than their girl infants. In other words, mothers were less relaxed with their boy babies than with their girls. In sharp contrast, the only thing mothers did more of with their girls was to imitate them. One does not need to be a psychoanalyst to interpret these findings as meaning that mothers were less easy with their infants of the male sex and expressing their sense of sameness with their girls by imitating them more.

By the time these same infants were three months old, an important difference had emerged in their interaction with their mothers. The male infants, even at three weeks of age, had cried more, fussed more, and been more irritable than the girls. Girl infants slept more and cried less than the boys. As the observer put it, there was "more happening with male infants." [62] For males, who were more irritable to begin with, the correlation between the total time they cried and the amount of attention they got from their mothers was negative: The more the infants cried, the less their mothers attended them. For the girl infants, in contrast, the relationship between the amount of crying and the amount of attention they got was positive. Trouble pacifying their little boy babies had led their mothers to attend them less; girls being easier to pacify led their mothers to mother them more. As the observer points out, the evidence on this point joins a number of other studies which show that male infants are more subject than females to "inconsolable states." The female organism "responds better to maternal intervention." [63] There is a clear picture, in other words, of what folk wisdom has known for a long time— there is a smoother interaction between mothers and their little girls than between mothers and their little boys.

Not only do American middle-class mothers get along better with their girl infants than with their boys, but they get along better with girl infants who are affectionate to begin with.[64] Some years ago, infant watchers found it very easy to confirm what mothers have known for centuries—babies differ in their response to cuddling. Once again it is amusing, in passing, to see how scientists have to struggle to incorporate the phenomena of affectionateness into their calculations. Infant cuddliness was established in a variety of self-evident ways. As one mother put it, a non-cuddler is "restless when you cuddle him. A cuddler cuddles you back." [65] Clearly, cuddliness is not something just within the infant, but it is the result of an interaction. Maybe some non-cuddly infants would have become cuddlers if cuddling had been offered them earlier than they got it. Boy infants, interestingly enough, are only a little less often cuddly than girl infants.[66]

One dissertation has the following findings on how mothers interacted with cuddly and non-cuddly infants of both sexes.[67] Mothers held, patted, and talked most of their cuddly girl infants. Female non-cuddlers got the least of these ministrations, even less than male non-cuddlers. Mothers not only imitate their girl infants more than their boys, as we have just seen, but they cuddle most those girls who cuddle back. The affectionate relationships to mothers paid off for cuddly girl infants. By the end of the first year, they were ahead in their general intellectual development.

But perhaps the most fascinating evidence that little girls are organized to respond positively to people (more than little boys) has developed in the last few years, in findings that were not expected by researchers who were not even looking for sex differences. One researcher was curious about whether or not infants can hear the difference between the cry of another infant and a non-human sound.[68] It has been common lore in infant nurseries that when one infant cries, all the others follow suit. The question is: Are the infants responding to a noise, or "in sympathy" somehow with another infant? Nearly one hundred newborns were studied—no infant more than seventy-two hours old. Each infant was studied in a special comfortable crib, but with the surroundings soundproofed, so that only the noises introduced by the experimenter would be heard. The sound of a newborn baby's cry was compared in its effectiveness to an artificial sound quite similar in all physical properties. The results showed without doubt that newborn infants are more responsive to the cry of another newborn than they are to an artificial sound with similar physical properties. Newborn crying in response to another newborn's crying is thus sympathetic. Furthermore, although he was not looking for sex differences, the experimenter found that girl newborns were even more responsive to the cry of another newborn baby than newborn boys!

Not only do newborn girls respond more than boys to the cries of another infant, but even two-to-three-day-old girls "smile" more than boys.[69] This finding was actually obtained in the course of observing the inherent organization of a newborn infant's functioning. Even in its very earliest encounters with the environment the infant shows rhythmical patterns of behavior which seem to be inborn. For example, one study [70] showed that the sucking behavior of infants has such an internally regulated pattern. During sleep, infants show groups of spontaneous bursts of sucking, separated by rest intervals. These patterns are relatively constant for a given infant. Infants with cleft palate suck at the same rate as normal children, while infants with brain damage show disorganization of sucking rhythms, indicating that these patterns are biologically given.

In the course of the study of the spontaneous behavior of two-to-three-day old infants during twenty-four-hour continuous observations in the nursery, not only sucking patterns, but "startles," "smiles," and "erections," were recorded from thirty-two infants. An unexpected sex difference was observed. Boy infants "startle" more in both waking and sleeping states. Female infants show more reflex smiles and bursts of regular mouthing (sucking). This two-day-old smile is, of course, *not* a social response, but it can be thought of as a forerunner.

This reflex smiling in newborn infants (which used to be thought of as "gas") now goes by the rather formidable name of the "endogenous smile." This means that it is not a response to an external stimulus, but is an expression of ongoing internal processes in the newborn. These processes we now know to be highly organized, rather than chaotic. The presumed biological function of regularly recurring smiles, sucks, and startles is the maintenance of something like "homeostatic" balance in the level of infant activation, and as an aid in the development of the nervous system.

In a follow-up study of newborn sucks, smiles, and startles, Korner [71] discovered a most interesting sex difference in what she calls "oral organization." By a detailed, carefully controlled analysis of films of infants' mouthings, Korner discerned a sex difference in the style of hand-to-mouth approach. For girls, a "mouth-dominated" pattern was more frequent. As Korner puts it, the female infant emerges as "orally more sensitized" although in no way less active or expressive than the male infant. Korner hypothesizes that the androgens which circulate in fetal life to produce maleness and are responsible for males' greater muscular strength may also suppress his responsivity and sensitivity, especially in the mouth and skin.

That newborn girls suck more than boys is a forerunner of the fact that girls suck their thumbs more often than boys and continue to do so longer in their lives than boys.[72] Thumb-sucking is, as everyone knows, an expression of longing for mother. Breast-fed babies of happily married mothers suck their thumbs *more* than babies in less happy circumstances.[73] The infant's first smile, fully developed at three months of age, is a landmark in the development of its affectionateness. That little girls suck more, smile more, and are more "orally sensitized" even at two days of age fits the picture of their having some kind of slight edge over boys in affectionateness.

That boys startle more fits with the picture of their greater irritability. That they have periods of regular erections of their penes goes somehow with the finding that mothers hold their boy babies farther away from their own bodies. It also connects with one experimenter's [74] finding that boys, not girls, have a "constitutional level of fearfulness" which follows them from infancy until they are at least eight years old. Things are more peaceful from the beginning for girls.

So the answer to our question whether women are more affectionate than men from the beginning may be yes. Girl babies bring something to the interaction with their mothers which is a forerunner of their greater sociability later on. Mothers respond to this something, so that they have a smoother and easier time of it with their girl babies. The result is a girl's earlier preference for mother and a stronger tie to her by the end of the first year.

Let's briefly recapitulate the evidence. Even at two or three days, little girls are more responsive to another infant's cry than little boys. Little girls smile more and suck more than little boys. These are precursor signs which have other expressions at six months of age: Little girls babble more upon seeing the human face. They suck their thumbs longer than boys. Mothers have an easier time of it with their girl babies, especially cuddly girls. By the time their infants are three months of age, mothers are having a harder time and give up more easily on pacifying their little boys, and an easier time pacifying their girls.

Mothers who were enthusiastic about having a baby see eye-to-eye more often with their girl infants and the girls in turn look longer at human faces. None of these relationships between maternal attitude, dyadic gazing, and preference for faces holds for boys. Little girls in general pay more attention to the human face. And by the second half of the first year, girls show earlier signs of stranger anxiety, that is, preferential attachment to their mothers. By the time they are a year old, girls give evidence of more separation anxiety.

What are the results of this difference between the sexes in the precursors of affectionateness? One important kind of result anticipates some of the story about intellectual functioning which we shall see in the next chapter. Girls have a clear advantage over boys in language development, and part of the reason may lie in girls' closer tie to their mothers.

Dorothea McCarthy, a specialist in the development of lan-

guage in children, suggested some twenty years ago that girls'
consistent advantage over boys in langauge development results
from the fact that the girl "more readily identifies with her
mother." [75] McCarthy suggested that there is an "echo quality"
in girls picking up language because they are interacting with a
same-sex caretaker. Boys, in contrast, are treated more harshly in
their families (as we shall see in Chapter 14) so that they are more
aggressive and so at a handicap in picking up a "communication"
skill. Boys also do less echoing of their fathers who are not around
to be echoed as much as mothers. McCarthy's pinpointing of
aggression as a hindrance to boys' intellectual development was
confirmed in Maccoby and Jacklin's recent comments on the
subject (as we shall see in Chapter 7).

Leaving aside the question of intellectual development, the
greater affectionateness of women has very different consequences in childhood than it does in adulthood. In areas of life
which are still relatively remote from the direct influence of an
exploitative society, one can see a picture of boys and girls as-
sorting differently but without harmful consequences. In well-run
nursery schools where the shadows of hatred and domination are
still quite distant from the benign atmosphere, observers tell us
that little girls are more nurturant and helpful than little boys.[76]
When little boys gather in nursery schools, they tend to be in
groups of three or more, and their attention is focused on some
object or activity. Little girls assort in pairs (one-to-one) and the
interaction between the two people is apparently the central
point. Such differences between the sexes arouse smiles in us. We
like the picture of an object-oriented male and a person-oriented
female. So far, no one is doing anybody else any harm.

Just one study of "person-orientation" in little boys and girls
may be taken as a model of its kind.[77] Its results, as we shall see in
Chapter 14, are repeated time and time again. Twenty boys and
twenty girls from middle-class white families were studied obser-
vationally at two years of age and repeatedly until they were four
years old. Parents were interviewed; a variety of behavior ratings,
drawings, and "spontaneous" behaviors of both parents and children were studied. It was established that parents expect their
girls to be more interested in persons than their boys. Fathers, in
particular, more than mothers, tend to differentiate the sex roles.
Girls at both two and four years of age clearly showed more

interest in other persons than did boys. Girls drew pictures of more persons and talked about more persons than did boys. This difference was significant even at two years of age. The investigator cites an interesting study in 1911 by Ballard, in England, in which 20,000 drawings made by nine-year-olds were examined. Girls drew human figures much more frequently than boys.

But when it comes to the effects of an exploitative society which spreads its gospel of domination even into the family, the picture of the greater affectionateness of women changes from its charming character. When little girls become aware of their gender—surely no later than when they are two years old—they become aware that theirs is the devalued sex. Mother, whom they are "like," who has imitated them, whose self is so intertwined with their own self, is someone to be scorned as weak and powerless. No wonder girls have trouble sustaining hatred for their mothers. No wonder they often behave as if the person they hated is themselves. They are so close to their mothers, it's hard not to get mixed up. No wonder, as we shall see in Chapter 16, women are more prone to depression than men.

Little boys, by the time they are two, have become aware that they are not like their mothers, but different from them. They have also had to work a little harder at getting her affection, just as she has had to work harder and has been a bit less successful at pacifying them. And soon they have to renounce all that as "unmanly." When they do long for their mothers, they find themselves in conflict with a paternal authority which says: "That's mine, not yours." Little boys have usually not been that close to their fathers. Little boys can contemplate father's destruction and "taking his place" without the self-searing conflict that little girls experience when they hate their mothers. But boys have to give up affectionateness in order to become *like* the powerful owner of mother, the source of supply. No wonder they often find themselves in a state where their longing and their fury fuse into sadism. No wonder, as we saw in Chapter 4, they have more trouble with their gender identity than little girls. And no wonder, as we shall see in Chapters 18 and 19, men are more prone than women to obsessional neurosis and schizophrenia.

These connections between sex differences in early infancy, and proneness to mental illness in later life can be made at the moment only in the form of an intuitive leap of understanding. At one end of the life span, in infancy, we find girls are attached to their mothers earlier and perhaps more deeply than boys. At the other end of the life span, there is evidence that bereavement in life plays a significantly greater part in proneness to psychiatric disturbance in women than in men. And women are more prone to depression than men (see Chapter 16). These observations, at two points in the life-span, fit together. They can be reflections of something genetic or "given" about women's greater affectionateness. But they also fit together because we can see that women's greater affectionateness would make them more prone to suffer loss. We see an exploitative environment which fosters and then scorns women's attachments, making them more prone to shame.

In the same way, men's proneness to obsessional neurosis and schizophrenia, illnesses which involve severe loss of emotional experiences, can be seen as fitting boy infants' lesser affectionateness and the fact that as infants they have had a somewhat harder time of it with their mothers. It also fits the slight evidence that boys are more attached to complex visual forms (to things) than to faces.° What needs to be spelled out, however, are the many steps by which an exploitative society pushes men to make things out of people, thus distorting their affectionate natures.

References

1. L. J. Stone, H. Smith and L. B. Murphy, eds. *The Competent Infant* (New York: Basic Books, 1973), p. 6.

2. David Pilbeam, *New York Times*, 3 September 1972.

3. Ibid.

4. P. Jay, ed., *Primates: Studies in Adaptation and Variability* (New York: Holt, Rinehart and Winston, 1968).

5. W. Hartup, "Aggression in Childhood," *American Psychologist* (1974), 336-341.

6. Ibid.

7. Ibid.

° Eleanor Maccoby, in her review of Bardwick's *Psychology of Women*,[78] warns that the evidence for a perceptual style in infancy is flimsy. In passing she suggests that there is more evidence for infant sex differences in sociability.

8. J. Garai and A. Scheinfeld, "Sex Differences in Mental Traits," *Genetic Psychology Monographs* 77 (1968), 169-299.

9. R. D'Andrade, "Sex Differences and Cultural Institutions," ed. E. Maccoby, *The Development of Sex Differences* (Stanford, Calif.: Stanford University Press, 1966).

10. J. Garai and A. Scheinfeld, op. cit.

11. R. D'Andrade, op. cit.

12. J. Garai and A. Scheinfeld, op. cit.

13. J. Garai and A. Scheinfeld, op. cit.

14. J. Garai and A. Scheinfeld, op. cit.

15. J. Garai and A. Scheinfeld, op. cit.

16. J. Garai and A. Scheinfeld, op. cit.

17. J. Garai and A. Scheinfeld, op. cit.

18. J. Garai and A. Scheinfeld, op. cit.

19. J. Garai and A. Scheinfeld, op. cit.

20. H. Jost and L. W. Sontag, "The Genetic Factors in Autonomic Nervous System," *Psychosomatic Medicine* 6 (1944), 308-310.

21. J. Garai and A. Scheinfeld, op. cit.

22. N. Berrill, *Sex and the Nature of Things* (New York: Dodd, Mead, 1953)9

23. J. Garai and A. Scheinfeld, op. cit.

24. G. Engel, cited by A. Korner, note 71.

25. J. Garai and A. Scheinfeld, op. cit.

26. J. Bowlby, *Attachment and Loss,* vol. 1 (New York: Basic Books, 1969).

27. J. Kagan, "Continuity in Cognitive Development During the First Year," *Merrill-Palmer Quarterly* 15 (1969), 101-119.

28. J. Kagan, "On the Meaning of Behavior: Illustrations from the Infant," *Child Development* 40 (1969), 1121-1134.

29. W. J. Meyers, "Observing and Cardiac Response of Human Infants to Visual Stimuli," *Journal of Experimental Child Psychology* 5 (1957), 16-25.

30. M. Lewis, "Infants' Responses to Facial Stimuli During the First Year of Life," *Developmental Psychology* 1 (1969), 75-86.

31. M. Lewis, J. Kagan and E. Kalafat, "Patterns of Fixation in the Young Infant," *Child Development* 37 (1966), 331-341.

32. Harriet Rheingold, "The Social and Socializing Infant," ed. D. Goslin, *Handbook of Socialization Theory and Research* (Chicago: Rand McNally, 1969).

33. K. Robson, F. Pederson and H. Moss, "Developmental Observations of Dyadic Gazing in Relation to Fear of Strangers and Social Approach Behavior," *Child Development* 40 (1969), 619-627.

34. S. Goldberg and M. Lewis, "Play Behavior in the Year Old Infant: Early Sex Differences," *Child Development* 40 (1969), 21-32.

35. H. F. Harlow, "The Heterosexual Affectional System in Monkeys," *American Psychologist* 17 (1962), 1-9.

36. K. Robson, "The Role of Eye-to-Eye Contact in Maternal-Infant Attachment," *Journal of Child Psychology and Psychiatry* 8 (1967), 13-25.

37. M. Ainsworth and B. Wittig, "Attachment and Exploratory Behavior of One-Year Olds in a Strange Situation," ed. B. M. Foss, *Determinants of Infant Behavior*, vol. 4 (London: Methuen, 1969), 111-136.

38. John Bowlby, op. cit.

39. I. Eibl-Eibesfeldt, *Love and Hate* (New York, Schocken Books, 1974).

40. Harriet Rheingold, op. cit.

41. Peter Wolff, paper read at the Edmund Weil Memorial Meeting of IPTAR, New York, June 1972.

42. C. Darwin, *The Expression of Emotions in Man and Animals* (London: John Murray, 1872).

43. E. Kaila, cited in H. R. Schaffer, *The Growth of Sociability* (London: Penguin Books, 1971), Chap. 3.

44. D. Freedman, "Smiling in Blind Infants," *Journal of Child Psychology and Psychology* 5 (1964), 171-184.

45. I. Eibl-Eibesfeldt, op. cit.

46. D. Freedman, "Hereditary Control of Early Social Behavior," ed. B. M. Foss, *Determinants of Infant Behavior*, vol. 3 (New York: Wiley, 1965), 149-159.

47. A. Korner, "Neonatal Startles, Smiles, Erections and Reflex Sucks as Related to State, Sex and Individuality," *Child Development* 40 (1969), 1039-1053.

48. E. Maccoby, and C. Jacklin, *The Psychology of Sex Differences* (Stanford, Calif.: University of Stanford Press, 1974).

49. K. Robson, op. cit.

50. M. D. S. Ainsworth, *Infancy in Uganda* (Baltimore, Md.: Johns Hopkins Press, 1967).

51. K. Robson, F. Pederson and H. Moss, op. cit.

52. K. Tennes and E. Lampl, "Stranger and Separation Anxiety," *Journal of Nervous and Mental Disease* 139 (1964), 247-254.

53. S. Goldberg and M. Lewis, op. cit.

54. K. Tennes and E. Lampl, op. cit.

55. K. Tennes and E. Lampl, op. cit.

56. J. Kagan, "Continuity in Cognitive Development During the First Year," *Merrill-Palmer Quarterly* 15 (1969), 101-119.

57. W. Meyers and G. N. Cantor, "Infant's Observing and Heart Period Responses as Related to Novelty of Visual Stimuli," *Psychonomic Science* 5 (1966), 239-240.

58. S. Goldberg and M. Lewis, op. cit.

59. H. A. Moss, and K. Robson, "Maternal Influences in Early Social-Visual Behavior," *Child Development* 39 (1968), 401-408.

60. K. Robson, F. Pederson and H. Moss, op. cit.

61. H. A. Moss "Sex, Age and State Determinants of Mother-Infant Interaction," *Merrill-Palmer Quarterly* 13 (1967), 19-36.

62. Ibid.

63. Ibid.

64. Brenda Ball, "Some Relationships Among Infant Preferences for Tactile Stimulation, Infant Developmental Level and Maternal Behaviors," *Dissertation Abstracts* 29 (1969) (12B), 4838.

65. H. Schaffer and P. Emerson, "Patterns of Response to Physical Contact in Early Human Development," *Journal of Child Psychology and Psychiatry* 5 (1964), 1-13.

66. Ibid.

67. Brenda Ball, op. cit.

68. M. Simner, "Newborn Response to the Cry of Another Infant," *Developmental Psychology* 5 (1971), 136-150.

69. A. Korner, op. cit.

70. P. Wolff, "The Causes, Controls and Organization of Behavior of the Neonate," *Psychological Issues* (1966), V, No. 17.

71. A. Korner, "Sex Differences in Newborns with Special Reference to Differences in the Organization of Oral Behavior, *Journal of Child Psychology and Psychiatry* 14 (1973), 19-29.

72. M. P. Honzik and J. P. McKee, "Sex Differences in Thumb-sucking," *Journal of Pediatrics* 61 (1962), 726-732.

73. M. J. Heinstein, "Behavioral Correlates of Breast-Bottle Under Varying Infant Relationships," *Monographs of the Society for Research in Child Development* 28 (1963).

74. Gordon Bronson, "Sex Differences in the Development of Fearfulness: A Replication," *Psychonomic Science* 17 (1969), 367-368.

75. Dorothea McCarthy, "Some Possible Explanations of Sex Differences in Language Development," *Journal of Psychology* 35 (1953), 155-160.

76. Corinne Hutt, *Males and Females* (Middlesex, England: Penguin Books, 1972).

77. E. E. Goodenough, "Interest in Person as an Aspect of Sex Differences in the Early Years," *Genetic Psychology Monographs* 55 (1957), 287-323.

78. E. Maccoby, review of Judith Bardwick's book *Psychology of Women, in Contemporary Psychology* 17 (1972), 368-372.

CHAPTER 7

Intellectual Functioning:
The Importance of Things Over People

Experiences of the self may be classified in many ways, but two dichotomies are most obvious. One is the dichotomy between experiences with other people as compared with things.° There is some evidence that even two-month-old babies respond differently to things than to people.[1] Specifically, babies continue to gaze at the place where a person (mother) has just been; under the same conditions they do not seem to miss an inanimate object.

A second dichotomy is between satisfying and frustrating experiences, both with others and things. Since in infancy the maternal behavior of the caretakers is the most powerful agency governing these satisfactions and frustrations, the infant's self first assimilates its relationship to others. These frustrations and satisfactions with others, while very powerful organizers of the self, are not, however, its only determinants. Infants are also interested in things, especially novel things, and are clearly pleased to inspect them, provided needs for food and sleep have been met. The organization of the self as it assimilates its environment involves two independent although interacting systems: the self in relation

° Since plants are phenomenally things, this distinction is better than the distinction between the self in relation to animate and inanimate objects.

90

to others and the self in relation to things. As we saw in Chapter 6, there is some slight evidence that girl infants may have an edge over boys in person-orientation, while boy infants may have a slight edge over girls in being interested in things, especially in novelty.

Let us consider, briefly, some differences in the organization of the self when it is engaged in transactions with others and with things. In the first place, the clear distinction between things and others is as important to the perception of reality as the distinction between the self and others. Schizophrenics, who are characterized by an apparent lack of emotional depth, are often bizarrely preoccupied with things. Such symptoms give us an insight into the fact that transactions with things can take place without emotional involvement, while transactions with people more often involve feelings.

In dealing with others as human beings (not as objects or things) the self necessarily engages in the vicarious experiencing of the others' feelings. Encounters with people involve an animate feedback, and the use of language of some sort in two-way communication. The transactions involved in dealing with people require a self with permeable boundaries. By contrast, when the self is engaged in grasping and changing the properties of a *thing*, the self is not ordinarily even aware of itself, except as an automatic reference point.

Things, especially novel things, have a "demand-character" which invites exploration and mastery. Although things are intrinsically interesting, they require a self which is active in approach to them. Mastery of things, involving approach and active manipulation of them, increases the experience of the self in the three-dimensional world and particularly with relation to space, in which things reside. It requires the capacity to locate the self in space and in turn accurately improves this capacity. In dealing with things, the self is often required to adopt a field-independent or analytical cognitive style.

There is, moreover, an interaction between the experiences of the self in relation to others and its experiences in relation to things. Therese Benedek, a psychoanalyst writing about the infant's adaptation to reality, suggested some years ago that the state of expectation which a three-month-old infant can display in waiting for mother to come with food is a relationship to the environment based on "confidence that the instinctual need will be gratified really and pleasurably." [2] Infants who have their "expectations" disappointed do not develop confidence. Infants without confidence develop anxiety and turn to material objects in the outer world in an attempt to control things. Moreover, they tend to mechanization of their behavior in reflex attempts to control their anxiety.

Melanie Klein has also described how an unsatisfying early relationship with the mothering person is experienced by the infant as a "bad world"; while satisfying relationships are experienced as a "good world." [3] Somewhat later in infancy, unsatisfying relationships with the caretaker have been assimilated as a "bad me"; while satisfying relationships become a "good me." This is not to suggest that mastery of things in the environment is motivated or developed only by frustrations with the mother in infancy, but rather to indicate that unsatisfying mother-infant experiences may push the self away from others and toward the mastery of things. Our exploitative society particularly emphasizes any differences which may exist between the sexes in their orientation toward persons versus things. In this respect it follows the general tendency which we saw in Chapter 5 for "high accumulation" societies to emphasize sex differences more than "low accumulation" societies.

Men, in keeping with the expectation that they will go into the world to earn their livelihood, are trained more frequently than women to understand the workings of inanimate objects or things. But more important, they are expected to accept, without thinking much about it, the idea that people may be treated as if they were things. In the United States, for example, the people who could be mistaken for things were the slaves in the South. The majority of men also often take for granted that they themselves should be treated as if they were things, for example, units in a labor force.

Women, in keeping with the expectation that they will devote their lives to others, are trained—in fact, they train themselves—to understand other people. Men are also expected to understand other people (it's hard to prevent). But in our competitive, dehumanized, "business" society, men's dealings with other people are supposed to resemble their dealings with things and very often do. Some women find it necessary to understand how things work in the world, since at least in the lower socioeconomic classes, women must supplement the family income. But women learn about things only temporarily and often grudgingly, until they can find a man. Then a woman can turn her attention to the real "business" of her life which is taking care of her husband and children.

In our own exploitative society, a division of labor between the understanding of things and understanding people has been forced on the two sexes. In addition, the model of understanding people is often made to resemble the model for things. Men are pushed into the intellectual as well as emotional distortions which are required in order to treat people (including themselves) as if they were things.

Two hallmark symptoms of schizophrenia, the "thought" disorder that is men's more frequent illness, are: an intense, often bizarre preoccupation with things, and an apparently total lack of feeling. Women also become confused by the great importance of things in our exploitative world. But they are more prone to treat things as if they were poeple. Everyone is amused by the way in which a depressed woman tries to find a substitute for some lost person by going to the store to buy something. The "acquisitive" woman, proud of her "well-chosen" possessions, is often the object of pity or scorn, since it is easy to see that she is only trying to substitute things for missing emotional relationships in her life.

Men's wits are sharpened by their dealings with inanimate objects and by dealing with people as if they were things. Thus, men have invented great complicated engines of species destruction which there is so far not much evidence they will be able to control. These engines of destruction are designed for "overkill" of millions of units (people) in the "enemy" country. Women's intelligence has not been distorted in the same way. But it has become restricted in its scope. Women miss out on the chance to sharpen their wits in discerning the intricacy of the way things work.

Understanding the workings of inanimate objects requires the functioning of a self which is very different in its organization from a self engaged in understanding other people. In dealing with others (as people, not as things), the self is engaged in a necessarily vicarious and empathetic experience. When it is in vicarious experience, the self is aware of itself, as if it were the other person. This kind of empathetic transaction requires, at least for the moment, a self with permeable boundaries. It requires a self which can become involved in someone else's experiences without losing its own identity. Encounters with other people usually involve an animate feedback from them. These two-way transactions take place principally through the use of language.

When the self is engaged in grasping (or changing) the properties of a thing, the self must be active in approaching it. Active physical manipulation of the inanimate object is of great help in understanding it. In this kind of transaction, the self is in only *one* place, its own position vis-à-vis the thing. The self-boundaries are not particularly permeable, since there is no other actual person with whom to empathize. Approach to, and active manipulation of things increase the separateness of the self as an independent entity in the world and particularly in relation to space in which things reside. The self is an egotistical position with reference to mastering things. In understanding things, the self is indifferent to the object since it is a thing, not a person.

Any summary of the well-established differences between men and women in intellectual functioning reflects men's assignment to master things and women's to understand people. The psychologists who developed intelligence tests were quite well aware that differences in intellectual functioning reflect differences in life experience, and they made a particular effort to develop intelligence tests which would be "fair" to both sexes.

The story of how intelligence testing developed is itself a fascinating one. It reflects the way in which the needs of an exploitative society were met by a scientific enterprise which, however, attempted to retain an egalitarian attitude toward the two sexes. Let's take a moment to digress for the sake of this story, which forms a background for the results to come.

The psychological testing movement, while it started in France in an effort to predict which children would do well in school, was picked up and given great impetus in our own country. The impetus came from World War I. The army, engaged in the task of drafting millions of new recruits, needed a "sensible" means of evaluating the men (the "units") and placing them where they would be most effective. Psychologists were called in to help, and they came through with a carefully constructed instrument, the "Army Alpha" test, which could predict differences in intelligent behavior among men.

The psychologists who went on to develop intelligence tests for more general purposes understood that men's abilities and women's abilities would tend to be different, and they wanted a "general" test which would be broader in its scope. One way this could be done would be to eliminate any test items which favored one sex over the other. But if they did this, the psychologists discovered that they would soon eliminate too many items, leaving nothing much left in the way of a test. So they made the test "fair" to both sexes in another way. They put in an equal number of items on which men did better and on which women did better, thus "averaging" the total intelligence test score so that it canceled out differences between the sexes. This also gave an apparently egalitarian quality to the intelligence testing movement which could then report that the two sexes did not differ, on the average, in their intelligence. But the differences in intellectual functioning which do exist between the sexes as a reflection of their different roles in an exploitative society have only been obscured, not eliminated. And when differences between the sexes which do reflect their different societal assignments are observed, there is a general assumption that these differences must be the "real" or innate ones, since, in general, the intelligence tests are "fair."

The following brief summary [4] * of agreed-on findings about sex differences in intellectual functioning is adapted from the 1966 summary assembled by Eleanor Maccoby, an expert in the field. Additional evidence has also been assembled from other sources. In every instance of a difference, its base in the sexes' different social roles can be seen. Because this is the case, however, there is a natural tendency to dismiss the whole question of sex differences in intellectual functioning as an artifact of our cultural order. But this at least partial truth also may obscure a further truth. It may be that there are some genetically determined differences in intellectual functioning between the sexes. Because our exploitative heritage has made the worst of these differences is no reason to deny them. On the contrary, denying them does an injustice to both sexes. As we shall see in a moment, the two sexes suffer from different intellectual "impairments" which need different correctives.

* Nothing in the recently published updated survey by Maccoby and Jacklin [5] contradicts this brief summary.

Verbal ability: I am following psychologists' custom in grouping language with other intellectual abilities. It should be
remembered, however, that language also reflects social ability.
Human beings have developed language because their social and
emotional communication is so highly developed (and vice versa).
In their updated review of the literature on language ability,
Maccoby and Jacklin [6] tell us the following: "Female superiority
in verbal tasks has been one of the more solidly established generalizations in the field of sex differences. Recent research continues to support the generalization to a degree."

Through the preschool years and in the early school years girls
exceed boys in most aspects of verbal performance. Girls say their
first word sooner, articulate more clearly and at an earlier age, use
longer sentences, and are more fluent. By the time school begins,
boys have caught up in vocabulary. But girls learn to read sooner,
and there are more boys than girls in special remedial programs.
Throughout all the school years, girls do better in grammar,
spelling, and word fluency.

Speech defects such as stuttering and language disorders of all
sorts are reported to be two to four times more prevalent for boys
than for girls, and boys are four times more frequently referred to
reading clinics for reading disabilities.[7]

Very clearly, there is a "language track" of intellectual
development which works better for girls than for boys. One clear
connection with girls' social role is the implicit assumption that
they will devote their lives to others. A self trained to understand
people is one which depends on and develops language skills,
since these are prime requirements in the two-way communication between people.

Not only are girls better earlier at verbal ability than boys, but
tests of language predict girls' future intellectual development
better than boys'. Little girls' babbling and vocalizations at six
months of age are good predictors of their later intellectual
development. [8] This consistencey of linguistic development in
girls suggests that language superiority may be a genetic given
which is not smothered but fostered by women's culturally
developed attachment to other people. The evolutionary advantage of the endowment of language to women is its value in what
one researcher calls the "vocal or non-harmful control" of the
infant.[9]

There is some evidence that girls have an innate advantage over boys in language. For women, for example, but not for men, a cluster of language-related items from tests of infant development shows substantial and increasing correlations with I.Q. through twenty-six years of age.[10] Language seems to play a different role in the intellectual development of girls than it does in boys. The "language track" of intellectual development is, of course, pushed by cultural expectations of women, as well as by some possible genetic factor.

Evidence exists that the dominance of the left cerebral hemisphere of the brain emerges earlier for girls than for boys.[11] The left hemisphere is the location of the language center. Establishment of the dominance of the left hemisphere is something which occurs normally in both sexes. One very ingenious study [12] measured the extent of dominance by sending sounds into the two ears simultaneously through two earphones. If the right ear is reporting more accurately, it is a sign that dominance of the left hemisphere has been established. At ages six, seven, and eight, boys and girls were no different in the accuracy of their reports from the right ear. But at age five, little girls were clearly superior. indicating that the left-hemisphere cerebral dominance had already been established for them and was still to come for boys.

It has been shown that boys with reading difficulties lag even further behind girls in the establishment of hemisphere dominance.[13] This and other evidence has led to the hypothesis [14] that girls' earlier verbalization is based on their earlier and stronger development of cerebral dominance.

Number ability: Girls also learn to count at an earlier age than boys. (My guess is that this early age counting depends heavily on verbal ability.) Through the school years, there are no consistent sex differences in skill at arithmetic. Some studies show that boys begin to get ahead on tests of "arithmetical reasoning" during grade school, but the results are not conclusive. By the time of high school, however, there is a clear result which continues into adulthood: Men are superior in arithmetical reasoning. Again, there is a clear connection between these results and boys' expectations of going out into the world of things and the marketplace, where ability to reason sharply about things count. Girls "drop out" of this arena. They don't think they'll need the skills, and besides, being clever can be felt as a handicap to their femininity. But notice: Girls' superior linguistic ability makes itself known very early—before the age of two. Boys' superior ability in sharp arithmetical reasoning does not make itself felt until much later—when girls have dropped out of the competition. This again makes it look as if superior linguistic ability might be a given for women, while arithmetical reasoning is not a given for either sex. We'll come back to this point in a little while.

Spatial ability: Spatial ability is a general term for such different tasks as aiming at a target, arranging objects according to a two-dimensional pattern, or having a good sense of direction. A capacity for organizing information about objects in space is a basic requirement for dealing with inanimate objects which derive some of their properties from their position in space. Very young boys and girls do not differ in spatial tasks. But by the time of early school years, boy do consistently better, and this difference continues into adulthood. As suggested earlier, the organization of the self so that it is sharply bounded is fostered by undertaking to master inanimate objects. That men have a better capacity than women to organize the space around them is a reflection of their assigned role of mastering things. Again, let's note that boys and girls when they are very young do not differ in this respect. That speaks against this capacity being given to men.

Analytical ability: There are two meanings commonly associated with this term: The first is the ability to keep an "object" separate in perception from the context in which it is embedded. For example, if a simple geometrical figure is surrounded by lines which blur its contours, it takes analytical ability to see the "hidden figure" anyhow. The same holds true if the item to keep separate is the upright perception of the position of one's own body when the whole surrounding room is tilted. This capacity has also been called "field-dependence" or "field-independence," since it requires "disembedding" an item from the context which surrounds it. Men are better at this than women—in part because the capacity to visualize space is involved. Also involved is the capacity to keep the visualization of space in mind when ordinary cues are not immediately available. For example, men fly airplanes better than women because (for one reason) they know better when they are flying upside down. The difference between the sexes in field-dependence is clearly established, however, only in late adolescence.[15]

The story of research about field-dependence in young children is itself instructive. That adult and late adolescent men are more field-independent than adult and late adolescent women had been clearly established. The question then arose: How early is this sex difference established? The tests of field independence which had been suitable for adults were not usable with children under the age of eight: The instructions were too complicated for one to know whether the child understood the task to be performed. With great ingenuity, researchers therefore set about to develop tests of field independence which were suitable for both young school-aged children and pre-schoolers. Results with these instruments, recently summarized by Susan Coates,[16] suggested that there may be a relatively brief period, at around age five, when girls are demonstrably superior at the disembedding skill. These results, which came as a surprise, were not easy to reconcile with the well-established male superiority by the time of late adolescence. As a consequence, there has been some tendency to treat the finding that girls are superior at age five as some kind of artifact, or else a relatively unimportant exception to the more general rule that, during childhood and early adolescence, there are either no sex differences in field dependence, or if there are, the difference favors boys.

Coates has suggested that the early superiority of girls is a phenomenon to be seriously explored. She suggests that it may be a resultant of the fact that in early childhood girls advance, physiologically, at a more rapid rate than boys. Or it may come about because boys are more aggressive than girls, and, at least among pre-schoolers, aggressiveness is a hindrance to analytic functioning. Both these factors may, of course, be operating together to produce girls' superiority at age five. Whatever the final outcome of the research on the question of little girls' superiority in field-independence, the tendency to dismiss the finding was an illustration of androcentric bias.

The second meaning of analytical ability is the capacity to group different objects according to an element they have in common. Boys generally use analytic groupings more often than girls. The age at which this difference first becomes apparent is not a settled question, since one study showed no difference in four- or five-year-olds, while another showed older boys better at analytic groupings than girls. The tests of capacity to group objects according to an essential common element overlap with the tests of field-independence, indicating that there are common requirements in the two kinds of analytical ability.

Creativity: There are relatively few studies comparing the sexes on creativity, although a great deal has been written insisting that men are inherently more creative. If creativity is defined as the ability to break an existing "set" or to restructure a problem, there is some tendency for boys to be superior, especially when the problem is perceptual, that is, spatial. If creativity is thought of in terms of divergent as compared to convergent thinking, there is some evidence that girls are superior, although the findings are inconsistent. A task requiring children to think of ways in which toys could be improved showed that in the first two grades of school, each sex was superior in dealing with the toys usually given to their sex. By the third grade, boys were better at thinking of ways of improving both kinds of toys. But girls and women do better than the opposite sex on a battery of divergent tasks if the problems are verbal. Once again, boys, especially older boys, become more adept than women at understanding things. Girls and women have a special affinity for intellectual functions involving language.

Achievement: Throughout school years, girls do better than boys even in subjects in which boys ordinarily excel on standard achievement tests. Girls try harder—so they get better grades. After graduation from school, men achieve more than women because *they* try harder. A follow-up study of gifted (middle-class) boys and girls showed that boys tend to achieve their intellectual potential; girls do not. Small wonder, since the culture discourages women's independent functioning!

Thus, the known differences in intellectual functioning between the two sexes tell us the following: Men become adept at what is required of them—mastering things in the world. Women are adept at language from their earliest years. Language is the species' unique mode of communication and understanding between people, which women's childbearing and child rearing function requires of them.

It is when we examine the way in which cultural pressures, operating through the family, mold the intellectual functioning of the two sexes that we get some idea of the different kinds of injuries that are inflicted. Men and women are not only on different intellectual tracks, but they differ in the way in which their childhood experiences and personalities are connected to their intellectual functioning.

Let's look first at the pattern of childhood experience and personality which is associated with "good" intellectual functioning in boys.[17] (The studies which have been done on this question mostly use the overall intelligence quotient for comparative purposes.) For men, being treated with warmth and attentiveness which their mothers gave them when they were little, predicts a high I.Q. in later years. When they were little however, it was the boys who were specifically anxious about their own aggressions who had the higher I.Q.'s. Aggressive little boys tended to have lower I.Q.'s. Little boys who are "cautious" and boys who have good control over their impulses tend to have higher I.Q.'s. So the picture emerges of maternal warmth toward a boy child responding in kind who is then likely to develop good intellectual functioning. So far, so good. But then we remember that it is the anxious, unaggressive men who are also ultimately more likely to be schizophrenic! [18] Men pay a heavy price for the good affectionate experience with their mothers which underlies their developing intelligence.

Now let's look at the corresponding picture for girls. It's quite a different picture. For girls, the crucial experience fostering their intellectual development is having a mother who allows them relative freedom from restrictions—freedom to wander and explore. It is the timid, fearful little girls who have the lower I.Q.'s. Impulsive little girls are better, for example, at a "grouping" task involving analytical ability. For girls, having to fight against the pressures which tie them to their mothers' apron strings is the price paid for the intellectual development. So the more aggressive girls turn out smarter.

Clearly, something is wrong on both sides. Girls are too timid and unassertive for their intellectual development to flower; boys need to control their aggressivity for optimum growth of their intelligence. Both sexes thus need to struggle against the different cultural pressures on them generated by an exploitative society.°

° In her earlier work, Eleanor Maccoby (1966) had put forward a hypothesis which suggested that "for optimal development most girls need to become less passive and inhibited, while most boys need to become less aggressive." [19] In the

The story of field-dependence and field-independence is a most illuminating one, not only because the sexes differ in this respect, but because field-dependence has been found to be connected to different forms of mental illness, to differences in personality, and even recently to differences in proneness to shame or guilt, as we shall see in Chapter 13. The connections between field-independence, mental illness, conscience mode, personality characteristics, and sex all fit together in the way one would expect. So, for example, paranoid schizophrenics and obsessionals are field-independent and more likely to be men. At the other end of the spectrum of mental illness, depressed and hysterical patients are field-dependent and more likely to be women. Field-independent patients are more prone to guilt; field-dependent patients are more prone to shame. Each package of connections represents the workings of a cultural order which straitjackets men into becoming egotistical exploiters and women into becoming their loving dependents.

The story of how Witkin came to discover that people differ in their ability to maintain the sense of themselves in space is itself fascinating. Its sequel now involves more than thirty years of research [21,22] by Witkin and his associates, of whom I have been one. It is a story which starts in opposing theories in psychology about whether the self is inherently egotistical or not. The great Gestalt psychologist, Max Wertheimer, believed that the human self is not egotistical. As a first step in trying to put his own theories to experimental test, Wertheimer decided to study the way in which a human being "knows" whether he or she is standing or sitting "straight" and how we know that things in the world are vertical and horizontal. This is a fundamental kind of knowledge which we all take for granted and at which we are all very accurate. If a picture hanging on the wall is only very slightly

---

1974 book, Maccoby specifically retracts the "passivity to impulsiveness" dimension, on the basis of more recent evidence.[20] But Maccoby and Jacklin continue to believe that "intellectual development in girls is fostered by their being assertive and active and having a sense that they can control, by their own actions, the events that affect their lives." For boys, perhaps because they are "already sufficiently assertive," the important issue in intellectual development is "how well they can control their aggressive impulses." Maccoby and Jacklin thus appear to be revising their hypothesis so that its central dimension is timidity-aggressiveness: Girls need to become less timid; boys less aggressive for optimum intellectual development.

tilted, almost everyone can see the tiny deviation. If we tilt our bodies even a very little bit to one side or the other, we know it at once. We know so instantaneously and accurately because ordinarily we get two sets of messages: one from the force of gravity acting on our bodies, and the second from the many verticals and horizontals in the buildings in the world around us. These two ordinarily go together to make us good perceivers of the uprightness or tilt of either objects or our bodies in space.

But suppose our perception of the surrounding world were interfered with, and we could go only by our own bodies? Would we still be accurate? Wertheimer's idea was that the self alone was not enough. With great ingenuity he proceeded to devise an experimental situation which could test his belief. He asked people to look through a tube into a mirror in which there were reflected some ordinary objects—a table and chair. As the people looked into the mirror through the tube, Wertheimer quietly tilted the mirror without telling them. He argued that if the upright perception depended mainly on the self alone, the objects in the mirror should continue to be seen as tilted, but if the surrounding framework were more important, the objects reflected in the mirror should gradually right themselves in their appearance and come to be seen as straight. This is just what happened in Wertheimer's experiments.

Wertheimer's experiments had been done in Germany before World War I. When he arrived in the United States in the late 1930s, a refugee from Hitler, American experimenters had a chance to become acquainted with his thinking and they took up and extended his work. New and less cumbersome methods of separating the influence of gravity feedback from the influence of the surrounding field were devised. One of these methods was to put people into a totally darkened room in which they could not see the floor and walls but only a luminous square frame with a stick inside the frame. Both the frame and the stick inside it could be tilted. Looking at the tilted frame, the person was asked to adjust the stick until it seemed "straight." Another method was to seat people in a special room, this time perfectly well-lit, but a room which could be tilted from side to side. People were asked to say when they saw or felt themselves to be seated "straight" within the tilted room. In the course of these experiments Witkin found that on the average people tended to adjust their perception of the upright in space to fit a surrounding framework. Within a tilted luminous frame, a luminous stick looks straight when it is actually tilted a few degrees. The body seems straight to the person seated in a tilted room when the body is actually tilted quite a few degrees. Thus, Wertheimer's idea that people's perception takes account of the framework and is not just egotistically determined was generally confirmed.

Witkin's discovery, however, was that people differ in the extent to which they are influenced by the surrounding framework and that they are very consistent in this respect. Some people see the stick as straight within the tilted framework when it is practically at the true vertical. They are the same people who say their bodies are straight when they sit at a 350-degree angle in a room which is tilted 56 degrees. Witkin called these people field-independent, while the people more heavily influenced by the surrounding framework were called field-dependent.

As I indicated earlier, women as a group were significantly more field-dependent perceivers than men. This difference between the sexes has been observed in many studies in our country and in many different countries of Europe and in Asia. But what is also true is that the extent of people's field-dependence varies with cultural conditions, specifically with methods of child rearing. As we saw in Chapter 5, in an agricultural community in Africa where children are raised to be obedient and are heavily punished if they are not, the children were much more field-dependent, as a group, than in a nomadic group where obedience is not inculcated and the children are not severely punished. And among the Eskimos, who are also a nomadic group, and where the world does not consist of well laid-out fields of clear boundaries but of vast homogeneous expanses of snow and ice, there is no difference between the sexes in field-dependence. The children have to organize the world more for themselves, and so they do. In addition, the Eskimos foster their children's initiative and independence and treat them gently. Thus, in a part of the world where people of both sexes have to organize the world of space because there are few ready-made landmarks to go by, the sexes are more alike.

There are probably few psychologists who would disagree with the notion that men and women's intellectual functions develop differently because they are coordinated to the different psychological "ecologies" which are contained in our society. Men are forced to mature in the impersonal milieu generated by the importance of things over people which in turn is generated by the profit motive. Women are forced to take second place because the profit motive gives people second place and women "only" grow people. So men grow sharp in analytical ability—they have to. Women's intelligence flowers along the language track, in keeping with women's orientation toward people.

How much of this two-track system of intellectual development is genetically determined? The superior linguistic competence of women over men starts very early. This may be an indication that it is genetically determined. Men's superior analytical ability does not start early. If anything, little girls at five years of age are more field-independent than little boys. There may, however, be an indirect connection between men's superior analytical ability with things and a genetic factor. The male hormones are activators; female hormones are gentling in their effects—they reduce activation. As we saw earlier, mastering inanimate things requires an active approach to them. Men may have a greater proclivity to activity, and this may bring them into readier contact with things and help to foster their mastery of them.

There may be an equitable distribution of nature's gifts between the sexes—such that women had more language ability and men more analytic ability in mastering things. It does not necessarily follow that sex-linked skills need to become the base for male exploitativeness.

References

1. P. Wolff, paper read at Edmund Weil Memorial Symposium, IP-TAR, June 1972.

2. T. Benedek, "Adaptation to Reality in Early Infancy," *Psychoanalytic Quarterly* 7 (1938), 200-215.

3. M. Klein, *Envy and Gratitude* (London: Tavistock Publications, 1957).

4. E. Maccoby, *The Development of Sex Differences* (Stanford, Calif.: Stanford University Press, 1966).

5. E. Maccoby and C. Jacklin, *The Psychology of Sex Differences* (Stanford, Calif.: Stanford University, 1974).

6. Ibid., p. 75.

7. J. Garai and A. Scheinfeld, "Sex Differences in Mental and Behavioral Traits, *Genetic Psychology Monographs* 77 (1968), 169-299.

8. J. Kagan, "Continuity in Cognitive Development During the First Years," *Merrill-Palmer Quarterly* 15 (1969), 101-119.

9. J. Kagan, ed. H. R.Schaffer, *The Origin of Human Social Relations* (New York: Academic Press, 1971), p. 69.

10. J. Cameron, N. Livson and N. Bayley, "Infant Vocalizations and their Relationship to Mature Intelligence," *Science* 157 (1967), 331-333.

11. A. W. H. Buffery and J. A. Gray, "Sex Differences in the Development of Spatial and Linguistic skills," eds. C. Ounsted and D. C. Taylor, *Gender Differences: Their Ontogeny and Significance* (Baltimore: Williams and Wilkins, 1972).

12. Ibid., D. Kimura.

13. Ibid., D. Kimura.

14. Ibid., D. Kimura.

15. Personal communication from H. A. Witkin.

16. Susan Coates, "Sex Differences in Field Dependence Among Preschool Children," eds. R. C. Friedman, R. M. Richart and R. L. Vande Wiele, *Sex Difference in Behavior* (New York: Wiley, 1974).

17. E. Maccoby, op cit.

18. F. Cheek, "A Serendipitous Finding: Sex Role and Schizophrenia," *Journal of Abnormal and Social Psychology* 69 (1964), 392-400.

19. E. Maccoby, op. cit., p. 133.

20. E. Maccoby and C. Jacklin, op. cit., p. 133.

21. H. A. Witkin, H. B. Lewis, M. Hertzman, K. Machover, P. Meissner, and S. Wapner, *Personality Through Perception* (New York: Harper, 1954).

22. H. A. Witkin, R. Dyk, H. Faterson, D. Goodenough and S. Karp, *Psychological Differentiation* (New York: Wiley, 1962).

PART III

Human Culture: A Janus-Face

CHAPTER 8

Exploitative Society: An Historical Given

The origin of the exploitativeness in economic and social systems is unknown. We know only that since ancient times the oppressors and the oppressed have been a given of civilized human existence. And, as we have seen, "civilized" humanity has no monopoly on exploitativeness, which some "primitive" peoples live by as well.

Why it is that men rather than women are the exploiters in an exploitative society is another problem. Why it is the women rather than the men who are assigned a position of social inferiority in so many societies throughout the world is a related puzzle. Even if one assumes that exploitation was invented by men, it does not follow that they invented it *because* they were male. Exploitativeness may have been an adaptation (now outmoded if we are to survive) to some ancient conditions of human life. Because exploiters are male does not make exploitativeness intrinsically masculine.

It is sometimes said that when human beings first emerged on earth they earned their livelihood as hunters and that the hunters were males rather than females because males are physically stronger than females, and females were busy caring for the young. Hunting (especially of large animals) does require physical strength, and as we have seen (in Chapter 5) in primitive societies where hunting large animals is the economic base, it is always the men who hunt. Hunting does require aggressiveness enough to kill, as well as physical strength. The increase in muscle size and strength which happens to boys at puberty and makes them physically stronger than girls can specifically adapt the male primate animal to his "*primate* role of dominating, fighting and foraging." [1] It is not, however, a specific adaptation to a man's role in *human* society.

Did Tarzan, as he came down out of the trees and became acculturated, automatically convert his superior strength and aggressiveness into an exploitative rather than a cooperative model of a hunting society? The answer is that a cooperative model of an ancient hunting society is by no means excluded from speculation. In fact, recent work in anthropology suggests that early men and women may have shared power.[2] This suggestion comes from recent studies of the nomadic !Kung society ° in Botswana, Africa. In this society, which is thought to be a model of how earliest human society was organized, men are hunters while women are gatherers of plant food and fish. Neither sex is economically or politically dependent on the other. Here men and women are relatively equal in power. (This is also how Engels imagined earliest society to be, although without modern anthropological evidence.) Lee, one of the anthropologists who studied the !Kung, does not generalize his evidence, but he does caution that early man's hunting cannot be used to "prove" his early supremacy over women.[3]

The !Kung people are of particular interest to anthropologists and social scientists because there is archaeological evidence that they have lived as nomadic hunters and food gatherers in the Kalahari Desert of South Africa for at least 11,000 years.[4] Recently, however, they have begun to lead a sedentary existence in agrarian villages near the Bantu people. Investigators who are documenting this change find that the settled !Kung women are losing their egalitarian status, and the children are no longer being brought up to be nonaggressive.

° The exclamation point refers to a "click," a hollow popping sound, which is part of the pronunciation of the name of the people.

Patricia Draper, an anthropologist at the University of New Mexico, attributes these changes in part to the difference between the social structure of a nomadic rather than a sedentary economy.[5] Among the nomadic !Kung, at least 50 percent of the food is produced by the women. Women leave camp as often as men to obtain food. Both men and women who do not seek food on a given day remain in the camp and share in taking care of the children.

The women in sedentary !Kung society have far less mobility than men and contribute less to the food supply. The men leave the village to clear fields and raise crops and to care for the cattle of their Bantu neighbors. The women remain in the village where they prepare food and take care of the children. Since the men work for the Bantus, they learn the Bantu language. Thus, when the Bantus deal with the !Kung, they deal exclusively with the men. This practice, together with the !Kung's emulation of the male-dominated society, contributes to the increasingly subservient role of !Kung women.

Another reason for the loss of equality between the sexes is the different way that agrarian as compared to nomadic !Kung bring up their children. Draper points out that nomads live in bands consisting of relatively few people so that a child generally has no companions of the same age. Play groups consist of children of widely varying ages and of both sexes. This discourages the development of distinct games and roles for boys and girls. Unlike nomadic children, the sedentary children play in groups consisting of the same sex and similar age. The boys leave camp with their fathers; the girls stay with their mothers helping with women's chores. Sex differences are thus emphasized rather than muted as they are among the nomadic !Kung.

The nomadic !Kung also actively discourage aggression and competition among their children. Their children were not observed by Draper to play competitive games; the wide age range makes competitive games difficult. The children also rarely witness physical aggression among the nomadic !Kung. It is tempting to assume that when egalitarian relationships exist between the parents, the children experience less aggression and so are less aggressive in turn.

The solution to women's inferiority in our own society is not, of course, a return to existence in nomadic bands of hunters and food-gatherers. (Fantasies of what life may be like if there are any survivors after a nuclear holocaust often envisage humanity starting all over again in this way.) Rather, it lies in extrapolating from such comparative studies as the nomadic versus agrarian !Kung the social forces which foster rather than inhibit egalitarian sexual attitudes: that the sexes share equally in economic productivity and in child rearing.

It is also possible that the engagement of prehistoric men in hunting fostered some unknown, hypothetical genetic determinants of a capacity to deal effectively with spatial relations. Having good geographical orientation is a capacity needed to stalk and kill animals in the wild. Effectiveness in dealing with large animals in the wild fosters an independent and egotistical self, accustomed to using itself as a silent reference point in making spatial and other judgments. Hunters have to take care of themselves. Hunting also fosters a self which is accustomed to dealing with *things* in the physical world. It fosters perceptual field-independence among the Eskimo, as we saw in Chapter 5. Effectiveness in dealing with infants, in contrast, fosters a self which is empathetic and sympathetic: an "other-directed" self (to use a term which sometimes evokes derision for its dependency connotations). But there is a vast difference between being empathetic and being submissive, just as there is a vast difference between being independent and being exploitative.

Hunting was not invented because of anyone's maleness, but because it filled some need of a human society. Given its physical requirements, it makes sense to suppose that hunting was more congenial to the men in a society than to the women. Hunting, however, does not require either male domination or exploitativeness within the culture. The ancient hunting economy which we know characterized primitive human society cannot be made the reason for the development of exploitativeness, although it was the men who hunted. No one really knows why exploitativeness developed; among civilized peoples it has just always been so, and it is the men who are more often the exploiters than the women.

The picture of prehistory is unclear. Without documents to go by, prehistory is reflected mainly in archaeological remains, which do not tell about the social fabric of existence. The archaeologists' division of Homo sapiens's prehistoric existence in Stone, Bronze, and Iron ages is based on an assessment of their tools of production. The historical development of a cultural tradition cannot be inferred, however, as a direct consequence of developments in material culture alone. As an example, the cave paintings of Paleolithic times (Old Stone Age) are justly celebrated as great artistic creations. In the 2,000 years before the development of cities (before 3000 B.C.) relatively poor and illiterate communities had made great contributions in the application of science to life on earth. In his classic book, *Man Makes Himself*, V. Gordon Childe lists: artificial irrigation; the plough; the harnessing of animal motive-power (including slavery); the sailing-boat; wheeled vehicles; orchard husbandry; fermentation; the production and use of copper; bricks; the arch; glazing; the seal; and—in the earliest stages of the (urban) revolution—a solar calendar, writing, numerical notation and bronze.[6] By contrast with these fifteen scientific discoveries, only two first-rate discoveries can be discerned in the 2,000 years following the urban revolution (2600-600 B.C.). Childe attributes this arrest in growth to internal contradictions inherent in the urban revolution: the economic degradation of the masses. The urban revolution had reduced the actual producers to the position of the "lower classes." The principal beneficiaries from the scientific achievements of the farmers and artisans were the priests and kings who emerged with the accumulation of wealth which characterized the urban revolution. These rulers had no need for the invention of labor-saving devices: human labor was abundant and cheap. Advances in the level of material culture thus occurred alongside the degradation of many human beings, as our own modern experience still attests.

In interpreting the history of civilization from archaeological remains, it is usually taken for granted that men were the prime movers. This seems to fit a historical picture which is derived in such large part from studying material culture—tools, buildings, and all manner of artifacts. The exploitative character of society is also taken for granted. The reader will have noted that Childe lists slavery as just one invention among the fifteen which occurred before the urban revolution.

Faced with a uniform picture of civilized human society as exploitative, the Marxists, while profoundly critical of exploitativeness, concluded that exploitation was an historical necessity in the development of civilization. And they, particularly Engels, suggested that women, being the weaker sex and burdened by children, were one group among the many groups which fell victim to exploitative power. We'll come back to Engels's views shortly.

Many social historians, critics of the existing social order, have been caught by the contradiction between the exploitativeness of human civilized society and the natural affectionateness of human beings. In his inquiries into the inequalities to be observed in civilized society, Rousseau, a philosopher of the Enlightenment, saw "at first ... only the violence of the powerful and the oppression of the weak." [7] "Throwing aside ... scientific books, which only teach us how to see men such as they have made each other," [8] Rousseau found the principle of *pitié* or compassion to be a "natural feeling, which, by moderating the violence of love of self in each individual, contributes to the preservation of the whole species." [9] As Rousseau conceived of *pitié*, it was the characteristic of primitive human beings which was suppressed or cut off by the development of civilization. Primitive human beings, seeing another person suffer, identified with that suffering and went to help. In civilized society, one human being sees another suffer and is indifferent; unconcern is codified by laws which distinquish human beings according to rank or wealth, and the unconcern is thus granted moral justification. Our own civilization, in other words, has arranged itself so that compassion is no longer required of human beings since some people have been "rationally" discriminated as different and inferior.

Rousseau's noble savage is, of course, a myth. But his comparison between natural human beings and civilized ones can be transposed into a comparison between the early social interactions which occur in the human family and those which occur after human social nature has been distorted by exploitative social systems. Rousseau's *pitié* is the fundamental basis of each individual's personal development because this kind of human interaction is required for growth. Both males and females in their early social interactions readily exhibit *pitié*—an empathetic sense of the other fellow's experience and an impulse to reduce the other's suffering. The sensitivity of the self to the other's experience is a natural result of the thoroughly social nature of earliest human experience. A self which remains uncaring about others' suffering occurs only with indoctrination into a dehumanized world.

Engels described the trouble with human society a bit differently but with a passion equal to Rousseau's.[10] Reminding us that the exploitation of human beings by each other has been a dominant factor in the history of civilization, Engels tells us that civilization's achievements occurred as a result of:

> setting in motion the lowest instincts and passions in man and developing them at the expense of all his other abilities. From its first day to this, greed was the driving spirit of civilization, wealth and again wealth and once more wealth, wealth, not of eociety but of the single, scurvy individual— here was its one and final aim.[11]

Engels also conjectured a prehistoric time in human life when things were not like that. As he read the minimal signs of earliest human history, there was a time before class-divided human society arose. In this prehistoric, primitive time, kinship ties played the important role in social organization. Division of labor was equal between the sexes.

> The man fights in the war, goes hunting and fishing, procures the raw material of food and the tool necessary for doing so. The woman looks after the house and the preparation of food and clothing, cooks, weaves and sews. Each is the owner of the instruments he or she makes and uses: the man of the weapons, the hunting and fishing implements, the woman of the household gear. Under conditions of equality of ownership of tools and in the mastery of tasks there is equality between the sexes.[12]

It is amusing to note, in passing, how taken-for-granted are stereotyped ideas of women's occupations. Even Engels, writing a treatise which is mainly about the oppression of women, imagines his mythical noble savage to be a warrior and hunter, while Ms. Noble Savage, although equal in rank, still minds the house. As we shall see later in this chapter, many primitive societies do follow the stereotype, but the nomadic !Kung do not.

Engels theorized that as the efficacy of tools developed and there emerged the possibility of exploiting the labor of others for the accumulation of wealth, kinship ties were replaced and superseded. Even within the biological family, relationships became exploitative; women became the property of men; children the property of their parents.

Engels's view, however, is not directly a view of human nature or of women's nature. It is a view of what human nature need not be—that is, greedy—provided exploitative social systems are abolished. And it suggests that the oppression and inferior social position of women are fostered by exploitative social conditions prevailing in general.

Freud also was critical of human civilization in its relations to human nature. He supposed that civilization was built on the suppression of human sexuality, an idea which bears considerable resemblance to Rousseau's idea of the suppression of *pitié*. Freud's insights are of particular value because they help to spell out the actual psychological processes by which cultural myths of women's inferiority develop out of contradictions between affectionateness and exploitativeness. We'll deal with Freud's views more fully in Chapter 12.

Engels's idea that there is a connection between a high level of technology and an exploitative social order has found some confirmation in a cross-cultural study of the relationship between technology and moral order.[13] Gouldner and Peterson, two sociologists, reviewed seventy-one different cultures which had been well.enough studied by anthropologists so that they could be scored on specific traits. Fifty-seven different traits were scored, each on a four-point scale ranging from the trait's being very much present—"dominant" in the culture—to absent. The fifty-seven different traits were such important characteristics of a culture as, for example, patrilineal inheritance, polygyny, level of technology, caste system, codified laws, elaboration of death ceremonies, government by restricted council (which means relative autocracy), and subjection of women. Gouldner and Peterson intercorrelated the scores on the fifty-seven traits for the seventy-one cultures and then performed a factor analysis of the matrix of intercorrelations. They came up with four important factors in describing the cultures: (1) "father right or mother right," (2) sex dominance, (3) level of technology, and (4) "Apollonian norms."

The last factor turns out to bear a striking resemblance to Nietzsche's comparison of Apollonian and Dionysian models of society, this is in turn the same set of models which Ruth Benedict found so useful in her book, *Patterns of Culture*.[14] Briefly recapitulated, Apollonian norms include: elaboration of ceremony and ritual; power vested in a chief; attractiveness of a future life; organized priesthood; marriage by capture; metals secured from outside the culture; codified laws; elaboration of mortuary ceremonies; authority vested in judges; government by restricted council; domesticated animals other than herded; legendary heroes; patripotestal descent; and patripotestal authority. Except in a few details, Apollo still guides us in our own society as well!

Gouldner and Peterson found a relationship between the level of technology and an autocratic pattern of societal functioning. And they found, further, that the subjection of women was correlated to the autocratic nature of society—the more autocratic, the greater the subjection of women. A correlation, of course, does not tell us that there is a causal relationship between two factors, but it does give a strong hint about a good place to look for causes. As we shall see in Chapter 10, women are better off where people in general have more freedom.

A cross-cultural study of the family yielded similar results.[15] This study was able to trace a connection between the development of civilization and the development of autocratic political states. And it was able to demonstrate that autocratic power structure usually entails the greater subjection of women. The study found that autocratic political structure is associated with greater deference required of people in the culture generally. Greater deference is expected from women than from men. There is also greater sexual restrictiveness in autocratic societies, and, as might be expected, the greater sexual restrictiveness is exercised even more against women than against men.

Simone de Beauvoir, reviewing Engels's notion that the subjugation of women is a category of the exploitation of human beings in general, has raised the very provocative question of why the development of division of labor, and of the possibility of exploiting human labor for the acquisition of wealth should have had as its result the subjugation of women. De Beauvoir wonders why the originally friendly, equal relation between the sexes could not have survived the division of labor, the exploitation of labor, and the acquisition of wealth. She grants that the division of labor according to sex and consequent oppression bring to mind in some ways the division of society by classes, but it is impossible, she thinks, to confuse the two. For one thing, there is no biological basis for the separation of classes. She solves this question by assuming that the "original relation" between a man and his fellows is a "result of the imperialism of the human consciousness, seeking always to exercise its sovereignty in objective fashion. *If the human consciousness had not included the original category of the 'other' and an original aspiration to dominate the other, the invention of the bronze tool could not have caused the oppression of women"* [16] [italics mine].

De Beauvoir is here making use of existentialist assumptions that (1) the category of the "other" is as primordial as consciousness itself. She writes: "Primordial consciousness of the Self and the Other is (as Lévi-Strauss would put it) an immediately given datum of social reality." (2) "Every individual concerned to justify his existence feels that his existence involves an undefined need to transcend himself, which it does in part through the domination of the 'other.' " . . .

Further, de Beauvoir says:

> To accept the position of "otherness" is to submit to a duality in which the Self is Absolute, the reference point against which the Other is perceived. Throughout history, women have always been subordinated to men, not because like proletarians they lost the competitive struggle for acquisition, but because they are women in their physiology and anatomy and because the bond which unites woman to her male oppressor is biological. The couple is a fundamental unity with its two halves riveted together, and the cleavage of society along the lines of sex is impossible. Here is to be found the basic trait of women: she is the "other in a totality of which the two components are necessary to each other." [17]

In her assumption that "man" has a need to transcend himself by dominating the "other," de Beauvoir is employing a number of related assumptions. In the first place, she implies that there is an interent hostility of one human consciousness to another, out of which the self derives its selfhood. In the second place, although she says that it is every individual who has an intrinsic need to transcend himself, it is clearly the male to whom she assigns this intrinsic need for transcendence. (Women are "immanent" beings; men "transcedent.") There is thus a contradiction between the assumption that the need to transcend is human, and the assumption that it is characteristic only of men. If the former were the case, it should be equally possible for women to adopt the position of the self which transcends by dominating the "other."

Perhaps a closer look at the origins of the self and its need for transcendence is in order. It is possible that it is the assumption that transcendence involves domination which is creating difficulties. If we turn our attention to the first occasions when human beings begin to develop a self, it occurs, as we saw in Chapter 6, in the course of the mother-infant interaction. During this interaction, and including the interaction between father and infant, the self appears to become transcendent as a result of what has been described as "mutual delight" in each other's being. This is not to say that anger generated in the infant in response to frustrations does not also play a part in fostering the autonomy of the self. But the impression is clear that infants who at one year were able to use their mothers as "secure base" for exploration of the environment (thus expressing de Beauvoir's transcendence) were those infants who had mothers who delighted in their being, and who evoked delight in their infants.

We can assume, with de Beauvoir, that the self originates in interaction with the "other," but we do not need to assume that this interaction is inherently one of domination. The self is nourished by affection as well as delineated by blows from the "other." It is of interest to observe, in passing, the extent to which the prevailing exploitative milieu influences even de Beauvoir's conception of the "original relation" between the self and the other. What may be at issue here is a failure to distinguish between the development of the self as it differentiates out of experiences with environmental *things*, and as it differentiates out of experiences with *others*. Mastery of things is the goal of the self in relation to *things*. Domination thus comes close to describing the relationship between things and the self. The self which is formed to deal with others performs its differentiation best (in dialectical fashion) when the relationship between self and other is closest. A self organized to respond affectionately to other *people* finds it hard to tolerate exploiting them, treating them as if they were things.

Both male and female selves differentiate out of an affectionate mother-infant interaction. When, however, the cultural arrangements are such that the originally affectionate relationship between caretaker and infant (for both sexes) is succeeded by exploitative institutions, women become the exploited because their maternal function carries with it a self more attuned to positive feeling for others. Exploitative cultural institutions are taken over by men, and thereafter expressly sanction women's inferiority. The contradiction between both sexes' earliest affectionate experiences with women, and women's social inferiority then becomes a major problem as well as a major theme of the culture's rationalizing myths, as we shall see in later chapters.

Not all feminists agree, of course, that the profit system and the exploitativeness it generates are the principal sources of women's subjugation. Feminists who minimize the role of exploitativeness in society believe rather that it is men who are the enemies of women. They believe that the central difficulty with society is the need for domination which is inherent in men's natures. Juliet Mitchell, without taking sides herself, summarizes the issue clearly in her book, *Woman's Estate*. "For radical feminists . . . the oppression of women is the *primary oppression* in all societies, whatever their mode of production" [18] [italics mine]. Mitchell quotes from a radical feminists' manifesto as follows:

> The purpose of male chauvinism is primarily to obtain psychological ego-satisfactions, and . . . only secondarily does this manifest itself in economic relationships. . . . For this reason we do not believe that capitalism or any other economic system is the cause of female oppression, nor do we believe that female oppression will disappear as a result of a purely economic revolution.

Furthermore, the manifesto reads: ". . . male need, though destructive, is . . . impersonal. It is not out of a desire to hurt the woman that he dominates and destroys her; it is out of a sense of power that he necessarily must destroy her ego and make it subservient to his." As Mitchell points out, pure or radical "feminism" is the "belief that women's oppression is first, foremost and separable from any particular historical context." [19]

The reader will have observed that this book, although revolutionary in its political and economic outlook, is reformist in its

attitudes about sex. There are many ways in which the two sexes
are hurt by each other, and men do more hurting. But since these
hurtful ways are attributable to interactions between exploitation
and the psyches of both sexes, the remedy seems to me to be to
change the exploitative system. Radical feminists, paradoxically,
are radical only with respect to altering the relationship between
the sexes. They are, if anything, reformist or even accepting of the
profit system, since they believe that women will be oppressed
whatever the prevailing eronomic system.

We can agree with the radical feminists' manifesto when it says
that men's need to dominate women is impersonal, growing out of
a need for power. The need for power is just what an exploitative
society generates. Without this larger source of energy behind it a
man's (or a woman's) need for power could find more than
adequate expression in the mastery of things which exist in the
world, as we saw in Chapter 7. As Freud has shown (Chapter 12),
the sadistic need to hurt women is itself a product of a profound
conflict between men's affectionateness and the culturally fostered demand that they be powerful.

There is also a division of opinion among feminists about how
to deal with women's subjugation to men. Radical feminists, following their belief that the relationship between the sexes is
intrinsically subjugating to women, propose to struggle first
and foremost against the traditional assignment of women to
motherhood, against the nuclear family with its transmission
of patriarchal and exploitative values, and against the institution
of marriage. Each of these institutions in our society has indeed
been corrupted by exploitative values. Trenchant criticisms of the
hypocrisy which corrodes the institutions of motherhood, the
family, and marriage, have come from many quarters: from Marx,
from Freud, and from the Marxist psychoanalysts, notably Fromm
and Reich. Contemporary women critics—for example, de
Beauvoir—have made use of insights from all these sources. They
have made use of Freud's methods while correcting Freud's mistakes (Chapter 12).

But the fact that our society has corrupted the institutions of
marriage, motherhood, and the family does not mean that these
institutions are not vital for human existence or that they cannot
function well in a peaceful society, as, for instance, among the
Arapesh or Zuni, as we shall see in Chapter 9.

Let's take the phenomenon of the family first. As it exists within our society, it is a transmission belt for patriarchal and exploitative values. Of the two evils, the second is greater than the first. As we shall see among the Arapesh, a patriarchal kinship-reckoning system, even one which determines inheritance, is not a barrier to an egalitarian society. But an exploitative system does inhibit equality between the sexes, as we shall see in Chapters 9 and 10. (I would not enjoy living in a matriarchal-exploitative society any more than I now enjoy living in a patriarchal-exploitative system.)

The nuclear family in our society functions as a haven—often false and unreliable, but a refuge still—from the profit-driven, aggressive world around it. Suggestions that the nuclear family become an extended family are welcomed by people who recognize how insufficient the haven is. Psychiatrists recognize how easily the affectionate bonds within the family are dissolved under the pressures of need for domination. So we shall see, in Chapter 18, how an army man became a rapist of his own daughter. These criticisms are essentially that the nuclear family is not loving enough and not powerful enough to protect us against a social order which is hostile to people. The remedy, it seems to me, is to change the hostile social order rather than to eliminate an admittedly inadequate refuge.

Some feminists have advocated the abolition of motherhood. Juliet Mitchell, again reporting the scene, tells us, for example, that woman "protests her submission to the arbitariness of conception." [20] Phyllis Chesler agrees with Shulamith Firestone that science must release women from biological reproduction.[21] Firestone [22] tells us, furthermore, that the sexual differentiation is the basis for women's oppression. The biological family involves keeping women at the mercy of their biological role in reproduction. She argues that the natural difference in reporductive function led to the first division of labor, which, in turn, led to women's subjugation. She therefore advocates that the "biological basis of oppression [be] swept away" [23] by the elimination of the sex distinction itself.

Woman's biological role has surely made it easier for her to be subjugated and exploited, as Engels has shown. But, as we have just seen, her biological role cannot account for why exploitativeness developed. As de Beauvoir points out, and the !Kung illustrate, the original division of labor between the sexes might well have been friendly and cannot alone account for the development of exploitativeness. Neither can we account for exploitativeness by some psychological factor, such as men's dread of women. This can account for a *wish* to exploit, but not the reality of doing so.

When it comes to freeing marriage from its function as a sophisticated form of wealth transfer among the bourgeoisie (Chapter 5), and to freeing women from the notion that marriage is their major fulfillment as human beings (Chapter 16), feminists of many persuasions tend to be in agreement. As in the case of motherhood and the family, however, the cultural institution of marriage, in spite of distortions, is an expression of the concept of long-lasting affectionate and sexual ties, which human beings can develop because they alone on earth have a self and a superego. Affectionate ties have bound people of both sexes to internalize images representing exploitative values. But they also bind people of both sexes to each other out of the profoundly affectionate relationships in which human life begins. Among human beings affectionate ties, including those in marriage, serve as a "defense" against threats from a hostile culture. Women cultivate both affectionate and ersatz ties to men in reaction to these threats. As we saw in Chapter 2, even among primate groups, the level of aggressivity determines the quality of the affectionate ties. But the solution to ersatz relationships seems to me to lie not in abandoning marriage but in removing threats to its affectionate qualities.

Human beings are profoundly attached to one another by nature, in spite of the fact that so many of them live in an exploitative world. Human survival in spite of the species' bloody history is a tribute to the strength of the affectionate ties which are implicit in motherhood, the family, and marriage.

On the other side of the feminist movement, more to the right, are the voices of women demanding integration into the mainstream. A bit of history may help to put this demand in perspective. As Viola Klein points out, before the industrial revolution there was hardly any job performed by men which was not also performed by women.[24] No work was too hard, no labor too strenuous to exclude women. Among the masses of people still emerging from serfdom and existing in terrible poverty, the family was an economic unit in which men, women, and children worked in order to survive. Marriage was not a favor bestowed upon women and an economic burden for men. It was an economic arrangement for their joint survival. Women were very much in the mainstream of backbreaking labor at starvation pay.

It was only with the industrial revolution and the creation of a middle-class that marriage itself became a career for women. While the increasing industrialization and specialization of labor created a multitude of new jobs (in factories and homes) with very low wages for women of the new proletariat, "it narrowed the lives of middle-class women and robbed them of their economic usefulness." [25] Within the new middle-class there was competition in conspicuous consumption, "in finery [and] in the idleness of women." [26] As a result, in the last century, the voices of women of the upper and middle classes began to claim political freedom, the right to work, and educational facilities, while working women wanted protection. While middle-class women were fighting for equality, working women demanded preferential treatment for their sex.

Thus it was no accident that the first historic examples of state interference with private enterprise were the laws protecting the labor of women and children. For example, the Mines Act, passed in England in 1842, made it illegal to employ women in the mines or children under the age of seven; the Ten Hours Act, a few years later, limited the hours of women and children in industry to ten hours a day. Flogging women had been prohibited earlier, in the 1820s.

As Viola Klein points out, there is a "peculiar affinity between the fate of women and the origin of social science, and it is no mere coincidence that the emancipation of women should have started at the same time as the birth of sociology." [27] Middle-class women actually slipped into public life through the back door of their humanitarian interests.

The economic mainstream of American life today is owned by a few giant multinational corporations which control enormous segments not only of our economy but of other countries as well. General Motors, for example, has annual sales which equal the GNP of some small nations. Yet this economic dictatorship calls itself the free enterprise system, hypocritically fostering the notion that there is freedom for all to participate equally in our economic life. Actually, both men and women are in bondage to the economic giants. As we shall see in the following chapters, both sexes therefore suffer, although differently, from the exploitative values which are distilled from the profit system.

References

1. J. M. Tanner, "Sequence, Tempo and Individual Variation in the Growth and Development of Boys and Girls Aged Twelve to Sixtee" *Daedalus* 100 (1971), 907-931.

2. R. B. Lee, quoted in *New York Times*, 30 March 1975.

3. G. B. Kolata, "!Kung Hunter-Gatherers; Feminism, Diet and Birth Control," *Science* 185 (1974), 932-934.

4. Ibid.

5. Ibid.

6. V. Gordon Childe, *Man Makes Himself* (London: NCLC Publishing, 1936), p. 257

7. J. J. Rousseau, *Essay on the Origin and Foundations of Inequality Among Men.*

8. Ibid.

9. Ibid.

10. F. Engels, *The Origin of the Family, Private Property and the State.*

11. Ibid.

12. Ibid.

13. A. Gouldner and R. Peterson, *Notes on Technology and the Moral Order* (New York: Bobbs-Merrill, 1962).

14. R. Benedict, *Patterns of Culture* (Boston: Houghton Mifflin, 1934).

15. W. Stephens, *The Family in Cross-Cultural Perspective* (New York: Holt, Rinehart, and Winston, 1963).

16. S. de Beauvoir, *The Second Sex* (NewYork: Alfred A. Knopf, 1957), p. 58.

17. Ibid.,

18. Juliet Mitchell, *Woman's Estate* (New York: Pantheon Books, 1971), p. 52

19. Ibid., p. 66

20. Ibid., p. 56.

21. P. Chesler, *Women and Madness* (New York: Morrow, 1972).

22. S. Firestone, *The Dialectic of Sex: The Case for Feminist Revolution* (New York: Morrow, 1970).

23. Ibid., p. 11.

24. V. Klein, *The Feminine Character, History of an Ideology* (Urbana: University of Illinois Press, 1971).

25. Ibid., p. 14.

26. Ibid.

27. Ibid., p. 17.

CHAPTER 9

Sex in an Exploitative Society: Bad for Men and Worse for Women

Although there is a popular stereotype which holds that the poor have no advantages *except* sexual freedom, sociologists' studies actually show that the quality of sexual relations is better among the rich than it is among the poor in our country.[1,2,3] And the most disadvantaged of all with respect to their sex lives are poor women. This is likely to occur in any exploitative society in which the poor get the least of everything except burdens. As we saw in the Introduction, the wealthier, less exploited "manly-hearted" North Piegan women are also known for their greater sexual enjoyment.

The sexual hang-ups of the cultivated middle- and upper-classes have often been described with great sympathy, especially in twentieth-century psychological novels and plays, so heavily influenced by Freud. The picture of the middle classes, bound by bourgeois morality, inhibited and conventional, invites the assumption that the poor are sexually free. The stereotype of the manual worker with unlimited sexual prowess is a pleasant sop to middle-class guilt about their own social advantages. It parallels the Southern White stereotype of the oversexed happy-go-lucky "darkie." It is amusing that these stereotypes are only about men and do not include a picture of the oversexed, happy-go-lucky poor woman worker. In fact, until recently, women's sex life was not a subject the public liked to read about. Kinsey's biographer tells us [4] that Kinsey discovered this to his dismay when he published his book on women's sexuality and was overwhelmed by the public's outraged reaction. A realistic look at the sex life of the poor, however, shows them disadvantaged sexually as well as economically, and shows the women to be even worse off than the men.

Lee Rainwater, a social psychologist, has done a careful study which he calls "Sex in the Culture of Poverty." [5] He compared the sex life of very poor people with the sex life of middle-class people in our Midwest. Depth interviews were conducted separately with husbands and wives and with men and women living together. They were asked about their gratifications and dissatisfactions with the relationship and about the meaning and importance of sex in their lives. The answers about sexual satisfaction ranged from double +, indicating great enjoyment of sex, to double −, indicating great aversion or outright rejection of sex. The number of people of both sexes who enjoyed sex was greater among middle-class people than among lower-class people. Within each class, however, women rejected sex more often than men. And the greatest frequency of aversion to sex came among the poorest women.

The level of sexual enjoyment for men was much greater among all the groups studied than it was for women. In fact, all the men's responses could be classified as + and + +. There were many more + + responses among middle-class men than among lower-class men, but there were *no* men who indicated negative attitudes toward sex. For the women, however, many answers fell in the − category, and 20 percent of the women in the poorest class had totally negative attitudes toward sex.

The following Table of results reproduced from Rainwater's study makes clear how being poor decreases the chances for a great amount of sexual enjoyment, and being poor and a women increases the chances of experiencing total aversion.

Alfred Kinsey and his collaborators had been telling us that there is less sexual enjoyment among the less educated.[6,7] The educational level of a group is in direct proportion to its economic level. The richer you are, the better your chances of going to

Table 1
ATTITUDES TOWARD MARITAL RELATIONS BY SOCIAL CLASS°
°(Adapted from Rainwater's Study.)

Attitude	Middle	Social Class Upper-lower	Lower-lower
Men (Number)	(56)	(56)	(59)
highly + +	78%	75%	44%
mildly +	22%	25%	56%
Women (Number)	(58)	(68)	(69)
highly + +	30%	53%	20%
mildly +	36%	16%	26%
mildly −	11%	27%	34%
highly −−	3%	4%	20%

college. And education works to improve the quality of sex if only because it helps to dispel anxiety and taboos. Sex education, along with the rest of our educational facilities is less available to the poor, in spite of the strong egalitarian tradition in this country.

The Kinsey studies tell us that among less educated men there is less freedom to experiment with varying ways of foreplay, particularly less oral foreplay. The Kinsey studies tell us, furthermore, that the difference between the more educated and less educated men increases with age. Less educated men abandon the idea of trying different coital positions earlier in their marriage than the more educated men. Rainwater's study also confirms that lower-class men give up on marital sex earlier than their more affluent fellows. He found that the longer the lower-class man is married, the more likely he is to describe a reduced interest in his wife and a reduced frequency of intercourse with her. Small wonder, if he has intercourse with a woman who has an expressed aversion to sex!

Kinsey also found that among women of lowest educational or socioeconomic class, the frequency of erotic arousal and the frequency of orgasm was much less than among more educated women. So Rainwater's findings amply confirm Kinsey's. The poorest, least educated women have the least fun in sex, and many of them have no fun at all.

Of course, it is not only increased opportunity for sex education which makes middle-class men and women have more fun in sex than their poorer brothers and sisters. Middle-class people are further away from the actual brutalities of economic struggle—from welfare rolls and unemployment. So they have more leisure to try to have pleasure in each other. They have breathing space within which to develop more jointly organized pleasures outside of bed—joint activities and interests both within and outside the home. When a husband and wife are not accustomed to dealing intimately and cooperatively with each other in their daily lives, it is hard to have a close and gratifying sexual relationship.

Rainwater also found that lower-class couples spent less time with each other than did middle-class couples. They went in less for jointly organized activities outside the home. Lower-class couples went their separate ways, in more rigidly segregated sex roles. The husband was the "boss" of the home; the wife was expected to submit. He kept his rights to nights out with his buddies, and to other "manly" recreations. If both were working, the money was kept strictly separate. Middle-class couples had a more conscious ideal of equality and cooperation between husband and wife. Dinner parties, the theater, and vacations taken together are a luxury middle-class couples can afford. And those couples whose marriages were organized more cooperatively did, in fact, report more sexual enjoyment.

The brutal consequences for the quality of sexual relations of being at the bottom of the economic heap are illustrated by the answers which the men and women in Rainwater's study gave to questions about what sex meant to them. Eighty-four percent of lower-class men, who described their idea of being a husband in the most rigid, sex-typed, "he-man" way, said that sex was for the purpose of relieving a physical urge. Even in sex, they treated women as if they were things. Only 64 percent of the women in the same marriage cited relief of a physical urge as their primary need in sex. Many more women than men in all classes said that sex fulfilled a need for emotional closeness. Thus, men and women facing the worst in our exploitative system go their separate ways even in their most intimate relationships. They have such rigidly defined concepts of themselves as people and so little empathy for each other's needs that their sexual relationship is too often barren of emotional meaning. And the women have an even worse time of it than the men.

The picture of premarital sexuality is no better than the picture of "marital bliss" by classes.[8] The double standard operates in all classes, oppressing women with particular cruelty. Among the lower class, boys openly value their sexual prowess and girls are strictly graded depending on their virginity. The middle-class tempers this double standard with some compassion for both sexes but without a real change in the competitive and exploitative quality which infects most sexual relationships, along with the rest of the people's activities.

How is it, then, for the quality of sexual relations in a non-exploitative society? In our times, the societies which hold themselves out to be nonexploitative, such as the Soviet Union and the People's Republic of China, are suffering from very recent and bloody revolutions. Even if we were able to do so, it would hardly be appropriate to study the quality of people's sex lives only one or two generations away from the competitive spirit of capitalism and from the days of mass slaughter. We can, however, seek some answers among primitive, nonexploitative societies which have been studied by anthropologists.

Zuñi and Arapesh societies have both had long traditions of peace and of nonexploitative, cooperative attitudes. The two societies are in very distant parts of the earth. Arapesh are a Papuan-speaking people living in New Guinea. The Zuñi are inhabitants of New Mexico, in America's Southwest. Neither society has any well-developed political system. Nor has neither any form of legal political "authority," a police or power structure governing the people's lives. Arapesh have a patriarchal system and it is patrilocal. This means that for purposes of inheritance descent is reckoned principally on the father's side and that girls go to live with their husband's family and place of residence when they are betrothed.

Arapesh girls and boys are betrothed as early as eight or nine years of age. Zuñi have a matriarchal and matrilocal system, which means that descent is reckoned principally on mother's side, and husbands come to live in the place of the wife's family. But despite these differences, both societies are noncompetitive and nonexploitative; and most important, for our purpose, they have been studied in some depth so that there is some evidence about the quality of the relations between the sexes.

As we shall see, even in these two nonexploitative societies, there is no absolute equality between the sexes. In the Arapesh patriarchal society, men have the privilege of having more than one wife and women pay a heavier penalty for their aggressions. The decision about infanticide is the father's. In the Zuñi matriarchal society, men have the disadvantage of being strangers in their wife's household. Men are still the ones who have been caught up in sheepherding, the only possible source of individual wealth. Despite these indications that real equality between the sexes does not exist, the Arapesh and Zuñi societies show us that in nonexploitative societies relations between the sexes are more peaceful than in exploitative societies.

Let us look first at the story of the Arapesh as told by Margaret Mead.[9] The Arapesh are very poor agricultural people, cultivating difficult, steep mountainsides in taro gardens, banana gardens, and yam gardens. They plant coconut trees and they hunt, but days of famine are not unknown.

Although food is scarce and of poor quality the people are not possessive about their gardens. Although the form of their society is patriarchal, there is no such thing as enforceable power. They have a "social order which substitutes responsiveness to the concerns of others and attentiveness to the needs of others for aggressiveness, initiative, competitiveness and possessiveness, the familiar motivations upon which our culture depends. . . ."[10]

The Arapesh do not conceive of themselves as *owning* their ancestral lands but rather as belonging *to* the lands. Their system of food-growing and gathering "is conducive to the warm cooperation and sociability that they consider to be much more important" than efficiency.[11] Planting and hunting are done, not individually, but together with friends. The same is true of house-building. Food-growing and gathering (hunting) and house-building—all men's responsibilities—are almost never done alone but in cooperation with other men.

Warfare is practically unknown among the Arapesh. The only time the society seems to need some leadership qualities is for the carrying out of large-scale ceremonials which occur every three or four years. For these ceremonials some men, whom the Arapesh call "big men," must be trained to become *"buanyin." Buanyin* is the term for an exchange-partnership between men of different clans. These exchange-partners have a duty to be insulting to each other and demanding sneeringly whether the other *buanyin* ever means to get started organizing a feast or ceremonial. It should be noted that *buanyin* do not challenge each other to build up individual hoards of yams or pigs, which would imply an increase of power. Instead, they spur each other to organizing a community event. Within this context, Arapesh society fosters some competitive behavior on the part of some of its males. They urge each other to "get going." But the larger context for this much aggressiveness, which the Arapesh regard as an unpleasant duty, is a set of attitudes in which the "lowest man in the community, the man who is believed to be so far outside the moral pale that there is no use reasoning with him, is the man who eats his own kill . . . " [that is, does not share it].[12]

The Arapesh cooperative spirit pervades all parts of life, but it is particularly apparent in their views on raising children. This is a central task of the society and is considered to be equally the responsibility of fathers and mothers. Arapesh behave in this respect as if they had heard some of us deploring the way in which fathers are excluded from child-rearing.

The care and growing of the children is the work of both men and women among the Arapesh people. When the Arapesh are asked questions about the division of labor, they answer: "Cooking everyday food, bringing firewood and water, weeding, carrying—these are women's work; cooking ceremonial food, carrying pigs and heavy logs, house-building, sewing thatch, clearing and fencing, carving, hunting, and growing yams—these are men's work; making ornaments and the care of children, these are the work of both men and women." [13] Arapesh children are not considered to be the product of a moment's passion, but a child "is made by father and mother carefully, over time." [14]

Not every infant born is reared. In a few cases, if there are several other children in the family, if the father is dead or food is scarce, the newborn will not be kept alive. The Arapesh prefer boys, because, they say, a boy will stay with his parents and be a comfort to them in their old age. Since girls go to their fiancé's at betrothal, a girl will go to live elsewhere when she is quite young. The decision not to rear—that is, for infanticide—is the father's.

The father shares with his wife the task of rearing a newborn infant. He brings the leaves with which a net bag is made in which the infant is carried during most of its waking hours. He lies down by his wife's side shortly after the birth. The Arapesh say: "He is in bed, having a baby."

The father lies quietly beside his newborn child and its mother. Both he and the mother fast together for the first day following birth. Magical rites are performed which insure that the infant will be hospitable and kindly. Father and mother must sleep each night with the baby, but there is a strong taboo against intercourse. This lasts until the child takes its first step. The Arapesh are perfectly aware that this taboo acts as a brake against too many pregnancies. Arapesh feel that abrupt weaning is cruel and that it adversely affects a child. Fathers tend their children as patiently as mothers—show no embarrassment about handling bowel movements and much patience in getting children to eat away from the breast. If one comments upon a middle-aged man as good-looking, the people answer: "Good-looking? Ye-e-s? But you should have seen him before he bore all those children." [15]

Arapesh children are most gently and affectionately reared. A child's crying is a tragedy to be avoided at all costs and the most trying period for parents is when the child is too old to be comforted by the breast and too young to make its needs known. Children remain nude until they are four or five years old, and there is no shame or embarrassment about their bodies. There are no competitive or aggressive games. Little girls have more actual experiences in groups, since they go in bevies to collect firewood. Boys go with their father, brother, or uncles in smaller groups to do hunting or house-building. By the time both boys and girls are seven or eight they have learned a "happy, trustful, confident attitude toward life." [16]

Arapesh have no suicides, as one might expect in a nonaggressive people. Not that there is no aggressive behavior at all among the Arapesh. Like us, they suffer frustrations, disappointments, jealousy, guilt, and shame. And there are differences in temperament among individuals. Some Arapesh people are more aggressive than others, some more possessive, more easily angered, or moved to physical violence. But their culture has not found a use for this kind of behavior in the sanctioned exploitation of some individuals by others.

When an Arapesh child is ornery, his parents will talk to him or her in the style we jokingly (and scornfully) call "Jewish mother."

Says the parent: "I grew you. I grew the yams. I worked the sago
. . . therefore, I have a right to speak like this to you." The Arapesh
are not ashamed that loving behavior is given and expected in
return. In our own society, in contrast, (as we shall see in Chapter
16) "Jewish mothers" are ridiculed, and are more often depressed
than other women.[17]

Arapesh, according to Mead, approve more of aggression in
men than they do in women. The *buanyin* insulting relationship,
for example, is prescribed for men, not women. Mead suggests
that Arapesh women who are more aggressive by temperament or
life experience suffer more often than men from social disapproval
of this kind of behavior. Since little girls leave their families at the
time of early betrothal, their temper tantrums are likely to be less
indulgently endured than those of boys, who are kept among their
own parents and blood relatives. Little girls more often than boys
experience the pangs of feeling hateful in a relatively strange
environment. Thus they pay a stronger penalty for their aggressions.

When the first signs of puberty appear, both sexes have initiation rites which are considered by the Arapesh as necessary in
order that the child may continue to mature. Initiation rites are
not a means of maintaining the authority of older men over the
younger men or over women. There is no spirit of hazing or of fear.
For the boy the essential of the initiation rite involves segregation
from the company of women, incisions made in the boy's skin,
eating a sacrificial meal, and being shown various secret, "marvelous" things. It is also revealed to the boy that these marvelous
things are done by men, not by gods. These are the forms of
initiation rites which are prevalent in this area of the world. While
in many places—some quite near the Arapesh—initiation rites are
performed with great cruelty, among the Arapesh the forms have
been maintained but the quality is gentle.

Arapesh girls also undergo initiation rites, the purpose of which
is to foster child-rearing. Even before puberty, however, a girl
may be living in her betrothed's house. An Arapesh boy regards
bringing food for his betrothed as his responsibility, just as an
Arapesh man regards it as his responsibility to rear and nurture his
children. No girl is unwed in Arapesh society. Every girl, unless
she is horribly deformed or diseased—and few such people can
actually survive—will be married at least once.

An Arapesh girl has the same attitude of trust and expected love toward her betrothed in whose family she is living as she had at home. When Margaret Mead asked these girls if they did not cry on leaving home, their answer was surprise and a clear negative. So, there are long years during which the future husband and wife live together as brother and sister. Arapesh attitudes toward sex reflect this fact. "Intercourse does not spring from a different order of feeling than affection. . . . It is simply a final and more complete expression of the same kind of feeling. . . . No definite day is set for intercourse . . . . Some day the two will consummate their marriage . . . without haste . . . in response to a situation in which they have lived comfortably together for years in the knowledge that they belong to each other." [18]

The Arapesh do not seriously conceive of sex outside marriage. Passion is suddenly aroused—but this happens to a man who is in a strange village and therefore frightened. It is considered by the men to be the result of their having been sorcerized and seduced by the women in the strange village. Arapesh fear of their immediate neighbors is not paranoia. It is based on their neighbors' warlike attitudes. Of rape the Arapesh know only that it is an unpleasant custom among their neighbors. The Arapesh presume monogamy, but they permit polygyny—that is, they permit a man to have more than one wife. Since the death rate for men is higher than for women, this happens more often in the case of women being widowed. Three-quarters of the widows remarry within their husband's group, among whom they already have many lifelong friends.

In describing their sexual relations, the Arapesh emphasize gentleness. Either a man or wife may make the tentative advances, and it is as customary for women as men. "They played together" is a term they use for intercourse. The emphasis on mutual ease and readiness is the dominant one. Neither men nor women are explicit about orgasm. Men refer to it as the time after which the penis is no longer erect. But neither sex complains of "trouble."

Margaret Mead sums it up:

Arapesh married life . . . is so even and so contented that there is nothing to relate at all. . . . The ethnologist cannot be forever recording: The two wives of Biamal with their two small daughters came into the village today. One of them remained to cook dinner, and the other took the two children and went for firewood. When she returned the dinner was cooked, Biamal came in from hunting, they all sat around the fire until chilliness drove them inside, and from within the house where the whole family sat together came the sounds of low laughter and quiet conversation.[19]

With this almost rhapsodic description of marital happiness by Mead, we can answer in the affirmative the question whether marital relations are any better in a nonexploitative society. And this despite the fact that the Arapesh are poor. Mead's own comments on Arapesh views of human nature are a measure of the extent to which the values of an exploitative society can invade our thinking. Mead writes:

> The Western reader will realize only too easily how special an interpretation the Arapesh have put upon human nature, how fantastic they have been in selecting a personality type rare in either men or women. . . . It is hard to judge which seems to us the most utopian and unrealistic . . . to say that there are no differences between men and women, or to say that both men and women are naturally maternal, gentle, responsive and unaggressive.[20]

By our ways of reckoning, Arapesh ways seem like a tour de force in which *they* have somehow managed to mold human beings against their inherently evil natures. Evil is taken for granted by us, since we are raised in a competitive, aggressive, and exploitative environment. By our reckoning, the Arapesh are "fantastic." But are they?

Let us look at another nonexploitative society, the Zuñi, and see how things go among them with respect to the relations between the sexes. The Zuñi, although like the Arapesh in their nonexploitative, noncompetitive existence, are an important contrast in several respects. In the first place, they are poor neither in food nor in worldly goods. In the second place, they are a matriarchal and matrilocal society, in which the theoretical position of women is in some respects superior to men. The Arapesh, it will be remembered, are a patriarchal and patrilocal society, in which the position of women is theoretically inferior. Nevertheless, as we shall see, the relation between the sexes in Zuñi society seems excellent, if the frequency of stable, tranquil lifelong marriage is used as the criterion.

Let us briefly examine the Zuñi story, as told by the anthropologist Irving Goldman.[21] Zuñi depend on agriculture and sheep raising for their subsistence. As with the Arapesh, the physical environment in which they live is difficult, since the high New Mexican plateau is arid. Prayer for rain dominates Zuñi religion.

The mechanism of social control among the Zuñi is not in the hands of any central authority, but in the subtle sanctions of public, that is, group censure. In their agricultural economic life, the Zuñi are a cooperative, noncompetitive people. Like the Arapesh, they also have no suicides.

Fields used for cultivation belong either to an individual man or to a matriarchal household, but in either case they are worked by all the men in the household who are assisted by friends and relatives. "All produce of the fields is pooled in one common storeroom to become the common property of all the women in the household." [22] Although differences in wealth do exist, every principle of Zuñi social organization is opposed to an excessive concentration of surplus in the hands of any one individual. Wealth which has been accumulated is redistributed among the members of the village either during the winter-solstice ceremonies, or in spontaneous gifts.

Sheepherding was introduced into culture by the Spaniards, and the attitudes of Zuñi toward sheepherding represent a foreign complex grafted onto their ancient economic attitudes. Sheepherding has become a major source of individual wealth. Sheep are now a means of trade for such contemporary luxuries as guns, kitchen equipment, and automobiles. Thus, it is only in connection with sheep-owning that precise ideas of property, acquisitiveness, and prestige attached to material possessions have developed among the Zuñi. Before the establishment of trading in sheep, cooperative attitudes were predominant. Although capital in sheep was individually owned by men, profits were shared by all in a group which shared the work of herding, lambing, and shearing. Even now, few Zuñi know how many sheep they own.

Nor do they compete with one another for sheep. Rather, those who are already established help the young get started.

House-building is likewise a collective undertaking in which all men of a ceremonial group share the labor, assisted by the women (who are the plasterers). When the house is built, it becomes the property of the women even though they were only assistants in building. Yet the men do not seem to feel that they have wasted their labor in building the house. Both sexes are skilled in artistic craft: Women create highly-decorated pottery; men work in turquoise and silver.

Zuñi children are very gently reared. They are nursed a long time and in a affectionate way. Zuñi children grow up under little restraint; they face no stern disciplinarian in the house. Rather, parents are all kindness to the child. Zuñi parents invoke the sanction of shame. Zuñi children are expected to grow up as fast as possible and are shamed by being called "childish." But both men and women shower affection upon any child in the house.

For girls, puberty passes unmarked, without any of the ceremonials which mark it among many other peoples. For boys, however, there are initiation ceremonies. Again, as with the Arapesh, the forms of the initiation rites are similar to those of other cultures throughout the geographical areas. The forms also include culturally sanctioned cruelty. But the Zuñi administer the initiation rite in the gentlest spirit. It is "not meant as punishment . . . not part of a process of breaking the boy. It is to purify, to bring good luck. . . ." [23] Boys are initiated between the ages of five and nine and again at fourteen, according to customs generally prevalent in the Southwest. At the second initiation, they learn that the masked gods who are initiating them are human beings impersonating gods. It is then the boys' turn to don masks and perform the initiation rites on their elders. They are thus initiated into the "realities" of the culture's ceremonials and into a sense of the equality of human beings. Girls are not forbidden to enter ceremonial societies, but it is not considered customary.

Zuñi are a monogamous society. Marriages are made by personal choice and are initiated by either sex. Since women are not dependent upon a husband for economic security, girls exercise considerable personal choice in marriage. Marriages are very simply arranged between the parties and involve no property transactions beyond a formal exchange. Girls who are very "choosy" about marrying are admonished, but that is the extent of cultural sanction against them. Zuñi mythology, however, is full of stories about girls who are punished by the supernatural because they will not accept the first man who comes along.

At marriage, a man leaves the household of his mother to join the communal economic unit of his mother-in-law's household, without, however, relinquishing his ceremonial obligations in his mother's house. The matriarchal household is the economic unit, cooperatively organized. It is a group of variable composition: a mother, her husband, her daughters and their husbands, and a fluctuating group of divorced or unmarried sons. In the things that count most, that is, in matters of ritual, a Zuñi man is an outsider in the house of his wife. A man finding himself out of harmony with this group, quietly withdraws. A Zuñi woman who finds living with her husband uncongenial places his "small bundle of belongings on the threshold of the home as a sign that he is no longer desired." Divorce is thus easy. The Zuñi do not like bickering and quarreling and if a marriage becomes too unhappy it is easily remedied when the man moves out. Still, "a very large proportion of Zuñi marriages endure through the greater part of a lifetime" and the great majority of Zuñi marriages remain peaceful.

In this society, where there is no exploitative class and no established power backed by physical force, it is also the case that women are in a position of social equality with men. In fact, although the ownership of food is collective, it is legally the property of women. A man is a relative stranger in his wife's household (which is also his mother-in-law's household). Among the Zuñi, the tables are thus turned a bit against men. Like women in so many parts of the world, it is the men who have to leave their loving households to enter a strange household on marriage. In Zuñi rape tales, the sexual roles are reversed. There are even tales of young husbands who have run away and are afraid of their wives.

Arapesh and Zuñi cultures show us that where relations among the people are generally peaceful and non-exploitative, sexual and marital relations are also peaceful. Long-term, monogamous marriages are thus not an "achievement" made by striving after moral excellence. They are an understandable product of loving feeling which experience no stress from the culture's oppression of either partner. They teach us, furthermore, that even in these "utopias," where growing up occurs in a loving atmosphere, sexual maturity is understood to be a time for renunciation of some childhood loving. There are initiation rites which signify the end of childhood and the beginning of adult sexuality. But in a peaceful society, this renunciation need not be violent nor need it be effected by force. Zuñi and Arapesh people both seem to assume that human nature is gentle among both sexes. And their sexual and marital relations seem to prosper under this assumption.

References

1. A. Kinsey, W. Pomeroy and C. I. Martin, *Sexual Behavior in the Human Male* (Philadelphia: Saunders, 1948).

2. A. Kinsey, W. Pomeroy, C. I. Martin and P. Gebhard, *Sexual Behavior in the Human Female* (Philadelphia: Saunders, 1954).

3. L. Rainwater, "Sex in the Culture of Poverty," eds. C. Broderick and J. Bernard, *The Individual, Sex and Society* (Baltimore, Md.: The Johns Hopkins Press, 1969).

4. W. Pomeroy, *Dr. Kinsey and the Institute for Sex Research* (New York: Harper & Row, 1972).

5. L. Rainwater, op. cit.

6. A. Kinsey, W. Pomeroy and C. I. Martin, op. cit.

7. A. Kinsey, W. Pomeroy, C. I. Martin and P. Gebhard, op. cit.

8. I. Reiss, "Premarital Sexual Standards," eds. C. Broderick and J. Bernard, *The Individual, Sex and Society* (Baltimore, Md.: The Johns Hopkins Press, 1969).

9. M. Mead, *Sex and Temperament in Three Primitive Societies* (New York: New American Library, 1953), p. 23.

10. Ibid, p. 23.

11. Ibid., p. 25.

12. Ibid., p. 31.

13. Ibid., p. 38.

14. Ibid., p. 33.

15. Ibid., p. 39.

16. Ibid., p. 53.

17. P. Bart, "Depression in Middle-aged Women," eds. V. Gornick

and B. Moran, *Women in Sexist Society* (New York: New American Library, 1971), pp. 163-186.

18. M. Mead, op. cit., p. 77.

19. M. Mead, op. cit., pp. 92-93.

20. M. Mead, op. cit., p. 118.

21. I. Goldman, "The Zuñi Indians of New Mexico," ed. M. Mead, *Cooperation and Competition Among Primitive Peoples* (New York: McGraw-Hill, 1937).

22. Ibid., p. 315.

23. Ibid., p. 341.

CHAPTER 10

Woman Power: A Corollary of People's Power

We have seen how sex in an exploitative society is bad for men and worse for women. Now let us look at how men and women fare earning their livelihoods in exploitative and nonexploitative societies. It stands to reason that in nonexploitative societies, where the people have more power over their own economic destinies, both sexes should be better off. But, as it turns out, not in equal measure. We shall see that even in socialist societies with a stated commitment to the equality of the sexes women are "less equal" than men.

Some recent comparative studies of the economic and political role of women in differing societies help us to document the notion that the absence of an exploitative system fosters woman power. The studies were conducted in very different parts of the world and with very different techniques of investigation, yet they point to a similar conclusion: Women have more economic and political power in a less exploitative society.

One study is by a group of French women anthropologists who set out to study the lot of women in the primitive (precolonial) societies of tropical Africa.[1] Another study of women in Africa was done by an American anthropologist, Karen Sacks.[2] It is a careful comparative study of the position of women in four African societies (also precolonial) which differed in the degree of egalitarian or class-based structure. In contrast to these studies of women in precolonial and precapitalist times, there are two studies of women under a present-day socialist system, that is, in a highly industrialized, technologically advanced society. One is by an American economist, N. T. Dodge, and it details the role of women in the Soviet ecomony.[3] Another study, by Hilda Scott, is of women under socialism in Czechoslovakia.[4] While both these studies describe the ideal of the sexes' equality under socialism, both make it clear that the ideal has not been attained. Scott's book documents a "lag in [socialist] consciousness" which sees nothing wrong in equating one poor job plus household chores for women with one good job for men. In spite of this cultural lag, however, women under socialism are at least the constitutional equal of men, while in our own country they are still fighting for the Equal Rights Amendment.

Let's look first at the French study of women's role in differing primitive societies of tropical Africa. It should be noted that all the societies were studied as they were in precolonial days, that is, before French or Belgian colonial oppression was superimposed upon whatever indigenous oppression already existed. The societies studied included the Dakar, Coniagui, Fulani, Nzakere, and Burundi people. These were varied in their organization; some were agricultural peoples; some nomadic herding peoples; some possessed very complex, stratified social systems based on absolute monarchical power; some were less stratified societies based on kinship ties.

Certain common features, all reflecting a bleak picture of social inferiority of women, were clearly apparent in the life in all these societies. First, all the societies were patriarchal and patrilocal. Marriage was polygamous, which meant that a man could have more than one wife. A girl was considered "on loan" to her husband by her parents until various economic transactions attached to marriage could be completed. Since the societies were all patriarchal and patrilocal, girls had to leave their homes for their husbands' families in which they were the strangers, often with no emotional ties to their husbands to ease their adjustment. Typically, there was a relative absence of any friendly intimacy between husband and wife.

Pubertal initiation rites involved removing a girl's clitoris and a long period of seclusion thereafter. Premarital sexual freedom was the norm for both sexes but could hardly be much pleasure to a woman without her clitoris. And since marriage meant leaving home, as well as the end of any sexual freedom, marriage was considered an evil by women, but a lesser evil than being without marital status, and particularly without children. A mother was a figure of prime importance in her new household once she had children. Women thus set much greater store by their children than by their husbands. In fact, the relations between the sexes were expected to be more hostile than not, since marriage was more of a social duty to be performed than a personal undertaking connected with individual preference or emotional fulfillment.

This is the kind of picture of women's inferior status in patriarchal and exploitative societies which we are accustomed to learning about not only in Africa, but in India, Australia, and many other parts of the world, including our own. It tells us that civilized societies have no monopoly on the oppression of women, and that some primitive societies can be equally brutal. But even within this grim context, the study of women in tropical Africa has turned up some instances of very real authority exercised by women. As we would expect, these instances occurred particularly in those societies with a system not based on the profit motive.

One of the anthropologists, Annie Lebeuf, studied the extent of women's authority in two main categories of African societies.[5] The first category comprised societies in which there was a highly organized state, and in which the economy was based on the profit motive. In these societies, social classes existed between which there was an unequal distribution of wealth and a corresponding difference in status. The second category of societies were those in which the social structure was mainly based on kinship organization, with kinship ties being the main basis of social relations. Authority rested with various heads of lineages and families (always a male authority), but patriarchal authority based itself on age differences and on ritual functions rather than on economic power. It is in this second category of societies that women could be found to have real authority.

In both groups of patriarchal societies, women attained positions of authority only when a male was not available. Although they did not normally hold authority, women in kinship-based patriarchal societies formed strong "unions." Such women's groups were unknown among the class-based hierarchical systems. These women's unions elected their own heads on the basis of personality and ability. They became extremely powerful politically. As an example of their organization and their power, in 1929 they involved more than 2 million people in a struggle against the colonial government over the government's placing a tax on women's property. This struggle resulted in the "Aba riots" which spread through a large area of surrounding country. Nothing like this kind of initiative and strength among women has ever been reported as occurring in the more hierarchical societies. Thus, even when women are in socially inferior positions, there is more room for their freedom where there is more freedom in general.

Karen Sacks's study of four precolonial, noncapitalist African societies documents this point in greater detail.[6] Sacks chose to compare the position of women in the Mbuti, Lovedu, Pondo, and Ganda societies. These four societies form a continuum from egalitarian to class structure. The Mbuti, of Zaire, were a band society, with subsistence based on communal net hunting and gathering of vegetable food. The Lovedu, in South Africa, were principally hoe agriculturists, with production for use rather than for profit. Pondo combined agriculture with livestock and had the beginnings of production for exchange, principally of cattle. Ganda, a class society in Uganda, based subsistence on hoe agriculture, with production for exchange, and the productive resources under male ownership.

Sacks compared the position of women in these four societies, using a variety of indexes of women's status. Among the Mbuti and the Lovedu, women were the equals of men, whereas Ganda women were subordinate and Pondo women fell somewhere in between. Sacks writes that "women in general stand in more equal relationship to men in nonclass societies than in class societies." [7]

The story of women in the Soviet economy makes the same fundamental point, as well as providing a very illuminating contrast to the story of women in the economic life of our own country. In the Soviet Union, as in the People's Republic of China, economic and political power both theoretically reside in the people. In neither place can it be said that power has settled into being taken for granted as belonging to the people, since both countries have been at war, repelling invaders, until as recently as twenty-five years ago. In both countries, grave violations of individual liberty have occurred in the name of "national security," and this excuse sounds as suspect at a distance as it does at home.

But the collective ownership of the means of production is the law of the land in both the Soviet Union and China, and the forms of economic as well as political equality have also been officially proclaimed. The profit system has been officially abolished in favor of an economy planned to promote the general welfare. The equality of women and men has also been proclaimed. A conception of women's role as equal to men's is an integral part of the theory of both socialism and communism. It is thus well worth our while to see how things are for women, both according to principle and, as far as can be judged, according to reality.

Although reliable information about China is not yet available to us, there is very good information about the Soviet Union on which we can draw. A study of women in the Soviet economy, published in 1966, was made by a distinguished American economist, N. T. Dodge,[8] working under the sponsorship of the Foreign Studies Group of the U.S. Office of Economic and Manpower Studies. The National Science Foundation contributed to the support of the study, which was made under the supervision of the Department of Economics of the University of Maryland. The study itself is a careful, objective account, based on evaluation of the best evidence available on the subject.

One outstanding conclusion of this study is that women in the Soviet Union "have come to occupy an extremely significant position ... particularly at the professional and semi-professional levels."[9] It adds: "Perhaps more than any other, Soviet society has developed and put to use both the strength and the genius of its women."[10] Dodge is also struck by "the difference in the utilization of women" in any comparison of American and Soviet "manpower resources." (Clearly Dodge is not familiar with feminist usage of terms referring to both sexes.) "For the most part," he writes, "Soviet women appear to have won the battle for equality."[11]

Not all of the impetus for this utilization of women had come from the ideals of socialism and communism. Women were badly needed in the Soviet Union both after the revolution and particularly after World War II. In 1946, at the end of World War II, women outnumbered men by 25 million! Only a slight change in population ratio had occurred by 1959. In 1959, women comprised 54.9 percent of the total population in the U.S.S.R., and 63.4 percent of the population over thirty-five. The comparable figures for the United States are women making up 50.8 percent of the total population, and 51.9 percent of the population over thirty-five. So the ravages of war which decimated the men made women of increased importance as a labor source.

But the socialist program did also play a part. For one thing, full employment is the order of the day in the Soviet Union. Wiping out the profit system has wiped out the notion of an "acceptable" chronic level of unemployment which the United States takes for granted as inevitable. Along with the full employment of men, participation of women in the labor force especially in the age group twenty to thirty-nine is 80 percent—a "phenomenally high rate in a country as industrially advanced as the Soviet Union." [12] In addition, Dodge shows that the pattern of entry into the labor force at age twenty and withdrawal from it at age twenty-five and reentry at age thirty-five, which characterizes women in our country, does not occur in the Soviet Union. In our country, women enter the labor force, leave to get married and raise children, then reenter the labor force after the children are grown. In the Soviet Union the participation of women in the labor force stays relatively constant with age, as well as phenomenally high.

A second reason why women participate so much more fully in the economic life of the Soviet Union is that the working woman is culturally approved. According to Dodge, "the Soviet Union has succeeded in creating an atmosphere in which a woman feels apologetic if she does not work." [13] The strong propaganda machinery of the government and the educational atmosphere and the law of the land are all geared to increase women's participation in all sectors of the labor force. Dodge emphasizes this point and tells us that we can gain "some comprehension of the forces which the party and government have brought to bear in mobilizing female talent . . . if we consider what would happen in the United States if the resources employed to sell soap and cigarettes . . . were used to promote the idea of women as engineers and doctors." [14]

A third reason why so many Soviet women work is that there is "legislation which could serve as a model" [15] which provides women with necessary government support for their efforts. Equal pay, equal job opportunities, paid maternity leave, old-age security, and protection from injury on the job are all part of the law of the land. Nursery facilities are provided for young children. Dodge estimates that facilities are provided to take care of 12 percent of all the children in the whole country and 20 percent of all the children in the area around Moscow as compared to an infinitesimal percentage of the children in our country. Even in the Soviet Union the demand for these facilities outruns the supply, but the contrast with our own country where even pitifully inadequate appropriations for day care centers are vetoed by the President is striking.

Still another reason why so many women participate in the professional life of the country is the emphasis on equality between the sexes of vocational choice and in educational opportunity. Soviet girls in school through the tenth grade receive as much training in the sciences and mathematics as do boys. Dodge tells us that the Soviets have been "remarkably successful in efforts to educate women and in particular to interest them in fields of science, technology, and medicine." [16] While women comprise only 7 percent of the physicians in the United States, they are 75 percent of the physicians in the Soviet Union. In engineering, the contrast is if possible even more striking. "Over a quarter of a million Soviet women are engineers, and make up a third of the profession while in the U.S., female engineers account for less than 1 percent of the total." [17]

It is unlikely that Soviet girls have recently acquired the genes which make them able to master enough mathematics, chemistry, and physics to become engineers or physicians. But it is likely that an atmosphere which fosters women's participation in the world's work makes it possible for women to develop their intellectual capacities without so much conflict as women experience in our country, where a woman participating as a man's equal is a bit suspect as to her femininity. Eleanor Maccoby, an expert in the field of sex differences in intellectual functioning, reminds us that in the United States a girl who cultivates good analytic thinking is "defying the conventions for what is appropriate behavior for her sex." [18] Maccoby tells us that it is a "rare intellectual woman who has not paid a price for it: a price in anxiety." Her comments only underscore the sad picture of women's self-destructive anxiety which we shall see in Chapters 16 and 17.

Note, however, that women are still not in positions of power in the Soviet government. Nor do they occupy positions of power in the universities and professions in which they play so much more numerous a part than women do in our country. The Soviet Union is still a male-dominated society in which the prospects of women's equality in actual power are still dim. Fewer women than men occupy high-ranking positions, even in the fields of education and health, where women participants are the majority. And there are no women in the high Soviet government hierarchy. In other words, the battle for women's full equality of participation has still to be fought even in a country professing socialist ideas. Old patriarchal attitudes die hard.

Hilda Scott's [19] study of women under socialism in Czechoslovakia illustrates just how hard it is for patriarchal attitudes to die. Scott had two reasons for choosing Czechoslovakia as the socialist country in which to study women's position. First, she had lived there for many years and so was witness to the sociological trends she describes; second, because Czechoslovakia, in contrast to the Soviet Union, had had a long-standing democratic tradition and was a highly developed industrial nation before the advent of socialism.

"By 1972," she tells us, "the image of the beautiful tractor driver as a heroine had receded so far into the distant past that a top official of the Czechoslovak Communist party, on a visit to a cooperative farm at harvest time, was captured on the TV screen expressing astonishment when he was introduced to two young husband-and-wife combine-operator teams. 'And do you let them drive?' he inquired of the husbands? 'They know the job,' came the terse reply." [20]

One fascinating reason for this failure of the socialist ideal of women's equality was the indirect result of a tendency even under socialism for women to enter jobs conventional for their sex. Such fields as health, social welfare, and agriculture became "saturated" with women between 1948 and 1958. An even more compelling reason for the failure of the socialist ideal was the failure of the ruling powers (mostly men) to recognize their rigidity in adhering to the rule: A good job for a man equals a poor job for a woman plus her household duties.

The professions of medicine and teaching, for example, became "afflicted" with what was considered the "blight of feminization." By the mid-1960s, women were about to become the majority of physicians. This was in part because the best male students went either into physics and chemistry or into heavy industry where the pay is higher than that of doctors. Moreover, it was discovered, belatedly, that the burden of women's work (the "second shift") was still afflicting women doctors, interfering seriously with their efficiency. They took their specialization exams, for example, later than men, and a smaller percentage of women rose to become heads of hospitals or clinics. Forty-one percent of women doctors, polled about their experiences, reported that they had had to exert "extraordinary effort" to combine their roles as physicians and homemakers, even though these women had fewer children than the national average. How did socialist Czechoslovakia deal with the problems of women trying to combine a career in medicine with a personal life? Not by additional child-care facilities or by a campaign to raise the consciousness of men to accept a role as caretakers of children and homemakers. But by increasing the strictness of admission requirements for women entering medical school so that fewer women would be trained!

The blindness of the Czech government to the discrepancy between the ideal of women's equality and the realities of women's inferior social position is clearly rooted in partriarchal attitudes which decree that homemaking and child rearing are women's work. Although feminists are scornful of such an attitude, the notion that child rearing is a sufficient occupation for women still has widespread appeal, not only among men, but among many women as well.

This is well illustrated by some comments which Dodge made in summarizing his study of Soviet women. While acknowledging the Soviets' enormous success in tapping talents which would otherwise be lost to society, Dodge finds the Soviet attitude toward women's economic productivity as rather inferior to our own. Our superiority is this: We view childbearing and the "raising of a family as a sufficient contribution to the welfare of society" [21] so that a woman need not feel pressed to do anything more. And there is something for the moment quite tempting about this existential view of women's immanent capacity for childbearing as contrasted to the Soviet's utilitarian attitude toward women as a productive force to be cultivated. But it is an existential (and romantic) view of women through a man's eyes. The moment one considers the question whether conceiving and rearing children should be enough of a raison d'être for both sexes, the picture changes.

Individual human beings of both sexes have many other reasons for living besides reproducing themselves. The assumption that species reproduction is a sufficient occupation for women dooms them to a narrowed participation in life's other experiences. It also transforms both sexes' experience of parenthood from a source of individual personal fulfillment into its most utilitarian function: species reproduction.

As we saw in Chapter 9, the Arapesh's socially advanced idea of child rearing as an important occupation for both sexes occurs in a nonexploitative economy, where there is no need either to penalize or romanticize having children. "Parenting" by both sexes is now also an ideal among many educated, liberal Americans. Its implementation, however, seems to me to require more than goodwill on the part of both sexes. A secure economic base in which both parents need not fear unemployment or suffer the indignities of being exploited is also required. That the idea of "parenting" has failed even to be acknowledged in an advanced socialist country, which could at least theoretically make provision for both sexes to share child rearing, is a measure of how deep-seated patriarchal beliefs can be. But an economy theoretically geared to people's needs rather than to profit-making at least has the potential for creating the economic conditions under which "parenting" could flourish.

References

1. Denise Paulme, ed, *Women of Tropical Africa* (Berkeley: University of California Press, 1963).

2. Karen Sacks, "Engels Revisited: Women, the Organization of Production, and Private Property," eds. M. Z. Rosaldo and L. Lamphere, *Woman, Culture and Society* (Stanford, Calif.: Stanford University Press, 1974), 207-222.

3. N. T. Dodge, *Women in the Soviet Economy* (Baltimore, Md.: The Johns Hopkins Press, 1966).

4. Hilda Scott, *Does Socialism Liberate Women?* (Boston: Beacon Press, 1974).

5. A. Lebeuf, "The Role of Women in the Political Organization of African Societies," ed. D. Paulme, *Women of Tropical Africa* (Berkeley: University of California Press, 1963).

6. K. Sacks, op. cit.

7. K. Sacks, op. cit., p. 219.

8. N. T. Dodge, op. cit.

9. N. T. Dodge, op. cit., p. 1.

10. N. T. Dodge, op. cit., p. 4.

11. N. T. Dodge, op. cit., p. 1.

12. N. T. Dodge, op. cit., p. 38.

13. N. T. Dodge, op. cit., p. 53.

14. N. T. Dodge, op. cit., p. 54.

15. N. T. Dodge, op. cit., p. 75.

16. N. T. Dodge, op. cit., p. 139.

17. N. T. Dodge, op. cit., p. 244.

18. E. Maccoby, "Women's Intellect," eds. S. Farber and R. Wilson, *The Potential of Women* (New York: McGraw-Hill, 1963) p. 33.

19. Hilda Scott, op. cit.

20. Hilda Scott, op. cit., p. 1.

21. N. T. Dodge, op. cit.

CHAPTER 11

Why Are There Culture Myths of Women's Inferiority?

Explicit and implicit myths of women's inferiority are needed in order to rationalize the injustice of women's subjugation. This is the same process with which we are familiar in myths about the intellectual inferiority of blacks. Culture myths operate at two levels: as "givens" in the social milieu, and as deeply-felt personal attitudes. Myths, rituals, customs, laws, traditions, and religious teachings of a society contain explicit instructions about how to treat women. Myths about women are also implicit in the beliefs and personalities of both sexes.

Both explicit and implicit culture myths carry an aura of truth and rightness about them. Analysis of them is difficult from within the culture, not only because analysis questions fundamental traditions, but because the thinking and feeling of the analyst have been molded by his or her own acculturation. Analysis is difficult also from a cultural outsider's perspective because the outsider often cannot grasp the logical assumptions of a differently accultured people.

One of the most productive viewpoints in the analysis of explicit culture myths is that of the anthropologist, Lévi-Strauss, who uses a method he calls "structuralism." For example, Lévi-

Strauss analyzes an Australian creation myth as an expression of the rationally perceived contradiction between men's social power and women's natural fertility. He stops short of calling the creation myth a rationalization of injustice, a Freudian concept which emphasizes the emotional distortion in the myth. Lévi-Strauss's emphasis on people's rationality is an important supplement to Freud's emphasis on their irrationality. Let's look briefly at the structuralist approach to the analysis of myths before turning, in the next chapter, to Freud's concepts.

Structuralism assumes that "history organizes data in relation to conscious expressions of social life, while anthropology proceeds by examining its unconscious foundations." [1] Lévi-Strauss assumes further that the "unconscious activity of the mind consists in imposing form upon content," [2] and further, that "these forms are fundamentally the same for all minds—ancient and modern, primitive and civilized (as the study of the symbolic function expressed by language so strikingly indicates)." [3] It is thus the anthropologist's task to "grasp the unconscious structures underlying each institution and each custom, in order to obtain a principle of interpretation valid for other institutions and other customs." [4]

Lévi-Strauss's search for the structures unconsciously underlying primitive institutions is thus a search which assumes that intellectual processes are the same in all minds. It also assumes that the unconscious processes create rational structures. Lévi-Strauss distrusts "affectivity ... as the most obscure side of man." [5] But he does assume (following Rousseau) that "compassion (pitié) ... the only psychic state in which content is indissociably both affective and intellectual" [6] enables a human being to identify with others. Identification with other creatures is a fundamental basis on which rational structures such as the consciousness of cultural contradictions can occur. It is also the basis for the feelings of injustice which arise from the contradiction, which must then be rationalized.

The process by which a perceived contradiction between men's social power and women's creativity is transformed into a rationalization is a very complicated affair. The term "rationalization" signifies an emotional defense, which means also that the thinking in it is distorted. Using this term makes it easy to assume that the contradiction is not really there at all but exists only in the mind of the perceiver. Lévi-Strauss does not deny the reality of power relationships and injustice, nor does he attempt to explain away the infrastructure underlying human psychic functioning as if the substructure were an illusion. "I do not mean to suggest," he writes, "that social life, the relations between man and nature, are a projection or even result, of a conceptual game taking place in the mind. . . ." [7] Lévi-Strauss does not question "the undoubted primacy of infrastructures." [8] His work develops a theory of the conceptual superstructures which people erect upon the infrastructures, a "problem scarcely touched on by Marx." [9]

The contradiction between men's social power and women's creativity can be experienced as neutrally toned perception of a phenomenon, or it can evoke passionate feelings of injustice. (Since men are its indirect rather than direct victims, perhaps they might be the cool perceivers of the contradiction.) Lévi-Strauss does not ignore compassion, which is the basis for feelings of injustice arising from the contradiction. He does, however, emphasize the rationality of people's thinking as they assimilate the conditions, including the contradictions existing around them. With this emphasis on rationality, it is easier to retain the importance of the infrastructure which gave rise to the contradiction. Freud emphasized the internalized emotional conflicts which the contradiction evokes, and the efforts people make to justify or resolve the conflicts by rationalizing them. In so doing, Freud tended to obscure or at least minimize the contradictions which inhere in the power structure, as we shall see in Chapter 12.

Dread of women or envy of women could not be such powerful psychic forces demanding denial or reversal into institutionalized inferiority of women if an exploitative, hostile milieu were not in the background. It is this background of oppression and violence which makes the stakes so high. Men in all societies have an opposite-sex caretaker in their mothers, and mothers have the power of life and death over their infants. But it is a society hostile to life which determines that having a cross-sex caretaker in infancy is a dangerous circumstance. Different-sex or same-sex gender identity could exist without such dangerous implications. Men and women could even envy each other's sex but without an oppressive power structure (behind both sexes) there is neither the need nor the possibility of institutionalizing revenge.

It is interesting to note, in passing, how insistently rational is

French thinking, as contrasted with the German tradition. In tracing the development of morality, Piaget also emphasizes the rational, charting the cognitive changes through which morality passes as children grow up and scarcely mentioning their affective basis. Freud, in contrast, emphasizes the emotional and conflictual basis of moral development.

Let's look now at Lévi-Strauss's analysis of a particular Australian creation myth. (Lévi-Strauss's analysis is based upon an account of the North Australian Murngin by Lloyd Warner.) This myth is also the basis for an important part of Murngin sexual initiation rites for the young men reaching puberty. Lévi-Strauss assumes that myth is a form of "code making it possible to ensure, in the form of conceptual systems, the convertibility of messages appertaining to . . . men's relations with each other on the one hand, or . . . men's relations with nature." [10] Here is Lévi-Strauss's account of the myth and its interpretation:

> At the beginning of time the Wawilak sisters set off on foot towards the sea, naming places, animals and plants as they went. One of them was pregnant and the other carried her child. Before their departure they had both indeed had incestuous relations with men of their own moiety [kinship group].
>
> After the birth of the younger sister's child, they continued their journey and one day stopped near a water hole where the great snake Yurlunggur lived who was the totem of the Dua moiety to which the sisters belonged. The older sister polluted the water with menstrual blood. The outraged python came out, caused a deluge of rain and a general flood and then swallowed the women and their children. When the snake raised himself the waters covered the entire earth and its vegetation. When he lay down again the flood receded . . . had the Wawilak sisters not committed incest and polluted the water hole of Yurlunggur there would have been neither life nor death, neither copulation or reproduction on the earth, and there would have been no cycle of seasons.[11]

Lévi-Strauss's interpretation of this myth rests first on a number of conditions prevailing in Murngin life. First, they live in an area of the world where there is a rainy season and a dry season, and this seasonal change is so regular that it can be predicted almost to the day. (Lévi-Strauss tells us that the graph of rainfall recorded at Port Darwin over a period of forty-six years might be a picture of the snake, Yurlunggur.) The rainy season causes the Murngin people to disperse and take refuge in small groups during which they are threatened with famine. A few days after the flood recedes, vegetation is lush and animals reappear. The rainy season is thus the bad season; the dry season is the good season.

Second, this Australian group shares with others of its neighbors a system in which old men enjoy sexual privileges and they also control esoteric and cruel initiation rites to which the young men in the tribe must submit. Women are excluded from these rites; women and the young men are in position of inferior social power in this and many other ways.

Lévi-Strauss's explanation of the Murngin creation myth is that it establishes "homologies between natural and social conditions." These equivalences are put together in order to manage contradictions in a reasonable way.

First, there is a homology between the snake and the rainy season. The snake and the rainy season are also equated with maleness. The Murngin consciously associate the snake and the rainy season on the basis that the rainy season is the fertilizing period; the snake is the (male) fertilizing agent. (Although Lévi-Strauss does not mention it, this concept fits Freudian theory in which the snake is the symbol of the phallus.) The "protagonists" of the great mythical drama, the snake and the Wawilak sisters, are associated with the rainy and the dry season respectively. The former represents the male and the initiated, the latter the female and the uninitiated. . . . The equivalences are roughly the following: [12]

pure, sacred; male, superior, fertilizing (rains), bad season

impure, profane; female, inferior, fertilized (land), good season

The contradiction embedded in this table is the equation of the bad season with the pure, sacred, superior, fertilizing male. On the natural plane, the good season is clearly superior to the bad; on the social plane, the good season is made inferior. The problem becomes how to interpret the contradiction: If the good season is said to be superior and male, then both social power and sterility would have to be attributed to the female element. This absurdity is disguised by making "a double division of the whole society into two classes of men and women (now ritually as well as sexually differentiated)." The young men are classed with the women and made inferior to the old men. And, "in consequence men forgo embodying the happy side of existence for they cannot both rule and personify it. Irrevocably committed to the role of gloomy owners of a happiness accessible to them only through an intermediary, they fashion an image of themselves on the model of their sages and old men . . . to attain full masculinity young men must . . . lastingly submit . . ." [13] to severe initiation rites at puberty.

Lévi-Strauss's interpretation thus follows the rational processes by which a people make sense of the conditions they find around them. The myth and the initiation rites for which it is the basis help to make sense of and to perpetuate the inferior social position of young men and of women, which the culture recognizes as a contradiction, if not as an injustice.

As we saw a few moments ago, Lévi-Strauss takes for granted the symbolic equation of snake and phallus. He also tells us that there is a "very profound analogy which people throughout the world seem to find between copulation and eating." He explains that the "lowest common denominator of the union of the sexes and the union of the eater and the eater is that they both effect a conjunction by complementarity." [14] He observes further that "the equation of male with devourer and female with the devoured is more familiar to us and certainly the more prevalent in the world but one must not forget that the inverse equivalence is often found at a mythological level in the theme of the vagina dentata." As we see, Lévi-Strauss emphasizes the rational basis for the simile between eating and intercourse; Freud would emphasize the affective foundation for the simile in the pleasurable memories and feelings of suckling at the breast which are revived during intercourse.

Lévi-Strauss ignores the guilt and the violence which abound in the Murngin creation myth. Violence and destruction are the part of the male (the snake), although the violence is then undone, and the snake's motion (his erection) becomes the source of the fertilizing rains. The Murngin creation myth reminds us of our own myth of Adam and Eve. It is Eve who is burdened by the guilt for Adam's fall from grace and Eve who had doings with (was tempted by) the snake. Among the Murngin the snake is outraged by the sisters' pollutions, innocent until provoked by women. Among ourselves it is also Adam who is the innocent, an "opposite" of men's aggressiveness in the real world.

Our own creation myths represent our culture's struggles with the contradiction between men's social power and women's childbearing. Even in otherwise egalitarian religious traditions, which profess the equality of all souls before God, there is a deeply rooted theme of women's inferiority. The psychologists, Sandra and Daryl Bem,[15] have brought together some quotations from Christian, Jewish, and Moslem bibles, which expose the ideology of women's inferiority. The following are the examples they cite:

> In the beginning God created the heaven and the earth . . . . And God said, Let us make man in our image, after our likeness; and let them have dominion over the fish of the sea, and over the fowl of the air, and over the cattle, and over all the earth. . . . And the rib, which the Lord God had taken from man, made he a woman and brought her unto the man. . . . And the Lord God said unto the woman, What is this that thou has done? And the woman said, The serpent beguiled me, and I did eat . . . . Unto the women He said, I will greatly multiply thy sorrow and thy conception; in sorrow thou shalt bring forth children; and thy desire shall be to thy husband, and he shall rule thee (Gen. 1, 2, 3).

Here is another citation from the New Testament:

> For a man . . . is the image and glory of God; but the woman is the glory of the man. For the man is not of the woman, but the woman of the man. Neither was the man created for the woman, but the woman for the man (1 Cor. 11).
>
> Let the woman learn in silence with all subjection. But I suffer not a woman to teach, nor to usurp authority over the man, but to be in silence. For Adam was first formed, then Eve. And Adam was not deceived, but the woman, being

deceived, was in the transgression. Notwithstanding, she shall be saved in childbearing, if they continue in faith and charity and holiness with sobriety (1 Tim. 2).

Another citation from Orthodox Jewish liturgy shows the rich heritage of ideology about women:

> Blessed art Thou, oh Lord our God, King of the Universe, that I was not born a gentile.
> Blessed art Thou, oh Lord our God, King of the Universe, that I was not born a slave.
> Blessed art Thou, oh Lord our God, King of the Universe, that I was not born a woman.

Here is an excerpt from the Koran, the sacred text of Islam:

> Men are superior to women on account of the qualities in which God has given them preeminence.

Symbolic transformations of contradictions are needed among ourselves as well as among the Murngin. Let's take the Biblical myth that Eve was created from the rib of Adam. Adam's rib is a symbolic equivalent of the penis and its central role in the myth is not only a denial of the importance of the womb, but a fusion of thoughts about the penis in the vagina: A rib is also long and stiff and inside the body cavity. There is a rational contradiction between the creation of women out of a male body part, when the actual gestation of men (and women) takes place within a woman's womb. The myth is a symbolic transformation of observations made about intercourse and birth, in a society where men were in a position of power over women. Myths reflect not only observations about nature of the world around people, and the contradictions in what is observed, as Lévi-Strauss showed, but people's feelings of injustice about these contradictions and their ways of rationalizing the injustice, as Freud showed.

The central point at issue is the basis for the feelings of injustice. Freudian theory, caught by the power of feelings to distort thinking, tends to obscure the fact that feelings of injustice are based on correct observations of social inequality. This is one important contribution of Lévi-Strauss's insistent rationalism. So, among some Freudians, for example, feelings of envy (including penis envy) are treated as if they were only irrational instead of having a basis in the actual conditions of social inequality. And in the case of penis envy, some Freudians (beginning with Freud) trapped themselves into the rational-sounding idea that it arose out of women's actual physical inferiority. Underlying this notion is the male-centered idea that a woman's penisless body is a poor replica of the superior male model. Although Freud's thinking was androcentric, however, his analyses of the mechanisms by which culture myths become implicit parts of people's personality are invaluable. We'll examine Freud's thinking in Chapter 12.

References

1. C. Lévi-Strauss, *Structural Anthropology* (New York: Doubleday, 1967), p. 19.

2. Ibid., p. 21

3. Ibid., p. 21.

4. Ibid., p. 22.

5. C. Lévi-Strauss, *Totemism* (Middlesex, England: Penguin Books, 1969), p. 140.

6. Ibid., p. 174.

7. C. Lévi-Strauss, *The Savage Mind* (Chicago: University of Chicago Press, 1968, p. 130).

8. Ibid., p. 130.

9. Ibid., p. 130.

10. Ibid., p. 90.

11. Ibid., pp. 91-92.

12. Ibid., pp. 92-93.

13. Ibid., p. 94.

14. Ibid., p. 106.

15. Sandra Bem and Daryl Bem, *Training the Woman to Know Her Place*, unpublished manuscript.

CHAPTER 12

Is Freud an Enemy of Women's Liberation?

With the revival of the feminist movement in recent years, Freud has been criticized, and justly, as a sexist. There is no question that Freud was androcentric in his thinking; he lamented it himself freely and often.[1] The very concept of sexism or sexist thinking, however, is something we owe to Freud's rich description of psychic defenses. Freud took for granted that his thinking about women was distorted by his own unconscious needs and that he was, in fact, as little able to escape his own personal blind spots as the rest of us. What he developed, however, in the major part of his work, are indispensable conceptual tools with which we can analyze the distortions in reality to which our own acculturation makes us prey.

Psychoanalysis was developed in a male-dominated exploitative atmosphere. Some of the ideas developed under its auspices contribute not only to women's subjugation but to the maintenance of an exploitative status quo. Nevertheless, I do not believe that psychoanalysis is an intrinsic enemy of women's liberation or of freedom from exploitation. On the contrary, one of the factors contributing to the resurgence of the women's liberation movement is the spread of psychoanalytic thinking during this century. A reconciliation of Marxist thinking and psychoanalysis has at least been attempted by such influential psychoanalysts as Fromm [2] and Wilhelm Reich.[3] Adler [4] was also critical of the social forces which emphasize people's inferiority feelings, and Horney,[5] in her *Neurotic Personality of Our Time,* was critical of the way society fosters competitiveness and hostility among its members. Fromm and Reich, however, were the most explicit in using Marxism as the base for their critique of society. We shall, therefore, look briefly at their formulations in this chapter.

Freud's discovery of the role of sexuality in neurosis and in personality has been a factor leading to the liberation of both sexes from oppressive sexual mores. Freud's originality lies also in describing the "primary-process" thinking which figures so heavily in the attitudes of us all. His brilliant dissections of such defense mechanisms as rationalization, projection, and reaction formation are so useful that these concepts have become virtually household words. Psychoanalysis has made it easier for all of us to "tell it like it is." Perhaps the most important of Freud's concepts which have attained everyday use is his concept of the superego. As a noted sociologist puts it, the idea of the [6] "internalization [into] the structure of personality of aspects of the normative culture of society in which the individual grows up" represents a remarkable confluence of the independent thinking of Durkheim and Freud (and, we should add, Marx).

Since Freud was focused at the beginning of his observations on the powerful effects of unconscious sexuality, he automatically considered sexual differentiation alone to be a powerful force for creating personality differences between the two sexes. Fromm and Reich emphasized, in addition, that the forces of social and economic repression operating through the family, push women in the direction of passivity and masochism, and men into sadism. Although psychoanalysis is such a revolutionary method of probing the human psyche, some analysts [7] have misinterpreted radical political action as the symptom of unresolved oedipal conflict, and some analysts [8] have assumed (Freud among them) that masochism in women is the natural order of things. These are mistakes in interpretation rather than intrinsic faults of the method of interpretation. Freud's insights into the intimate connection between social behavior and sexual behavior, via infant experiences in the family, offer us the basic understanding of how the family transmits cultural values. Before discussing the use which Fromm and Reich made of Freud's methods, let's look at how Freud began.

In Freud's earliest observations, the family was the source of powerful feelings generated within it. Attention to local family dynamics was forced upon Freud as he sought to understand and cure the neurotic symptoms of his patients who were mostly upper middle-class Viennese ladies and gentlemen. Before Freud suggested that neurotic symptoms were the resultants of repressed or throttled sexual wishes, neurotic symptoms had been regarded by the medical profession as the results either of neurological or intellectual degeneration. (Even enlightened French psychiatry which thought that neurotic symptoms arose in a hypnoid state did not attribute the hypnoid state to strong feelings, but rather to some lapse of the conscious mind.)

Freud also observed that children naively express sexual feelings and impulses which adults regard as impermissible and abhorrent. He also observed that many references to these abhorrent sexual impulses were in the stream of consciousness—the "free associations"—of his patients, and that his patients were too ashamed and too guilty to be able even to verbalize their sexual feelings except on Freud's insistence that they do so. He sensed that in some way their dammed-up feelings were transformed into symptoms.

Freud observed that human sexual development began not at puberty, but in infancy. He inferred that it followed a growth-sequence depending on the major source of the child's gratifications, taking first an oral, then an anal, and then a phallic form. Freud assumed that girls' sexuality was also phallic, and the clitoris was a girl's penis-equivalent. Each of these psychosexual stages represents a different kind of social (and affectionate) relationship between child and parents; hence, the term "psychosexual." The oral stage involves passive and dependent gratifications, in closeness to mother; the anal stage, gratifications in independence and mastery; the phallic phase involves gratification from the child's genitals and wishes for sexual union.

The threat of parental retaliation against the child for incestuous sexual wishes, however, causes the child to renounce the parents as sexual partners and instead to identify with them (I'll be like you when I grow up). Along with this identification, the child internalizes the parental figures, together with their castration threats and praises. The internalized system of prohibitions and ideals of conduct is each person's superego. Disturbances in the sequential pattern of psychosexual development, and disturbances in the parent-child affectionate bond result in unbearable conflicts during childhood. A cruel, archaic superego develops as defense against these unbearable affects and creates a personality vulnerable to neurotic and psychotic illness. But a superego, whether healthy or archaic, is an inevitable part of human acculturation.

Having first observed the noxious effects of sexual repression, Freud then justified it by considering sexual repression to be the necessary basis for the existence of civilization. Specifically, in *Totem and Taboo*,[9] he formulated a theory of the origin of civilization as an act of parricide and cannibalism by the male young in a nuclear family, who were denied access to the females by the father. The guilt which resulted from killing the father and eating him is carried in the unconscious of succeeding generations of (male) human beings. It is the source of the incest taboo and of the societal institutions through which civilization exerts its moral authority over human beings. This theory is not taken seriously by anthropologists in its literal form; Lévi-Strauss considers it a myth or parable about the origin of society [10] (something like the Murngin creation myth). Freud's theory of the origin of civilization was a simple extension into mythical primitive history of what he had observed on a smaller scale in Vienna. The parable clearly implied that the young had revolted against the irrational authority of the father; more important, it implied that both cultural institutions and moral values have irrational, unconscious roots. The reader will note that the parable is about men; the women are only sex-objects. So it is clear that Freud's critique of civilization needed re-working.

In one of his few excursions into psychology, Marx made the famous observation that capitalism, by making human labor a commodity, alienates the worker from his work.[11] But Marxism, since it is a theory of social institutions, has no theory of the psychological processes by which institutions come to govern human attitudes and behavior. Fromm and Reich, considering themselves Marxist psychoanalysts, extended and amplified the ways in which cultural institutions mold human personality. As

Fromm explained, human personality is the mortar which holds together the bricks of social institutions.[12] Fromm described, for example, how nineteenth-century bourgeois capitalism fostered a human being who is "competitive, hoarding, exploitative, authoritarian, aggressive and individualistic." [13] Fromm thus generalized Freud's clinical description of the "anal character" into a description of bourgeois character. Reich, similarly, wrote that "every social order produces in the masses of its members that structure which it needs to achieve its aims." [14] This statement implies, as does Fromm's, that both the ideology and human character structure generated by an exploitative social order operate so as to maintain its exploitative power.

Writing during the time of fascist power in Germany and Italy, Reich tried to comprehend the psychological basis for fascist political success, that is, the psychological basis on which so many German and Italian people accepted and approved fascist doctrine (leaving aside submission based on the terror of guns). Reich also asked the question "why man had allowed himself to be exploited and morally humiliated . . . for thousands of years." [15] Reich answered these questions by reference to Freudian theory. Specifically, he traced the mystical appeal of fascist ideology: "honor," "duty," "sacred motherhood," "purification of German blood" to psychic defenses against the sadism which is fostered by an exploitative society. Reich interpreted the ecstatic feeling which characterized fascist crowd behavior to the yearnings resulting particularly from inhibited orgasm. He commented on the "frequent cohesion of sadistic brutality and mystical sentiment" [16] in mass murderers (war leaders) throughout history. Reich thus interpreted the potency of fascist appeal on the basis of Freudian theory.

Both Fromm and Reich are in agreement that the patriarchal family, a reflection in miniature of exploitative power in the societal background, is the transmission belt for irrational guilt. They also share the conviction, which Freud did not have, that the abolition of exploitation would free human beings from the character deformations which they now suffer. Fromm, for example, envisages the sane society as one in which the central value is human growth, not the use of human beings as commodities. In such a society, individuals would develop so that conflicts between the self and others are minimal.

Reich suggests that "originally and naturally sexual pleasure was the good . . . which united man with nature in general." [17] Reich also believed that "work must be arranged in such a way that the biologic urge for activity is developed and gratified." [18] This includes both a "direct relationship between the worker and his product," [19] and the prevention of rigid character-armoring so that sexual energy can be converted into an interest in work.

It is thus implied by Fromm and Reich that human beings have a natural tendency toward peaceable relations with others, to enjoy work, and that the unrestricted gratification of sexual activity would find expression in "genital character . . . spontaneously pure and honorable." [20] Reich is most explicit in restricting Freud's critique of civilization to civilization's present forms. He follows Engels in assuming that the suppression of sexuality makes its appearance at the same time as the establishment of an authoritarian patriarchy.

Reich also explicitly disagrees with Freud in the theory of work. Freud thought that the erotic nature of both sexes makes them unwilling or unable to accept the restraints upon copulation and the discipline required to do the world's work. In this view, Freud did not distinguish between work of intrinsic interest and labor which is sold to the highest bidder. Freud thus implies that the human attitude toward work is intrinsically aversive, and that coercion which represses sexuality is the foundation upon which human work is done. He implies, moreover, that those who do the work, that is, men, need more coercion. Furthermore, men solve the problem of coercion by "internalizing" it more, in the form of a stricter conscience. We shall return to the question of women's and men's conscience later on in this chapter.

Now that we have looked at how Fromm and Reich used Freud's insights in their critique of an exploitative society, let's look more closely at the most important of these insights: the concepts of infantile sexuality; of "primary-process" thinking and psychic defenses; and the superego. Let's take infantile sexuality first.

The shocked and outraged reaction to Freud's concept of infantile sexuality, the derision and opprobrium with which Freud's work was greeted, are now a matter of history. Freud was treated as if he were defiling the sanctity and innocence of childhood. Another, even more deadly criticism was of the inaccuracy of

Freud's definitions. It is still true today that people who value strict definitions are quite dissatisfied with Freud. And it is true that infants' and children's sexual behavior is not strictly speaking the same as adult sexual behavior. But any unbiased observer of infants and children can see that there is enough similarity between adult and childhood sexuality to warrant Freud's hunch of a profound connection. For one thing, the passionate, affectionate feelings of childhood are revived when adults fall in love; for another, children have been masturbating long before they grow up to be adults. Cross-cultural studies make it clear that infantile and childhood masturbation are universal phenomena.[21] And as we saw in Chapter 6, two- to three-day-old infants have regular periods of penile erection.[22]

Let's pause for a moment to see (with hindsight) why Freud's choice of sexuality as the prime target of his research into neurosis was such an inspired idea. Sexual differentiation in a species structures events so that, even if no other activity of the animal is social, at least sexual activity will be. Once a species is divided into male and female, they must come together in order to unite. Sexual behavior is thus one of the quintessentially social phenomena in the animal world. Yet, we are accustomed to thinking of the human sex drive as an individual or egotistical affair, because it also does express the unique sense of self. Thus, in targeting sex as his area of research, Freud was tapping a profoundly social, affectionate human feeling, and discovering that people fall ill of the unresolved conflict between individualistic and social needs.

As Freud suggested in one of his earliest writings,[23] and a modern investigator into the sexual behavior of animals also remarks,[24] sex is not a drive in the same sense as hunger or thirst. No one ever dies for lack of sex (only a species would). Moreover, sexual appetite among human beings has very little direct relationship to biological or physiological need, rather it is a product of social experience, actual or vicarious. Although no one ever dies of lack of sex, thwarted or unrequited love turns into hate. So sexual life, both in childhood and adulthood, is a major source of human aggression. As one expert on the history of Freudian theory puts it, Freud had the greatest difficulty understanding how love turns into hate.[25] (This is still a major unsolved psychological puzzle.) But Freud was so impressed by the virulence of the hatred which is evoked in human beings that he thought people had a "death instinct," along with Eros. In his thinking, Freud was more often caught by the individualistic aspect of the sex drive than by its social aspect, although it was he who had also called attention to the latter.

Freud's original discovery was that faulty psychosexual development has a negative effect on social development, causing such symptoms as obsessions, phobias, and depression. Since this original discovery of a link between sexual and social development, evidence has been accumulating which not only confirms the link, but confirms a reverse link: Faulty social development results in faulty individual sexual differentiation. Thus, an expert on human genetic sex defects writes: "Any impedance of normal development and maturation, however seemingly remote from psychosexual identity, may have a noxious side-effect on psychosexual differentiation." [26]

Although sexual activity is grounded in infant *social* attachment, however, it is a paradoxical fact that sexual activity also has the meaning of *individual* assertion. A psychoanalyst has suggested that orgasm performs the function of affirming the reality of the individual's existence in terms of emotional conviction.[27] The orgasm thus serves the "ego function" of establishing the incontrovertible truth of the reality of personal existence. That human beings should need such an affirmation is a reflection of the complexity of the culturally developed sense of self which partly functions automatically, and at the same time requires "confirmation."

That sexual activity is assertive is again and again reflected in myths in which authority is thwarted in its attempts to restrain forbidden lovers. The myth of the Wawilak sisters, which Lévi-Strauss interpreted (Chapter 11), contains the same theme—of forbidden sexual activity. Children's naughtiness is often sexual, suggesting that not only adults but children find individual assertion in sexual arousal. Sexual activity is paradoxically both a social and an individualistic phenomenon. In sex, one is alone in the act of uniting oneself with another.

It is also a fact that, unlike hunger and thirst fantasies, sex fantasies actually work. As an extreme example, sex fantasies can produce false pregnancy, and they can produce orgasm, sometimes with minimal or even absent physical stimulation of the sexual organs. From early on, fantasies of gratification and warmth emanating from the "other" may be actually satisfying without the other's presence. Sexual activity is thus a developer of autonomy, but most especially because it is so responsive to fantasy involving others. This is another way of saying that the self plays a unique role in sexual activity, being at the same time in its own and in the other's place.

Let's look briefly at an example of infantile sexuality as illustration of how the self manages to be simultaneously in its own place and in communion with another. Some years ago, a distinguished psychoanalyst-researcher, René Spitz, set out to observe the sexuality of one-year-old infants living with their mothers in a reformatory setting.[28] All were without their fathers, and the mothers could be said to be living under the generalized stress of prison confinement, even though the physical conditions of the institution were adequate. One of the surprising observations from this study was that a small group of infants developed a (premature) form of highly pleasurable anal activity, namely, playing with their feces. From the dreamy expression on these infants' faces, as they handled and tasted their own feces, it was clear that they were in some kind of "way-out" psychic state. It was also observed that the mothers of these infants had (unwittingly) subjected them to an abrupt loss of previously stable maternal affection. For a relatively long interval of the infants' early life, the mothers had been very affectionate and sensitive with their infants; then, abruptly (because the mothers had fallen into depression or for other reasons were unavailable), the mothers had vanished from their infants' lives. Because the mothers had been consistently affectionate over many months, the infants had been able to develop at least a primitive image of "mother." When she vanished completely, they were enraged, but without a clear-cut target of their rage and without any power to effect a change, or to stop their longing for her. Spitz hypothesized that the fecal play had a symbolic meaning for the infants: I have taken you (mother) into me, and I have defecated you out and I am enjoying being with you, able to control you symbolically in my feces. Fecal play is a primary-process compromise formation expressing both the loving (I take you in) and the rageful (I expel you, and I control you). The advanced language which adults need to put these feelings into words does not do justice to the combination of primitive ideas, imagery, and feelings which constitute the infant's experience in fecal play.

This illustration from a study of infant sexuality brings us to the second of Freud's discoveries: that primary-process thinking comes into play in order to express people's unresolved conflicts. Let's take another, less primitive and therefore less complicated example of primary-process thinking, easier to follow than the hypothetical explanation of fecal play because language is more involved. Masturbating, that is, handling his penis is forbidden to a man by his conscience, which has incorporated his parents' threats of punishment and disapproval. But he masturbates anyway and falls asleep physically satisfied but with a guilty feeling. (In waking life, he is accustomed to project his guilt.) In sleep, he dreams that a snake (wearing eyeglasses) is on its way to attack him; it frightens him, but he strangles it with his bare hands. The dream is a primary-process formation of thoughts and images, in which the penis is symbolized by the snake. The threat of danger to himself is symbolic of his angry conscience (the eyeglasses are some reference to his punishing father), and the necessity of strangling the snake is a rationalization. He had to strangle the snake (he had to use his hands), or the snake would have killed him. A symbolic transformation of thoughts and feelings and images has taken place in which "I couldn't resist handling my penis" is transformed into "I had to kill the dangerous snake." And perhaps the most remarkable result of the dream's work in making a symbolic translation of waking experience is that the person can remain blissfully unaware that his dream of a dangerous snake has anything to do with his having masturbated.

Primary-process transformations have their own logic of representation. They do not involve random or senseless thinking, but rather a special mode of thinking which is encoding the experience of unresolved psychic conflict. Freud spelled out in marvelous detail the mechanisms of psychological defense against the unbearable affects which would otherwise be generated by unresolved psychic conflict. For example, he analyzed the mechanisms of identification, projection, reaction formation, and isolation of affect, all of which permit a person to express a part of his or her longing, and to remain unconscious of the rest. The mechanisms of defense were at first all subsumed under the general heading of "repression." Only as clinical material developed was Freud able to distinguish between mechanisms which blotted out feelings but left out some of the verbal content of longings, as in "isolation of affect," and mechanisms (now called repression), which blotted out the whole verbal content of an experience, leaving behind only a generalized feeling of depression and anxiety.[29] Isolation of affect is particularly prominent in obsessional neurosis and schizophrenia, while repression in the narrower sense is prominent in depression and anxiety. As we shall see in later chapters, men and women differ in their proneness to these different psychic illnesses.

Sexual intercourse and sexual anatomy are themes which evoke many symbolic translations especially when sex is subject to strong social taboos, and where men are expected to be in positions of superior power. Let's take the breast as an example of primary-process symbolism which can develop about this part of a woman's body. The breast is a symbol of milk and so of feeding and so of nurturing another human being. The breast can symbolize "dependency" on the body of another and become a symbol of past helplessness, or "symbiosis," especially in a world which values egotism. Or the breast can become a symbol of the commodity value of women—as food providers. So, in many primitive cultures, women are exchanged for cattle, another form of wealth and food provision. Lévi-Strauss, for example, interprets this cultural institution of bride price as a reflection of the symbolic equation between women and food (without commenting on the implied dehumanization of women).[30] In a social context in which mutual sharing and cooperation are valued, the breast can also (accurately) signify a symbolic gift which is mutually gratifying to the giver and the receiver.

When it comes to the penis, androcentric thinking has figured heavily in the interpretation of symbolic transformations. So, for instance, Freud suggested in his famous paper on the psychological consequences of the anatomical difference between the sexes,[31] that little girls interpret the absence of a penis as a "defect" of their bodies, a "scar" on the self. But then Freud went on to say that, in effect, the absence of a penis was a *real* deficiency, not a symbolic or primary-process interpretation of an anatomical fact. Horney and others, notably Ernest Jones, were understandably dissatisfied with this un-Freudian thinking on Freud's part. Horney, in fact, became so dissatisfied with Freud's theories about women that she formed her own psychoanalytic school. In a recent historical reconstruction of the events during the 1920s, when these questions of women's psychological development were being discussed within the psychoanalytic movement, Zenia Fliegel [32] has suggested that Freud's intransigence on the subject of women's constitutional inferiority developed after his first bout with cancer in the year 1923-24.

It must be remembered, also, that the intellectual atmosphere around Freud was completely male-dominated. For example, the then available evidence about human embryology made it a generally acceptable doctrine that the clitoris was a vestigial penis. Mary Jane Sherfey's efforts to get embryologists to take another look at this concept are a relatively recent story.[33]

Let's digress for a moment to tell it. Nineteenth-century embryologists showed that all mammalian embryos (including human ones) are sexually undifferentiated at conception (chromosomes were then unknown). Soon the embryo develops a genital tubercle which becomes the penis in the male and the clitoris in the female. Everyone immediately assumed (Freud included) that the clitoris was a vestigial or abbreviated penis.

By about 1930, sex hormones—the androgens and the estrogens—were discovered. It had also been established that the XX and the XY chromosomes start different hormones going into action, thus effecting the sexual differentiation into male and female. A widely held modern embryological notion is that the embryo is basically female at conception. Without the operation of the proper hormones, the embryo develops as a female. The Y chromosome, which only males have, starts androgens going. This effects the male differentiation out of a basically female "template." In other words, the modern theory says that Adam may come out of Eve, instead of vice versa.

Scientists, mostly male, were very resistant to this kind of theory when it first appeared in 1947. (As nearly as I can make out, the problem of whether the embryo is basically female or neuter is still an unsettled question.) But what is instructive is how difficult it was for the theory that the embryo is female to obtain credence, and how scientific jargon obscured the issue. Sherfey says that it was not until she had read the statement, "the neuter sex is female," that she got an inkling that some emotional problems might lie underneath such a strange sentence. Biologists were having trouble announcing to the world the possibility that the "rib belonged to Eve."

Freud's idea that the absence of the penis is women's constitutional defect was itself a rationalization of women's social inferiority. But it is an idea to which we have become profoundly accustomed. Recently, Theodora Wells, a psychologist, invited an audience to introspect their feelings if they were bombarded with information, both explicit and subliminal, which attested superior power and social status on the part of women. Here is an excerpt from Wells's reverse "propaganda": [34]

> Feel into the fact that women are the leaders, the power-centers, the prime movers. Man, whose natural role is husband and father, fulfills himself through nurturing children and making the home a refuge for woman. This is only natural to balance the biological role of woman who devotes her whole body to the race during pregnancy: the most revered power known to Woman (and man, of course). Then feel further into the obvious biological explanation for woman as the ideal: her genital construction. By design, female genitals are compact and internal, protected by her body. Male genitals are so exposed that he must be protected from outside attack to assure the perpetuation of the race. His vulnerability obviously requires sheltering. Thus, by nature, males are more passive than females and have a desire in sexual relations to be symbolically engulfed by the protective body of woman. Males psychologically yearn for this protection, fully realizing their masculinity at this time, and feeling exposed and vulnerable at other times. A man experiences himself as "whole man" when thus engulfed. If the male denies these feelings, he is unconsciously rejecting his masculinity. Therapy is thus indicated to help him adjust to his own nature. Of course, therapy is administered by a woman, who has the education and wisdom to facilitate openness leading to the male's growth and self-actualization. To help him feel into his defensive emotionality he is invited to get in touch with the "child in him." He remembers his sister's jeering at his primitive genitals that "flap around foolishly." She can run, climb and ride horseback unencumbered. Obviously, since she is free to move, she is encouraged

to develop her body and mind in preparation for her active responsibilities of adult womanhood. The male vulnerability needs female protection, so he is taught the less active, caring, virtues of homemaking. Because of his vagina-envy, he learns to bind up his genitals, and learns to feel ashamed and unclean because of his nocturnal emissions. Instead, he is encouraged to dream of getting married, waiting for the time of his fulfillment: When "his woman" gives him a girl-child to care for. He knows that if it is a boy-child he has failed somehow—but they can try again. In getting to the "child in him" these early experiences are reawakened. He is led by a woman. In a circle of nineteen men and four women, he begins to work through some of his deep feelings.

Theodora Wells's statement of what things might be like if the power structure were turned upside down is an amusing example of how Freudian concepts can be used to counter Freud's mistakes.

When it comes to the superego concept, there is also a woeful gap in thinking about the superego of women, but the concept can be amended to make it even more useful than it has been in helping us to understand psychic illness. Freud's superego concept was originally developed about men, and he frankly stated that it must be inadequate because its author was a man.

Let's first review the story about men. The culture's morality is internalized by the growing child at the time of the Oedipus complex (maybe also even earlier), under the threat of castration by the father. This threat breeds impulses to destroy the father, as does the boy's jealous longing for mother. Destructive wishes bring the boy into conflict between his love for his father and his hatred of father. This conflict the boy solves by "identification" with father; as he takes on father's role, he unconsciously internalizes father's values and father's person. These internalized prescriptions function as the child's conscience—his superego. Even when father is not literally there with threats, the superego now punishes and threatens in lasting identification with the punishing father.

Once having developed a male model of superego formation based on the castration threat, Freud had trouble with the model for women's conscience, since women have no penis and so could not be threatened with its loss. This makes the superego of women inferior; a less reliable kind of internalized morality.

In addition to the description of the boy's identification with his father under the castration threat, however, Freud had also described another, even earlier route of identification, and one which was equally open to boys and girls. This earlier route of identification with parents he called "anaclitic identification," by which he meant the child's wish to be in unison with, and later to emulate the nurturing, beloved parents (mostly mother, but not exclusively).

Anaclitic identifications lead to the formation of ego-ideals, which also function as internalized standards of conduct. One expert wrote that "in contrast to the pressures and threats of punishment which we relate to the superego, the ego ideal seems to exert its pull by holding forth a promise—it derives its strength mainly from positive libidinal strivings. . . ." [35] The ego-ideal dictates what kind of *person* one wants to be like, and it is as powerful a force as the dictates of *things* one ought not to do.

As psychoanalytic thinking has developed, it has become the convention to reserve the term superego for the identification with the aggressor route of conscience development and to pay less attention to the more benign route of loving identification with parental figures. Ego-ideals are much less discussed than the superego,[36] which has, in fact, become the overall term for both internalized threats and praises, but usually carries the meaning only of the former. In a male-dominated, exploitative society, the more relevant identification route for men is identification with the aggressor, although theoretically the benign route of identification is available to them. Women are actually pushed more into the benign identification route. As we shall see in later chapters, they make more use of the ego-ideal as their internal regulator. That women differ from men in their prevailing superego mode would follow from the fact that anaclitic identifications especially with mother, are more available to them than to men. Women's same-sex-as-mother gender identiy and their culturally sanctioned role as affectionate infant caretakers push them to develop personal ideals of goodness.

It is worth considering at this point why Freud paid so little attention to the anaclitic identification route. The trouble lies deeper than the fact that the castration model is a male model, not open to girls. It lies in the fact that defensive identification describes not only a male-model but a model suited to an exploitative society. There is an implicit equation of masculinity and power in the concept of defensive identification as a resolution of the castration threat. The conflict within the nuclear family is cast as a conflict over "possession" of the mother sexually. (Mother is the first love-object and sex-object.) This is the parable of *Totem and Taboo,* as we saw in Chapter 11. As Fromm and Reich taught us, however, the struggle is over patriarchal *power*—and the prize is power to exploit other people (not only to copulate with mother). Since the little boy cannot literally copulate with his mother—his genitals are not developed—sexual possession of the mother is a symbolic concept. The small size of the boy's penis as compared to his father's is also a symbol of inferiority of power. Power is what fathers either have or should have in an exploitative, patriarchal society. The identification based on castration threat is in the little boy's self-interest. It is the unconscious contract he makes with society: "I'll be good, so you won't hurt me."

This is an accurate description of the conflict between man's love for both his parents and the cultural requirement that he be powerful. The sexualizing of the conflict is a particularly accurate observation. "Sexual possession" symbolizes power, and the fusion of sex and power establishes sadism. But men are guilty for their sadism. How this can happen to men in our society becomes very clear when the process comes apart at the seams. Then, for example (Chapter 19), we have the picture of Dr. Schreber's paranoid illness—his personal religious myth that he became a woman with whom God copulated in order that their children could teach men to cultivate femaleness.

Of course, in a society where women take second place to masculine exploiters, girls cannot be "castrated," not just because they have no penis, but because they do not join the ranks of the exploiters. They approach the arena of power already feeling inferior to men. Since they are the inferiors, not the principals, they can afford to turn their eyes away from the bloody struggles in an exploitative society—to see no evil, hear no evil, and think no evil. By the same token, if women were the exploiters and had to learn the personal lessons of power, they would also learn to identify with (female) aggressors and develop a "strict" conscience based on the internalized fear of reprisal. A conscience based on loss of love in one's own and other's eyes is not so useful in an exploitative society.

In my book, *Shame and Guilt in Neurosis*,[37] I have suggested that it is useful to distinguish two different modes of superego functioning, shame and guilt, corresponding to the ego-ideal and the internalized threat of punishment. Shame occurs when there is a failure to live up to the ego-ideal, and the punishment is "loss of love" in one's own and the other's eyes. Guilt occurs when there is a transgression, and the punishment is fear of danger. (Both shame and guilt can be evoked by transgressions; and both can be evoked by the failure to live up to ego-ideals.) I have suggested that it is useful to regard both shame and guilt as equally developed modes of superego functioning, differing in their phenomenology along the lines of the identification routes which have been stirred. Shame is a highly personal experience in which the self-in-the-eyes-of-others is focal in awareness; guilt is a more "objective" experience about *things* which have been done or not done.

I have suggested also that shame is the more frequently evoked superego mode in women, while for men, guilt is the more frequently evoked state. It is a well-known fact, for example, that women blush more than men. Darwin had long ago observed that blushing with shame is the result of increased "self-attention," which in turn is the result of attention to the opinion of others about the self. Darwin observed, incidentally, that blushing is a uniquely human phenomenon.[38]

In their direct participation in an exploitative world, men commit more transgressions and are thus more prone to guilt. Women excluded from direct participation in the battle and pushed to fulfill themselves through others, are more prone to the experience of shame.

It does not follow, as Freud thought, that women's shame-prone superego is inferior to men's guilt-prone model. It will be remembered (Chapter 9) that among the Zuñi, who are a peaceful society without a power structure, shame, that is, loss of love in one's own and others' eyes, is the dread sanction. We can agree with Freud's statement that "for women the level of what is ethically normal is different from what it is in men. Their superego is never so inexorable, so impersonal, so independent of its emotional origins. . . ." [39] But it does not follow that an impersonal conscience is the only useful kind. As Martin Buber [40] suggests, in a world which tends to rationalize the greatest cruelties as inexorable, justified necessities, conscience may need to regain its personal, emotional roots. Women may be readier than men to confront the personal and emotional implications of ethical decisions. In a world faced with nuclear warfare, this is a needed antidote to abstract justice. In any case, the difference between men and women in their proneness to shame and guilt is one basis for the difference in the way the two sexes fall mentally ill.

References

1. S. Freud, *The Infantile Genital Organization of the Libido*, Standard Edition, vol. 19.

2. Erich Fromm, *The Sane Society* (New York: Rinehart and Co. 1955).

3. Wilhelm Reich, *The Mass Psychology of Fascism* (New York: Farrar, Straus and Giroux, 1971).

4. Danica Deutsch, *The Role of Women in Adlerian Psychology*, unpublished manuscript.

5. K. Horney, *The Neurotic Personality of Our Time* (New York: W. W. Norton and Co., 1937).

6. T. Parsons, "Social Structure and the Development of Personality: Freud's Contribution to the Integration of Psychology and Sociology," *Psychiatry* 21 (1958), 321-340, p. 322.

7. Gustav Bychowski, for example.

8. Helene Deutsch and Marie Bonaparte.

9. S. Freud, *Totem and Taboo*, Standard Edition, vol.13.

10. C. Lévi-Strauss, *Totemism* (Middlesex, England: Pelican Books, 1969).

11. Karl Marx, *The Class Struggle*.

12. Erich Fromm, "Psychoanalytic Characterology and its Application to the Understanding of Culture," eds. S. Sargent and M. Smith, *Culture and Personality* (New York: Viking Fund, 1947), pp. 13-30.

13. Erich Fromm, *The Sane Society*. (New York: Rinehart, 1955).

14. W. Reich, op. cit., p. 23.

15. W. Reich, op. cit., p. 25.

16. W. Reich, op. cit., p. 148.

17. W. Reich, op. cit., p. 296.

18. W. Reich, op. cit., p. 296.

19. W. Reich, op. cit., p. 169.

20. W. Reich, op. cit., p. 169.

21. C. Ford and F. Beach, *Patterns of Sexual Behavior* (New York: Harper & Bro., 1951).

22. A. Korner, "Neonatal Startles, Smiles, Erections and Sucks as Related to State, Sex and Individuality," *Child Development* 40 (1969), 1039-1053.

23. S. Freud, *Three Contributions to the Theory of Sex*. Standard Edition,vol. 7.

24. Frank Beach, "Characteristics of Masculine 'Sex Drive,' " ed. M. R. Jones, *Nebraska Symposium*, 1956.

25. Reuben Fine, *Freud: A Critical Re-evaluation of His Theories* (New York: David McKay, 1962).

26. J. Money, "Psychosexual Differentiation," ed. J. Money, *Sex Research* (New York: Holt, Rinehart, and Winston, 1965), p. 13.

27. H. Lichtenstein, "Changing Implications of the Concept of Psychosexual Development," *Journal of the American Psychoanalytic Association* 18 (1970), p. 300-317.

28. R. Spitz and K. Wolf, "Autoerotism," eds. R. Eissler et al., *The Psychoanalytic Study of the Child* 3 (1949), p. 85-120.

29. Peter Madison, *Freud's Concept of Repression and Defense* (Minneapolis: University of Minnesota Press, 1961).

30. C. Lévi-Strauss, *The Savage Mind* (Chicago: University of Chicago Press, 1968).

31. S. Freud, *Some Psychical Consequences of the Anatomical Distinction Between the Sexes*, Standard Edition, vol. 19, 248-258.

32. Z. Fliegel, "Feminine Psychosexual Development in Freudian Theory: A Historical Reconstruction," *Psychoanalytic Quarterly* 42 (1973), 385-408.

33. M. J. Sherfey, *The Nature and Evolution of Female Sexuality* (New York: Random House, 1972).

34. T. Wells, *personal communication*.

35. E. Bibring, "Some Consideration Regarding the Ego-ideal in the Psychoanalytic Process," *Journal of the American Psychoanalytic Association* 12 (1964), p. 512.

36. E. Turiel, "An Historical Analysis of the Freudian Concept of the Superego," *Psychoanalytic Review* 54 (1967), 118-140.

37. H. B. Lewis, *Shame and Guilt in Neurosis* (New York: International Universities Press), 1971.

38. C. Darwin, *The Expression of Emotions in Man and Animals* (London: Murray, 1872).

39. S. Freud, op. cit., pp. 257-258.

40. Martin Buber, "Guilt and Guilt Feelings," *Psychiatry* 40 (1957), 114-129.

CHAPTER 13

The Superego Experience: Shame and Guilt

A person's superego is twofold: It is value-system operating from within which works automatically to signal "guilt," stop wrongdoing, and it is a self-concept which works in a more personal, feelingful way to signal "shame," that the self has failed to live up to its ideals. Guilt and shame are internalized aggressions against the self, although shame feels as if it comes more from the eyes of other people. It is a commonplace of today's wisdom that too much aggression turned against the self produces mental illness. Popular books on how to cope with emotional disturbance lean heavily on teaching people to stop blaming and hating themselves. This prescription comes from Freud's concept that a malfunctioning superego creates mental illness. As he put it: "When the superego is established, considerable amounts of aggressive instinct are fixated in the interior of the ego and operate there destructively. This is one of the dangers to health by which human beings are faced on their path to cultural development." [1]

Although Freud's superego concept has been invaluable in unraveling neurotic and psychotic symptoms, there has been a relative neglect of the study of superego states—the phenomenology of shame and guilt experiences. And the more neglected experiential state has been shame. In the *Index of Psychoanalytic Writings*,[2] there are sixty-four citations under the heading of "Guilt" and only eight under the heading of "Shame." This is so even though once attention is called to shame, it is not hard to see that shame experience is practically identical with depression. Guilt, in contrast, has an obsessive quality.

The reasons for the neglect of shame in psychiatric and psychoanalytic research are numerous and varied. One reason is that shame is an acutely painful experience for both the person who suffers it and the sympathetic observer. Shame is, in fact, often contagious—one can feel oneself growing embarrassed at the "other's" discomfiture. Shame evokes a tendency for both the sufferer to hide and the observer to look away. Although shame is always evoked by being a patient in psychotherapy, it is often ignored because it is so painful and also because it is a relatively non-verbal state, easier not to talk about.

Another, and perhaps more important, reason why shame has been relatively neglected in psychoanalysis is that Freud originally developed the superego concept with men in mind. Because of his focus on the male model of superego, Freud's attention was drawn more to guilt than to shame. As we saw in Chapter 12, Freud was frank to admit that, being a man, he did not understand the superego of women.

In their very first work, on hysteria,[3] Breuer and Freud had suggested that neurotic symptoms resulted from "mortification suffered in silence," and in his last work, Freud was still using a similar formulation.[4] Yet, shame experiences have been neglected perhaps because it is so much easier to articulate a sense of guilt. As I have said in my book, *Shame and Guilt in Neurosis*,[5] I was forced to pay increasing attention to shame in my work as a psychoanalyst when it became apparent over the years that undischarged shame might be hindering a successful therapeutic outcome.

Another influence calling my attention to shame was the research in perceptual style in which I had also been involved for many years.[6,7,8] Thinking about superego states of shame and guilt in connection with perceptual style made me wonder whether there isn't also a superego style. Shame, the "other-connected" superego experience, seemed likely to be more frequent among field-dependent people; while guilt, the self-propelled and self-contained experience, seemed more likely to occur among field-independent people.

We already knew that women are more field-dependent perceivers than men. We knew also that women are more prone to depression than men, and that depressed patients are likely to be field-dependent. It is folk-wisdom that women are more prone to shame than men (although there is very little hard evidence). On the other side, men are more field-independent perceivers than women; more likely to be obsessionals; and obsessionals are more likely to be field-independent perceivers. In addition, there was information that patients suffering from conflicts over dependency needs—ulcer,[9] asthma,[10] obesity,[11] and alcoholism [12] —are all likely to be field-dependent perceivers. On the other side, there is a connection between field-independence and paranoia [13] and between field-independence and being delusional.[14]

So a network of connections was known to us which looked something like this:

Field-Dependence Related to Women	Field-Independence Related to Men
depression	obsessional
dependency needs: ulcers, asthma, obesity, alcoholism	paranoia; delusional
shame?	guilt?

As a first step in the systematic investigation into this network of connections with shame and guilt my colleagues and I chose to study field-dependent and field-independent patients in their first sessions of psychotherapy.[15,16] Our hypothesis was that field-dependent patients would be more shame-prone while field-independent patients would be more guilt-prone.

Let's look briefly at our investigation and what it revealed. First, this was our procedure: All patients applying during an interval of about a year to a large, urban, outpatient, mental hygiene clinic were given our tests of field-dependence in the initial screening battery. (It was necessary to test 172 patients in order to obtain two extremes of perceptual performance and to achieve a reasonable match between patients in the two groups of perceivers.) Four field-dependent and four field-independent perceivers were obtained (matched on a group basis) for age, sex, level of schooling, and occupation. A field-dependent and a field-independent patient were assigned to individual psychotherapy with each of four therapists. Having the same therapist for a "pair" was important, because the therapist's perceptual style has been shown to be an important factor in the patient-therapist relationship.

The therapists who took part in the research were simply requested to do individual psychotherapy with each patient in the usual way. They knew nothing of their patient's perceptual style, nor were they told the purpose of the style. The patients were informed that they were participating in a study, and their permission obtained to tape-record their therapy sessions. After therapy sessions had finished, but before the therapists were informed of their patients' perceptual style, an interview was conducted with each therapist about his or her experiences with each patient, particularly with respect to the therapist's own personal reactions to the patients.

In order to assess the therapy transcripts for shame and guilt, we made use of an established method of assessing verbal productions for implied affect which had already been developed. This method, developed by a psychoanalyst, Louis Gottschalk, and his colleagues,[17] had already been proven to be a reliable and valid instrument for measuring the feelings implied in what people say. Each phrase of a person's utterances is separately scored under two main headings: anxiety and hostility. And there are six subcategories of anxiety: death, mutilation, separation, shame, guilt, and diffuse anxiety. Three main categories of hostility are scored: outward-directed, inward-directed, or ambiguously directed hostility.

Guilt anxiety is scored whenever a phrase contains references to "adverse criticism, abuse, condemnation, moral disapproval, guilt, or a threat of such experience." Shame anxiety is scored whenever a phrase contains a reference to "ridicule, inadequacy, shame, embarrassment, humiliation, overexposure of deficiencies or private detail, or the threat of such experience." It is apparent that the criteria used for scoring follow common understanding of the two states.

The transcripts of patients' first two therapy sessions were sent to Gottschalk's laboratory for scoring, with all identifying material removed so that the scoring could be done by "blind" judges, that is, judges who did not know the purpose of our study or what we expected to find.

We found, as we had predicted, that the transcripts of the field-dependent patients had significantly more references to shame than to guilt, and conversely, our field-independent patients were talking more about guilt than about shame. We had also made predictions that the field-dependent patients would show more self-directed hostility, while field-independent patients would direct their hostility outward. Whether this resulted from their guilt-proneness or their field-independence we could not assess, but there was some indication of a strong association between shame and self-directed hostility, and that this association—between shame and self-directed hostility—was particularly strong in field-dependent patients.

We also observed a significant difference between field-dependent and field-independent patients in the rate of patient-therapist exchange. Field-dependent patients had a faster rate of exchange with their therapists than did field-independent patients, regardless of the patient's characteristic rate of speech. We were able to obtain the therapist's perceptual style and to show that the highest rate of exchange occurred between a field-dependent patient and his or her (relatively) field-dependent therapist; while the lowest rate of verbal exchange occurred between field-independent patient and field-independent therapist. Thus, a picture emerged of a field-dependent therapist-patient pair, interacting with each other at a great rate of exchange, while the field-independent pair were "cooler" and slower in their rate of interaction.

One very interesting aspect of our study was the way in which the therapists experienced their field-dependent and field-independent patients. One therapist, contrasting the two without knowing the basis for the contrast, spontaneously remarked on the way her field-independent patient went in for "distancing," while the field-dependent patient formed "this clinging transference—he would come and live with me if I would let him." Another therapist, commenting on his field-dependent patient, said: "She was always saying, is that what you want to know?" His field-independent patient, on the other hand, seemed to him to be saying: "Sit there and shut up and I will tell you what the whole thing is about."

In talking about field-dependent and field-independent patients, we are talking, although indirectly, about shame-prone and guilt-prone people. The patients who were more shame-prone seemed to develop considerable closeness to their therapists and wished to please them. Their superego was operating in the "other-connected" mode. The more guilt-prone patients, whose superego was operating along self-propelled lines, were more aloof and more hostile to their therapists.

Our success in predicting differences in proneness to shame and guilt between field-dependent and field-independent patients encouraged the idea that shame and guilt experiences are well worth systematic exploration.

Let us turn now to some highlights of the experiences of shame and guilt.° The reader is invited to introspect his or her experiences of shame guilt along with this description. My guess, based upon experience with people's feedback from this material, is that women who are more familiar with shame as well as guilt will be less troubled as they read along. A review of phenomenology leads to some formulations about intrinsic factors which make shame and guilt difficult to discharge, in different ways. These factors rest on both the dynamics of the self-evaluating function and the position of the self vis-à-vis the "other" in guilt and shame. Difficulties in coping with and discharging shame and guilt may be grouped under three main headings: (1) difficulties in identifying one's own state as shame or guilt; (2) difficulties in the smooth functioning of the self; and (3) difficulties in finding satisfactory means of discharging the internalized aggression evoked against the self. As a result, undischarged shame has a special affinity to depression, while undischarged guilt leads to obsessive and paranoid ideation.

(1) *Difficulties in recognizing one's psychological state in shame and guilt:* Shame and guilt are often fused and confused.

When shame and guilt are both evoked in the context of a moral transgression, the two states tend to fuse with each other, and to be labeled guilt. For example, in the wake of some transgression,

---

° The description has been adapted from *Shame and Guilt in Neurosis.*[18]

one can feel both guilty and ashamed of oneself. The self-reproaches that are likely to be formed as guilty ideation develops might run as follows: How could I have *done that;* what an injurious *thing* to have done; how I *hurt so-and-so;* what a moral lapse that *act* was; what will become of *that* or of *her (him),* now that I have neglected *to do it,* or injured *him (her).* How should I be *punished* or *make amends. Mea culpa!* Simultaneously, ashamed feeling says: How could *I* have done that; what an *idiot I am—*how humiliating; what a *fool,* what an *uncontrolled person—*how mortifying, how unlike so-and-so, who does not *do* such things; so-and-so must think *I'm rotten; how awful and worthless I am.* Shame! Since, in this kind of instance, the ideation of being ashamed of oneself is the same as that of guilty self-reproach, the shame component, although an acute feeling, is buried in the guilty ideation. A current of aggression, however, has been activated against the whole self, in both one's own and the "other's" eyes. This current of shame can keep both guilty ideation and shame affect active even after appropriate amends have been made.

Shame may be evoked in connection with guilt, as an acute form of it in the hypothetical instance we have just seen, or it may be evoked by sexual rebuff, failure, competitive defeat, social snub, invasion of personal privacy, or being ridiculed. When such "non-moral shame" [19] is evoked, it nevertheless readily connects with moral shame. For example, under the press of shame for sexual failure, one can begin an immediate search for moral lapses or transgressions which make sense of the personal injury one has suffered. Conversely, as we have just seen, moral shame is indistinguishable from guilty ideation. Shame thus has a potential for a wide range of associative connections between transgressions and failures of the self. "Stimulus generalizations" occur, such that shame for defeat or unrequited love evokes guilt for transgression. Shame and guilt states are thus easily confused with one another by the person who is in love, although an observer may have a clearer view of the immediate stimulus.

Because shame can merge with guilt (as in an alloy of metals), people are prone to a wide variety of variants of painful superego states, all of which are about the *self.* Feeling ridiculous, embarrassment, chagrin, mortification, humiliation, and dishonor are all variants of shame state. Each has its own admixture of guilt and self-directed hostility. Embarrassment or chagrin, evoked without much underlying guilt, can yield to good-humored laughter. When one has trouble righting oneself after feeling ridiculous or embarrassed, there is usually a conscious, underlying guilt. But the person who is thrown by embarrassment or ridicule is for the moment confused, being helpless to put the matter to rights and ashamed of it. Dishonor is the most serious shame state, because it has the most implication of guilt, signifying both a serious crime and a personal failure. In any case, recognizing precisely one's own psychic state of shame or guilt usually requires the help of a sympathetic observer who has also done some introspection.

(2) *Difficulties in the functioning of the self in shame and guilt:* Shame is about the *self;* guilt is about *things* done or undone.

Shame is about the *self;* it is thus a narcissistic reaction, evoked by a lapse from the ego-ideal. An ego-ideal is difficult to spell out rationally; shame is thus regarded as a subjective, irrational reaction. Adults regard shame as more appropriate to childhood, especially if it occurs outside the context of moral transgression.

Because shame is about the self, which is focal in awareness, shame experience has a way of reaching into the past, reminding one of similar painfully acute moments. Because shame feels childish and can have such direct connections to childhood experiences, it is, on the one hand, appropriate to denigrate shame experiences, as trivial or unimportant in reality. On the other hand, it is the self which has been attacked in shame, and the psychic importance of the shame experience refuses to subside. It is this very contradiction between how trivial shame events are in the real world and how important they can become to the self of the person which can drive people up the wall.

In shame, there is what Laing calls an implosion of the self.[20] The body gestures and attitudes include head bowed, eyes closed, body curved in on itself, making the person as small as possible. At the same time that it seeks to disappear, the self may be dealing with an excess of impulses from the autonomic nervous system: blushing or sweating or diffuse rage, experienced as a flood of sensations. Shame is thus regarded by adults as a primitive reaction, in which body functions have gone out of control. It is regarded as an irrational reaction for this reason also.

Except for times when the ideation is identical with that of guilt, shame is a relatively wordless state. The experience of shame occurs in the form of imagery, of looking at or being looked at by people. Shame may also be played out in imagery of an internal colloquy, in which the whole self is condemned by the "other." There is, however, a relatively limited vocabulary of scorn. The wordlessness of shame, its imagery of looking, together with the concreteness of the body activity make shame a primitive, irrational reaction, to which there is difficulty applying a rational solution. One is often ashamed of being or having been ashamed. Shame thus compounds itself out of an intrinsic difficulty in finding a rational place for it in the adult's psychic life.

Perhaps because it feels like so primitive and irrational a state, shame is connected to a specific defense of hiding or running away. It is a state in which the mechanism of denial seems particularly to occur. Denial makes shame difficult for the person experiencing it to acknowledge even though there is a strong affective reaction. The person is half-blind about what has hit the *self*.

Another kind of defense against shame appears to operate before any affective state is evoked. This defense, which is best described as "by-passing" shame feeling, does not obliterate the recognition of shame events, but appears to prevent the development of shame feeling. This "by-passing" of shame is accomplished by a "distancing" maneuver. The self views itself from the standpoint of the "other," but without much affect. The person wonders what he or she would think of himself (or herself) if he (or she) were in the position of the "other." The content of the ideation in question concerns shame events, but without shame affect. Shame affect is by-passed and replaced by watching the self from a variety of viewpoints.

Guilt is about *things*—acts or failures to act or thoughts, for which one bears responsibility. It is often difficult, however, to assess the degrees of one's responsibility or to assess the extent of injury which one has committed. It is also difficult to assess what reparation or amends one owes to balance the requirements of justice. Guilt is thus often defined as an obligation.

It is difficult, furthermore, to assess the extent of punishment which one ought to bear in retribution for one's guilty conduct. An "objective" assessment of the extent of responsibility and of punishment seems to exist and require adherence. The Gestalt psychologist, Heider, who investigated the phenomenology of guilt and punishment, describes punishment as "P harming O because O harmed or acted against the objective order as P understands it." [21]

When guilt is evoked, it can merge into a problem in the rational assignment of motivation, responsibility, and consequences. As the guilty person becomes involved in these problems, it can happen that guilty feeling subsides, while worrisome ideation about the events continues. Guilt thus has an affinity for "isolation of affect," leaving a residuum of "insoluble dilemma" thoughts, but without the person being necessarily aware that he or she has begun to transform guilt into worry.

Shame is an experience in which a source in the field seems to scorn, despise, or ridicule the self. The source in the field may be a specific significant "other," or it may be an ill-defined source. Shame like guilt may be experienced in private. But it may also be evoked by an actual encounter with a specific (or an ill-defined) "other." The self is acutely self-conscious during this encounter, whether the encounter occurs in fantasy or in reality. The self is thus divided in shame; it is experiencing condemnation from the other or from the field, and it is simultaneously acutely aware of *itself*. This complicated, divided activity of the self, which is "is in two places at once" and acutely self-conscious at the same time, makes it difficult for the self to function effectively. Although there is acute self-consciousness, the self is not otherwise functioning effectively as a perceiver. Perception of the self and the surroundings are notoriously unclear in shame.

Shame is an acutely painful experience. It can also involve bleeding, sweating, and trembling. Specifically, the gross body arousal, which involves an access of proprioceptive and kinesthetic feedback into awareness heightens the intensity of the affective experience, and heightens its painfulness. If accompanied by autonomic arousal, shame can reverberate over a period of time. Paradoxically, because shame can be evoked by the presence of an "other," it can vanish when the "other" is gone. Shame is also relieved by some reassurance from the "other." Autonomic stirrings, however, may continue to reverberate after the person is no longer ashamed. A split between autonomic state and cognitive state thus occurs in shame, in which the affective experience lingers behind the cognitive. The resulting incongruity within the self is a source of discomfort, which may in turn re-evoke shame.

The "split" functioning of the self thus also makes it difficult for the self to function effectively in finding a solution to shame. The dictionary definition of "embarrassment," that is, literally hampered or hindered in functioning, applies to the self in shame.

Shame is about the whole self. It is possible in moments when one is *not* ashamed to regret or grieve over a specific disfigurement or personal failing. At the moment when one *is* ashamed of specific shortcomings, shame affect involves the whole self. This global target of hostility makes it difficult to find a solution short of a sweeping replacement of the self by another, better one, or none at all, as in suicide. When shame recedes, it is possible, in retrospect, to specify more limited reforms.

The objective character of guilt and the affinity between it and rational assignment of responsibility can result in the person's becoming very busy in making amends for guilt or in an insoluble dilemma of thought about guilt. The self is active in this pursuit. It is intact and self-propelled, in contrast to the self's divided functioning in shame. The self is active in pity or concern for what it has done to the injured "other." But especially since affect may subside, leaving only the ideation of guilt, just amends may be made which do not, however, meet the emotional needs of the "other." The unconscious gratification of being in a morally elevated state also sometimes keeps the guilt active beyond the time of expiation. "He who despises himself," wrote Nietzsche,[22] "thereby esteems himself as the despiser. . . . When we train our conscience, it kisses as it bites." [23] The self, then, may be caught in its own unconscious pride in being guilty, thus prolonging guilt rather than discharging it. The unconsciously perpetuated guilt takes the form of obsessive ideation. The person cannot stop his or her ideational activity.

(3) *Difficulties in discharging hostility in shame and guilt.*

Whether it is evoked in the context of moral transgression or outside it, shame involves a failure by comparison with an internalized ego-ideal. There is thus an implied framework of negative comparison with others. In the painful experience of being unable to live up to the standards of an admired "imago," attention is often focused on the "other," admired figure. Shame is close to the feeling of awe. Fascination with the "other" and sensitivity to the "other's" treatment of the self can ease the acute feeling of shame, while at the same time it renders the self still more vulnerable to shame. It is the feeling state from which one is very susceptible to falling in love. And when one is in love, one is very susceptible to the shame of rebuff or rejection.

In shame, hostility against the self is experienced in the passive mode. The self feels not in control but overwhelmed and paralyzed by the hostility directed against it. One could "crawl through a hole" or "sink through the floor" or "die" with shame. The self feels small, helpless, and childish. When, for example, there is unrequited love, the self feels crushed by the rejection. So long as shame is experienced, it is the "other" who is experienced as the source of hostility. Hostility against the rejecting "other" is almost always simultaneously evoked. But it is humiliated fury, or shame-rage, and the self is still in part experienced as the object of the "other's" scorn. Hostility against the "other" is trapped in this directional bind. To be furious or enraged with someone because one is unloved renders one easily and simultaneously guilty for being (unjustly) furious. Evoked hostility is readily redirected back against the vulnerable self.

For shame to occur there must be an emotional relationship between the person and the "other" such that the person cares what the "other" thinks or feels about the self. In this affective tie the self does not feel autonomous or independent, but dependent and vulnerable to rejection. Shame is a vicarious experience of the significant "other's" scorn. A "righting" tendency often evoked by shame is the "turning of the tables." Evoked hostility presses toward triumph over or humiliation of the "other," that is, to the vicarious experience of the other's shame. But the "other" is simultaneously beloved or admired, so that guilt is evoked for aggressive wishes. Or the image of the "other" may be devalued; but in this case one has lost an admired or beloved person. Shame-based rage is readily turned back against the self, both because the self is in a passive position vis-à-vis the "other" and because the self values the "other."

The position of the self as the active initiator of guilt and the determiner or judge of extent of responsibility puts the self in charge of the hostility directed against the self. It also puts the self in charge of the distribution of hostility, as well as the assessment of the happenings in the field. This active role of the self in guilt opens the possibility that hostility may be directed not only in righteous indignation against the self, but in righteous indignation against the "other" and the forces in the field. Guilt thus invites cognitive distortions of the happenings in the field. As indicated earlier, the difficulties in making just amends for transgressions are an important source keeping guilt undischarged.

The sequences from undischarged guilt into psychic symptoms are more familiar in the clinical literature than are the sequences from undischarged shame. The sequence from undischarged guilt into obsessional neurosis was traced by Freud in the case of the Rat-Man [24] and has since been well documented. A specific sequence from undischarged guilt into obsessive ideation is apparent from the affinity between guilt and isolation of affect.

Similarly, the active role of the self in guilt makes it possible that hostility is discharged upon "others" as well as upon the self, creating an affinity between guilt and projection of hostility. This creates an easy sequence between undischarged guilt and paranoid ideas.

Undischarged shame, especially if it is not recognized by the person experiencing it, is experienced as depression. The simultaneous pull of undischarged shame toward depression, and toward turning the tables or humiliating the "other" can be experienced as excited or agitated depression. Undischarged shame, with its often florid imagery of the self being watched by the "other," has an affinity for the development of hysterical scenes. Since the target of hostility is the self in shame, and the self is not an easily specifiable object, there is also an affinity between undischarged shame affect and diffuse anxiety.

The following table summarizes a working description of shame and guilt.

Before we leave our review of the phenomenologies of shame and guilt, let us note that guilt is the more "respectable" affective state (for both sexes), as well as the more articulate. Shame for the failure of the self to live up to its ideals is respectable enough when it is spoken of in the abstract. When it is experienced in its concrete, living form—when the ideal is represented in consciousness as an actual "other" before whom one is ashamed—the experience itself evokes more shame. Shame is not only a neglected experience, it is a devalued experience because it is so feelingful and so "other"-connected. In our society, people are ashamed of themselves for being ashamed.

The great American psychologist, William James, understood

Table 1

SUMMARY OF WORKING DESCRIPTION OF SHAME AND GUILT°

° (Adapted from Lewis, *Shame and Guilt in Neurosis.*)

	Shame	Guilt
Stimulus	(1) Disappointment, defeat *or* moral transgression	(1) Moral transgression
		(2) Event, act, thing for which self is responsible
	(2) Deficiency or *self*	
	(3) Involuntary, self unable	(3) Voluntary, self able
	(4) Encounter with other	(4) Within the self
Extent of libidinal component	(1) Specific connection to sex	(1) Specific connection to aggression
Conscious content	(1) Autonomic nervous system reactions, blushing, etc.	(1) Autonomic reactions less likely
	(2) Connections to past feelings	(2) Fewer connections to past feelings
	(3) Many variants of shame feeling	(3) Guilt feeling is monotonic
	(4) Watching the self	
Position of self in field	(1) Self passive, unable	(1) Self active, able
	(2) Self focal in awareness	(2) Self not focal in awareness
	(3) Multiple functions of self at the same time	(3) Self intact, functioning silently
	(4) Vicarious experience of other's view of self	(4) Pity, concern for other's suffering
Nature and discharge of hostility	(1) Humiliated fury	(1) Righteous indignation
	(2) Discharge blocked by guilt and/or love of "other" Discharge on self	(2) Discharge on self and other
Characteristic defenses	(1) Denial	(1) Isolation of affect
	(2) Repression of ideas	(2) Rationalization
	(3) Affirmation of the self; "narcissism"	(3) Reaction formation: good action or thought
	(4) Affect disorder: depression; diffuse anxiety	(4) Thought disorder: paranoia; obsessions

very well the "other-connected nature" of the self, even in a competitive society. "Only a non-gregarious animal," he wrote, "could be without [an ideal spectator]. Probably no man can make sacrifices for 'right without to some degree personifying the principle of right for which the sacrifice is made . . . and expecting thanks from . . . the highest possible judging companion." [25] As we saw in Chapter 9, in a cooperative society, like the Zuñi, shame is the worst punishment for the adults and the children. Not to be loved and respected by one's neighbors is a worse penalty in a cooperative society than it is in a competitive one. (In competitive societies, the main point is not to love your neighbor but to put your neighbor down.) Even in competitive societies, however, ostracism is a terrible sanction, and this is, in itself, a tribute to the fact that men's affectionateness is not easily squelched. Societies in which aggression is the bread of life for men cause men to suffer, not so much the punishments of loneliness and depression as from internalized "foreign agents"—obsessive and compulsive thoughts which invade the self, and which the person cannot drive away.

References

1. S. Freud, *An Outline of Psychoanalysis*, Standard Edition, vol. 23, p. 150.

2. A. Grinstein, *The Index of Psychoanalytic Writings*, vol. 9 (New York: International Universities Press, 1966).

3. J. Breuer and S. Freud, *Studies on Hysteria*, Standard Edition, vol. 2, pp. 3-313.

4. S. Freud, op. cit.

5. H. B. Lewis, *Shame and Guilt in Neurosis* (New York: International Universities Press, 1971).

6. H. B. Lewis, "Over-differentiation and Under-individuation of the Self," *Psychoanalysis and the Psychoanalytic Review* 45 (1958), 3-24.

7. H. B. Lewis, "The Organization of the Self in Manifest Dreams," *Psychoanalysis and the Psychoanalytic Review* 46 (1959), 31-35.

8. H. B. Lewis, "A Case of Watching as Defense Against an Oral Incorporatation Fantasy," *Psychoanalytic Review* 50 (1963), 68-80.

9. H. A. Witkin, "Psychological Differentiation and Forms of Pathology," *Journal of Abnormal Psychology* 70 (1965), 317-336.

10. Ibid.

11. Ibid.

12. Ibid.

13. Ibid.

14. Ibid.

15. H. A. Witkin, H. B. Lewis and E. Weil, "Affective Reactions and Patient-Therapist Interaction Among More and Less Differentiated Patients Early in Therapy," *Journal of Nervous and Mental Disease* 146 (1968), 193-208.

16. H. B. Lewis, "Shame and Guilt in Neurosis," *Psychoanalytic Review* 58 (1971), 419-438.

17. L. Gottschalk and G. Gleser, *The Measurement of Psychological States Through the Content Analysis of Verbal Behavior* (Berkeley: University of California Press, 1969).

18. H. B. Lewis, *Shame and Guilt in Neurosis* (New York: International Universities Press, 1971).

19. D. Ausubel, "Relationships Between Shame and Guilt in the Socializing Process," *Psychological Review* 62 (1955), 378-391.

20. R. Laing, *The Divided Self* (Chicago: Quadrangle Books, 1960).

21. F. Heider, *The Psychology of Interpersonal Relations* (New York: Wiley, 1958), p. 273.

22. F. Nietzsche, *The Philosophy of Nietzsche* (New York: Modern Library, 1937).

23. Ibid.

24. S. Freud, *Notes Upon a Case of Obsessional Neurosis*, Standard Edition, vol. 10.

25. W. James, *Principles of Psychology*, vol. 1 (New York: Holt, 1890), p. 317.

CHAPTER 14

The Superego by Sexes: Shame and Guilt in Character-Formation

That men and women growing up in an exploitative society should differ in their superego style, with women more prone to shame and men to guilt, can be derived from two sets of related forces. First, as we saw in Chapters 4 and 5, the pattern of absorption of cultural values differs for boys and girls within the nuclear family. The loving identifications which little girls make with their mothers make them vulnerable to the threat of losing love, which in turn predisposes them to shame. In identifying with their mothers, little girls are also identifying with the devalued sex. The loving identifications which little boys make with their mothers have to be superseded by masculine identification with their fathers and the "defensive" identifications which little boys make with their fathers in order to avoid "castration threats" result in internalized guilt.

The second set of forces which push women and men toward different superego modes are in the exploitative society which forms the background for the nuclear family. An exploitative society, which trains men to aggression, going against the nature of their earliest experiences, makes it more likely that there will be more occasions when they will be in a state of guilt than is the case for women. A society which trains women to be loving, in keeping with their earliest experiences and their maternal function, and then devalues affection, makes women prone to shame on two counts: their greater use of loving identifications and their subjugated, inferior place in the world of affairs, in particular, vis-à-vis men. This profound difference in the mode of psychic war within each sex makes it hard for men and women to understand each other emotionally. It also makes them go "crazy" in different ways. Women collapse into depression and hysteria—into an abysmal state of sadness, fear, or helplessness. Men are more likely to develop compulsions and obsessions about *doing* "crazy" things which will change the world. These differences in characteristic ways of falling mentally ill will be discussed more fully in Part IV. In this chapter, let's look at the evidence which supports the difference between men and women in underlying superego mode and in their prevailing characters.

Men sell their labor in the marketplace. They thus learn that their economic survival rests upon their being aggressive, competitive, and self-sufficient, even though this means a renunciation of the affectionateness and attachments of their childhood. A man absorbs the notion that in order to be free he must submit himself and his labor to a market. Ethical values have to be developed which somehow make aggression and competitiveness in the market right. The values of self-sufficiency and, particularly, freedom and power, are thus established as ideals for a man. (Even today, our profit system is still known as the "free-enterprise" system in spite of the fact that a very small minority of persons monopolizes control of the means of production.)

Toughness may require a man to hurt other people; it places him in a position of guilt. It goes counter to a man's earliest identifications, especially those with his mother. In order to make this conflict bearable, toughness becomes sexualized in sadism, which is sexual pleasure in the cruel treatment or exercise of power over others. Sadism is a transformation of the conflict between toughness and loving into a fusion of them. Another way of justifying toughness is for it to be associated with masculinity; it becomes a man's "machismo." But sadism and machismo also bring men into a state of guilt because neither is a sturdy substitute for affectionateness.

Women do not need to learn the ethical lessons of the market-place directly. Their economic survival is still theoretically the responsibility of men. (This is still a cultural given even though more than 50 percent of American women go out to work. Theoretically, they are doing so for "pin money" or to "help out" their husbands, or because they have no man of their own.) Women have to learn the values of dependency and of taking second place to the main protagonists in the world—men. And they have to learn these lessons in a supposedly egalitarian world which preaches freedom and equality. Since responsibility for women's economic survival is assumed by men, women's ethical relationship to the marketplace is like that of an accessory before or after the fact. If the men they depend on are creating a world of horrors, it is easier not to look. Instead, women can cultivate their relationships within the family in an unbroken line of develop-ment from the affectionate experiences of childhood. Women give their labor to men and to the family as their own mothers gave them the breast. Women's dependency on men pushes women to develop the gentle values of conciliation, compromise, and ac-commodation. Above all, it requires them to renounce the values of independence, freedom, and self-sufficiency which only men require. Women sexualize their renunciation in masochism, in order to diminish their degradation. But they are prone to the shame of their helplessness. An exploitative society thus pushes to subvert men's affectionateness into sadism, and women's into masochism.

The psychological literature is full of examples of how the superegos, that is, the value systems and self-concepts of men and women are geared to different central problems because the sexes absorb an exploitative society in different ways.

Men and women clearly approach their jobs with very different motivations.[1] Men rate the important satisfactions in work as power, profit, independence, and prestige. Women prefer jobs offering them interesting work, social recognition, social interac-tion, and social service. Men have to "sell" their souls. Women can afford the "luxury" of cherishing theirs, since the world's work is not the main focus of their lives.

Even before they come into the marketplace to earn their livings, the primary concerns of boys and girls are very different. In exhaustive interviews dealing with their vocational choices, boys clearly based their identities on getting a satisfactory job. Girls' identities were based first on their affiliating with others (read: "getting a man"), and secondly, on what work it might be that they would do.[2] In one study, for example, approximately 4,000 boys and girls ranging in age from ten to nineteen years were asked: What is your biggest personal problem? The boys answered that their problems were financial and succeeding in school. Girls indicated that interpersonal and family problems were their biggest concerns.[3]

Another study [4] of nearly 500 high school seniors in the South asked that young men and women rate themselves and their ideal selves on an adjective checklist of personal qualities. Two major dimensions were scored from groups of adjectives—qualities of "dominance" and qualities of "love." The young men rated themselves and their ideals higher in dominance; the young women rated themselves and their ideals as high in love. As our cultural expectations predict, men have made "dominance" their territory of operations; women have made love their preserve.

One illuminating experiment [5] used a simple game—something like Parcheesi—to study the way the two sexes differ in their respective drives to win. The game involves pushing counters along a board from start to home, a certain number of paces on each throw of dice. If they want to, the players can made "coalitions"—they can team up to win. The game was played by a team of three same-sexed players. There were ten triads of each sex at ages seven and eight; ages fourteen to sixteen; and thirty triads of each sex of college students. The younger children tended to form "coalitions" in an accommodative manner in which they tried to come to terms which would be mutually satisfactory to all members. They often split "points" three ways. The older boys became much more exploitative and competitive, attempting to use power and coalitions to gain the most advantage for themselves. The women remained accommodative in their playing techniques! Thus, the adult men were different both from adult women and from younger children in their techniques of playing the game. Our exploitative society pushes men into exploitative techniques even in playing games. Women stay cooperative—it fits their early experiences, and society affords them the "luxury" of doing so.

Since women spend their lives devoted to others, loss of love in their own and others' eyes is what typically plagues women in the form of shame. One investigator set out to compare the extent to which men and women were subject to "castration anxiety" and anxiety over "loss of love." She predicted, of course, that women would be more prone to anxiety over loss of love, while men would fear castration. An intensive assessment of men and women of the same age and background, confirmed this prediction.[6] Anxiety of "loss of love" is the superego functioning in the shame mode, "castration anxiety" is the basis for guilt. We'll come back to other studies of the difference between men and women in anxiety later on in this chapter.

This is not to repeat the familiar canard that women's ethical development is inferior to men's. Proneness to a state of guilt is no direct measure of the rectitude of conduct. If it were, our jails would not be housing so many more men than women. Nor would the juvenile delinquency rate be so much higher for boys than it is for girls. There is evidence, in fact, that men's and women's moral code as expressed in *talking* about their ethical decisions is very much the same.[7] Both sexes have high ideals, although, as we have seen, the content of their ideals is very different. We'll come back also to empirical studies of the ethical behavior of the two sexes later on in this chapter.

One investigator made a survey of the attitudes of adolescent boys and girls in the United States by conducting a long, structured interview with many thousands of them.[8] She put together two composite scores from the interview responses. One composite score involved "internalization of moral standards"; the second comprised "development of interpersonal skills and sensitivity to others." These two composites were correlated with scores on "ego-development," that is, energy level, self-confidence, time perspective, achievement, and autonomy. The internalization index was correlated with ego-development in boys; the interpersonal index was correlated to ego-development in girls. Guilt, in other words, accompanies ego-development in boys; sensitivity to others, a shame experience, accompanies ego-development in girls.

We have said that women are more prone to shame because their sex is devalued. In fact, which sex do people say they prefer? One amusing study tells us graphically that men are "No. One" in minds and hearts of people of both sexes. A large number of men and women from the same background were asked to rate men and women on an adjective checklist containing both positive and negative qualities. These were not ratings to be made of particular men and women but of the two sexes in general. In addition, there was a separate, straightforward question: "Are men or women superior in worth?" Both the men and the women doing the rating felt that men were more worthwhile! [9]

This stated preference for the male is not present among very young children but is an accompaniment of growing up in our society. Children at three years of age, asked to choose their three most-liked playmates or asked to state which sex is better, choose their own sex. Boys keep right on choosing their own sex when asked to make value judgments on the subject of which sex is better. Beginning at about five years of age, girls begin to express a devalued opinion of their own sex.[10] No wonder women are prone to shame—they devalue themselves.

Up to this point we have been assuming that men in our society do become more aggressive than women, and that women do become more loving than men. As we shall now see, turning to this question, the evidence is overwhelmingly clear that this is the case.

The picture of an aggressive man and an affectionate woman has been overwhelmingly documented by psychological studies conducted over the last quarter of a century. A 1966 bibliography of the evidence on the question of which sex is more aggressive [11] turned up forty-nine separate studies by different investigators. Some studies used observations of children's behavior, some asked observers to judge behavior, others asked the people themselves to report about their behavior; still other studies used projective techniques such as the Rohrschach test or made analyses of people's fantasy productions. The people studied ranged in age from three years to adulthood. *All forty-nine studies showed that men are more aggressive than women!* Three-year-old boys in nursery school quarrel and fight more than three-year-old girls. College men are more aggressive than women toward someone who is frustrating them. College men form more "hostile sentences" when offered the beginning of a sentence and asked to complete it. Men sixteen to sixty-four years of age, asked to talk about themselves in a structured interview, described much more overt aggressive behavior than do women. Our society, which trains men to be exploiters and warriors, does a thorough job of inculcating the necessary level of aggression.

What is more, a man's level of aggression remains characteristic of him from earliest childhood until adulthood. Follow-up studies made of the same person later in his life show unequivocally that the more aggressive boys turn into the more aggressive men. And the more aggressive boys "choose" or "prefer" toys and activities which are assigned the "masculine" label by our society. The equation between masculinity and aggression equals "machismo." One investigator sums it up: "Aggressive adolescent boys become aggressive, easily angered men . . . appropriately sex-typed, they become 'instrumental,' i.e., self-sufficient, but lacking in sociability and introspection." [12]

When they become fathers, men continue their characteristic level of aggressive functioning. However much they may love their infants, their level of aggression remains higher than women's. A number of experimental studies asked the question: "Which sex is more punishing in the family? And to which sex child?" The answer is that fathers are more punishing than mothers, but *only* to boys, not to girls. When it comes to the way they treat girls, the two parents are not so different from each other.[13] Women not only give more love, they get more when they are children, and they do not have to renounce it on the way to growing up into motherhood.

The same bibliography [14] of psychological studies also documents the overwhelming evidence that women's attitudes toward other people are more positive than men's. These studies are important because they make this point *in addition* to the fact that women are less aggressive than men. Besides their lesser level of aggression, women, as the studies show, are more positively oriented to other people (including men) than are men. The finding is bolstered by forty-seven studies, listed in the aforementioned review, under the following headings: "interest in and positive feeling for others"; "nurturant behavior"; and "need for affiliation" (sociability, affectionateness, friendliness, and gregariousness). Once again, the studies covered people ranging in age from three years to adulthood and used a very wide variety of observational and experimental techniques. Forty-two out of the forty-seven studies showed that women were more "positive" in their attitudes toward others than men. The other five studies showed no significant difference between the sexes; in other words, no study showed that men had more positive attitudes than women.

On the basis of their recent survey of the psychological literature, Maccoby and Jacklin [15] have labeled as a myth the idea that girls are more "social" than boys. As I indicated in Chapter 4, I think this conclusion is too sweeping and overlooks a good deal of the evidence cited in their own pages. As Maccoby and Jacklin themselves recite their conclusions: "Women and girls [are] more interested in social activities, with ... tastes in books and TV programs ... more oriented toward the gentler aspects of interpersonal relations. . . ." [16]

Maccoby and Jacklin warn, of course, against the danger of overgeneralizing and concluding that girls have a "greater" capacity" for social responsiveness. As I suggested in Chapter 4, this idea, while very far from a proven conclusion, is nevertheless an hypothesis which on genetic grounds ought to have the same status with the hypothesis of men's greater capacity for aggression.

There are a number of findings in Maccoby and Jacklin's new book which rescue the idea that girls are more sociable than boys from its status as a myth. I shall briefly review some of this evidence, which may be of more interest to the professional psychologist than to the general reader, although the issues raised are themselves important.

As a first example, Maccoby and Jacklin review the evidence about sex differences in motivation to achieve success and in self-concept. They do not classify achievement-motivation or self-concept under social behavior. This itself reflects a theoretical bias toward regarding these psychological phenomena as individualistic. Their review of the evidence on the achievement motive shows that boys are more highly motivated when the circumstances are competitive, while girls are more motivated by "social goals." On the question of self-concept, Maccoby and Jacklin suggest that women and men have "different arenas of ego investment." [17] Women invest more in affiliative relations with others; men are more involved in status and power. Investment in affiliative relations with others is surely more social behavior than investment in status and power.

In their section on social behavior, Maccoby and Jacklin also underestimate some of their powerful evidence that women are more sociable than men. For example, the evidence is strong that girls' friendships are different in quality than boys. Girls develop "chumships"; boys develop "gangships." By definition, this makes girls' friendships are different in quality than boys'. Girls develop (and more aggressive.)

When it comes to helping and sharing behavior, Maccoby and Jacklin cite a cross-cultural study by Whiting and Pope which showed that in six different primitive cultures, girls offered help more than boys: food, toys, labor, advice, and support. Girls also "suggested responsibly" more often than boys, that is, made efforts to protect another child. Maccoby and Jacklin suggest that this greater responsibility for others arises out of girls' baby-sitting assignments, which is a reasonable explanation. It is an explanation, however, which also points to girls' maternal function which is both a biological and cultural source of girls' being more social than boys, more accustomed to positive attitudes toward others.

Let's look, briefly, at one important line of work on the relation between capitalism and idealized sex-roles. In 1966, David Bakan [18] suggested that there are two fundamental modalities of human experience: "agency," which refers to the self-preservation of the individual, and "communion," which involves the participation of the individual in some larger entity. Bakan suggested that men are trained toward agency, while women are trained toward communion. He suggested, further, that "unmitigated agency" is an evil, and that capitalism requires an exaggeration of agency. In a cross-cultural study of masculine and feminine ideals which included examples of both "agentic" and "communion" behavior, Block [19] found fewer sex differences and less emphasis on agency in Sweden and Denmark, two countries whose economies are much more socialized than ours.

Women show their greater closeness to others in a variety of ways. Some of the techniques which psychologists have devised to study this sex difference have been ingenious and amusing. One team of investigators set out to study the extent to which men and women are willing to disclose themselves to the important people in their lives. They asked unmarried college students to rate how much they tell about their disappointments and their feelings of self-dislike and failure. The students were also asked how freely other people confided in them. Women confided more in others than do men; and women said more often than men that others confided in them. Both men and women confided most in a same-sex friend and more in people they liked. But women by far had what the investigators called "input" and "output" of self-disclosure.[20]

One researcher has been engaged, along with collaborators, in a very interesting research on the extent to which men and women look into each others' eyes. This is, as we all know, an excellent indicator of the extent of good communication which is really going on. (Being unable to look into someone's eyes when one wants to is a symptom of shame—intense but negative communication.) Men and women were observed when they were in three-person discussion groups. During the discussion, observers spot-checked the instances in which two subjects look each other in the eye. Women did this much more than men. In a follow-up on this finding, the researchers studied eye-to-eye contact during different face-to-face interview situations. Sometimes the interviewer was asking embarrassing questions, sometimes the persons interviewed were asked to conceal their real feelings. Sometimes the interviewer was a man talking to a woman, sometimes vice versa. Under all experimental conditions, women looked into the other person's eyes more often than men.[21] Positive communication is hard to stop in women. Paradoxically, this openness to others makes women more prone to shame.

Just as aggressiveness is the most stable, enduring characteristic over the lifetime of men, so affectionateness, dependency, and timidity are the stable lifetime personality characteristics of women. Girls who are the more affectionate, dependent, timid of their sex during childhood grow up to have the same relative standing within their sex as adults.[22]

When the question is asked: "Are mothers more nurturant and affectionate than fathers within their own families?" the answer is no surprise. Mothers are more nurturant and affectionate than fathers in their behavior both to boys and to girls.[23] And so the scene perpetuates itself. Aggressive fathers make aggressive sons who turn into aggressive fathers. Nurturant mothers make affectionate daughters who turn into nurturant mothers. When fathers are dealing with their daughters, their aggression is muted so that women, treated more lovingly during their lives, return it to their children. And the women pay for this loving, which is incongruous with the values of a warring society, in "loss of love" anxiety and especially in proneness to shame.

It is interesting to observe in this connection that even in their dreams men and women show differences in both aggression and in positive attitudes toward others. One study [24] found a greater frequency and higher intensity of aggression in the manifest content of men's dreams than in women's. Another study showed that women's dreams more often contained a greater number of people than men's dreams, more familiar people, and a greater number of references to parents.

Even in their symbolic conceptions of the Deity, men and women have different modes of response. A Rorschach study [25] showed that fear of God was more characteristic of men, while benevolent representations of the Deity were more characteristic of women.

A psychoanalytic observation which by now has crept into general knowledge is that the end-product of conflict within the individual between love and hostility in which hostility loses (and is repressed) is anxiety. Women's lesser tendency to aggression and their greater lovingness push them into a greater proneness to anxiety. This happens even though they are called on to function less directly in the competitive world. In this same recent survey of sex differences from which I have been quoting,[26] twenty-six studies were listed comparing the level of anxiety in the two sexes, both children and adults. The measures of anxiety were all questionnaires (which means reporting about anxiety rather than living it). Of the twenty-six studies, fifteen showed that women and girls have a higher level of anxiety than boys or men; eleven studies showed no difference, and no studies showed boys higher in anxiety. It may be that these results reflect that women are talking about anxiety more—perhaps because they feel freer to express it. But the few studies [27] which try to observe anxiety in operation also agree that "real" anxiety—blushing, sweating, and rapid heartbeat—are easier to elicit in women than in men. That women blush more was observed long ago by Darwin.[28]

One investigation [29] has directly connected "femininity," suppression of agression, and anxiety. The more "feminine" people of both sexes felt themselves to be, the less agression they expressed and the more anxiety they showed.

Not only are women more anxious than men, but their anxiety plays more havoc with their performance in the world than it does for men. The study [30] which showed this compared the behavior of men and women solving anagrams. The men and women subjects were selected so that some were usually very anxious (by their own account), and others were usually not anxious. Men who were *very* anxious and women who were *not* anxious did better on solving the anagrams than women who were *very anxious* and men who were *not*. If you're a man, anxiety doesn't necessarily get in the way of your functioning; if you're a women, it does!

Another study observed children of both sexes at work solving puzzles. Boys tended to return to the puzzles they had failed to complete. Girls tended to ignore these—thus withdrawing from activity after failure.[31] But perhaps the more damning indictment of how anxiety works in men and women comes from a study [32] in which boys' and girls' expectations of success and failure were observed. The brighter the boy, the better he expected to do in future tests. Also, the brighter the boy, the more he thought that the good scores he did make were the results of his own competence. Just what we'd expect from a reality-oriented, self-assured male! The brighter the girl, however, the less likely she was to think that good performance was a reflection of her own capacity. Just what we might expect from people who, to begin with, accept that they are second-class!

Every time I have to speak at a professional meeting, I carefully write out my paper. I have always felt a little ashamed of this as evidence of my own excessive shame anxiety. I'd much rather speak extemporaneously. I enjoy it more and so does my audience, as I well know from long years of teaching. This is another source of both guilt and shame for me, since it indicates that I am afraid of my colleagues and not of my students—a distinction which (to my mind) I ought not to be making. I always envy my male colleagues, who less often read their papers (except if they are trying to convey complicated results in a short time). I have also observed that my female colleagues tend to be just like me—nervous and well-prepared.

At a recent symposium, which I organized, I had, as it happened, invited one woman and two men speakers (a pretty good reflection of the ratio of men and women in the field). The men both spoke extemporaneously. The woman psychologist read her paper. Of the three, all of whom are distinguished, she has the longest established reputation.

My most recent such experience was attending a professional symposium on women's role in society. As usual, the male participants all came without prepared text. All the women came holding their papers in their hands (and nicely dressed, with hair specially done). The organizer of this symposium was a woman and mindful of women's struggle for equality. Without particularly being aware, I think, that all the men were ready to speak extemporaneously, while the women were not, she urged "all" to throw away their texts and speak from their hearts. Although I agreed with her in principle, I found myself resentful at this assault on my anxiety. I also realized that we women were being covertly ridiculed for our nervousness and exhorted into instant self-assurance. So I remonstrated (rather meekly) and persuaded the authority to permit us "nervous nellies" to read our papers as we had planned. All my women colleagues were obviously relieved. They read their papers, which were all lively and informative, and the symposium remained a valuable experience.

I recount this little episode because I think it contains a moral for the women's movement. The moral is about shame, anxiety, and aggression. The resultants of women's second place in the competitive world are their lesser level of aggression, their greater reliance on others' approval, and their greater level of self-destructive anxiety. Of these three resultants, only the last is an intrinsic, unmitigated evil. Having a low level of aggression is not an evil; it is a deficiency in a warring world. Reliance on others is also not an evil, except that it doesn't work in an exploitative, warring world.

Cultivating aggressiveness will not reduce anxiety. The solution for anxiety is an awareness that it arises out of a long, cruel process by which women repress their need for freedom and autonomy. This awareness will not effect an instantaneous change. In order to get through the chronic, self-destructive anxiety which besets them, women must first stop being ashamed of the way they are. And a first step is to get over the unconscious male model of excellence: aggressive, egotistical, self-propelled, and self-contained.

In recent years, psychologists have developed a technique for studying people's reactions to moral transgression. This technique consists of asking people to complete a story involving wrongdoing. In one investigation,[33] this technique was combined with a study of actual cheating among boys and girls of school age. Although in this study the boys had actually cheated more than the girls, the girls were much more likely to include a "confession" of guilt in their stories. "Confession" of guilt in story completion was also a much better general indicator of resistance to cheating in girls than it was in boys. The psychologists who did this study interpreted the tendency of the girls to "confess" more than boys as an indication of girls' greater dependency on the approval of others. This is another way of saying that girls tend to feel ashamed of themselves and to attempt to discharge shame in confession: in making peace with others.

There is not much direct evidence from formal psychological studies about women's superego mode. But there are two recent studies which did some probing about conscience among men and women of college age. This is probing more into talk than into actions, but the results do confirm the relative shame-proneness of women, and the guilt-proneness of men.

One study [34] tried to get at the experience of conscience just by asking men and women about it. The question was asked: "When you are tempted to do something wrong, how do you know whether to do it or not?" This is a question aimed directly at the guilt side of conscience. As one would expect among verbal, sophisticated people, the similarities between the two sexes were, on the whole, greater than their differences on this question. But women gave as their most frequent answer that they would take into account all the circumstances. Men's most frequent answer was that they would consult their own standards. Women said they would consider the harm to others and the teachings of their parents, thus demonstrating their "other-connected" conscience. Men said they would consider the strength of their own desires and also consider whether they would get caught. Women mentioned this consideration least often. Men's conscience considerations were thus more egotistical and practical, as befits men of action.

This same study also used a list of metaphors for conscience which had been developed out of psychoanalytic thinking. The metaphors were designed to represent the conscience as an alien, threatening force (fear of castration) and as an attractive, guiding force (an ideal of good conduct). Women more often chose the metaphors representing conscience as an ideal of goodness. The metaphors they chose more frequently than men represented conscience as a "hidden lamp," a "seeing-eye dog," a "hidden camera," the "North Star." Women's conscience operates in terms of an internalized observer in whose eyes the self is judged. Both sexes actually preferred the metaphors representing the positive, ego-ideal side of conscience. But men also chose punitive metaphors more often than women: a "threatening father," a "concealed weapon," a "foreign agent." Men's conscience felt "ego-alien"—it is more like an internal enemy. Women's conscience involved an ideal of goodness—it was more benign. These findings on the metaphors men and women use to describe their conscience fit very well with the results of the study [35] which assessed the two sexes' conception of God.

Another study [36] assessed proneness to shame or guilt by making an analysis of people's earliest memories. Memories which involved being ridiculed, teased, ignored, or rejected were categorized as shame-memories. Memories of hurting other people, or making a "bad" choice were scored as guilt memories. Women had more shame-memories than men; and conversely, men had more guilt-memories than women.

Some researchers have developed a method of assessing the different kinds of anxiety which can be observed in a five-minute sample of people's thinking aloud. This is the Gottschalk method,[37] referred to in the preceding chapter. People are asked to talk about anything that interests them and each phrase of their free-wheeling talk is scored for whether or not it reflects guilt anxiety, shame-anxiety, death-anxiety, mutilation-anxiety, or separation-anxiety. In one study, women showed more shame-anxiety than men.

How does this difference in superego mode affect the relationship between the sexes? The stereotype is of a confident, down-to-earth no-nonsense man emotionally inarticulate about himself, but very articulate about things in the world. He is trying to understand and to be understood by a timid, sensitive, emotionally articulate woman, talking about herself (mostly about her anxieties of being unloved)—and both are getting nowhere! He makes her feel ashamed; she makes him feel guilty.

It is hardly necessary to document this accurate stereotype. Just one example of it comes from a sociological survey [38] of premarital dating habits among young people in our country during the fifties. Among men, the survey concludes: The degree of physical intimacy actually experienced or considered permissible "was inversely related to the intensity and familiarity and affection felt for the woman." The more he cared about her, the guiltier he would feel if he were intimate with her sexually, as if intercourse were aggression. For women, the more familiar and affectionate they felt toward the man, the more they felt it permissible to make love. As the survey put it, women were more liberal in their conduct with their lovers; men more conservative. Men were threatened with guilt if they "did something" to a woman they cared about. Women were ready to give themselves to a man they cared about, of course, expecting mutual commitment. Neither sex was really being any "nobler" than the other, but rather following different values and different self-concepts.

References

1. J. Garai and A. Scheinfeld, "Sex Differences in Mental and Behavioral Traits," *Genetic Psychology Monographs* 77 (1968), pp. 169-299.

2. J. Garai and A. Scheinfeld, op. cit.

3. J. Adams, "Adolescent Personal Problems as a Function of Age and Sex," *Journal of Genetic Psychology* 104 (1964), 207-214.

4. R. McDonald and M. Gynther, "Relationship of Self and Ideal-self Description with Sex, Race and Class in Southern Adolescents", *Journal of Personality and Social Psychology* 1 (1965) 85-88.

5. W. Vinacke and G. Gulliksen, "Age and Sex Differences in the Formation of Coalitions," *Child Development* 35 (1964), 1217-1231.

6. Jean Bradford, "Sex Differences in Anxiety," *Dissertation Abstracts,* 29 (1968), 1167.

7. L. A. Siebert, "Superego Sex Differences," dissertation, University of Michigan, 1965.

8. E. Douvan, "Sex Differences in Adolescent Character," *Merrill-Palmer Quarterly* 6 (1960), 203-211.

9. J. P. McKee and A. Sherriffs, "The Differential Evaluation of Males and Females," *Journal of Personality* 25 (1957), 356-371.

10. L. Kohlberg, "A Cognitive-Developmental Analysis of Children's Sex-Role Concepts and Attitudes," ed. E. Maccoby, *The Development of Sex Differences* (Stanford, Calif.: Stanford University Press, 1966), p. 120.

11. E. Maccoby, ed., *The Development of Sex Differences* (Stanford, Calif.: Stanford University Press, 1966), annotated bibliography by Roberta Oetzel.

12. P. Mussen, "Early Sex-Role Development," ed. Goslin, *Handbook of Socialization Theory* (Chicago: Rand McNally, 1969), p. 712.

13. E. Maccoby, op. cit., annotated bibliography.

14. E. Maccoby, op. cit., annotated bibliography.

15. E. Maccoby and C. Jacklin, *The Psychology of Sex Differences* (Stanford, Calif.: Stanford University Press, 1974).

16. Ibid., p. 214.

17. Ibid., p. 159.

18. D. Bakan, *The Duality of Human Existence.* (Chicago: Rand McNally, 1966).

19. J. Block, "Conceptions of Sex-Role", *American Psychologist*, 28 (1973), 512-526.

20. S. Jourard and P. Richman, "Factors in the Self-disclosure of College Students," *Merrill-Palmer Quarterly* 9 (1963), 141-148.

21. V. Exline, "Effects of Need for Affiliation, Sex and the Sight of Others upon Initial Communication in Problem-solving Groups," *Journal of Personality* 60 (1962), 541-546.

22. R. Sears, L. Rau and R. Alpert, *Identification and Child Rearing* (Stanford, Calif.: Stanford University Press, 1965).

23. E. Maccoby, op. cit.

24. A. Paolino, "Dreams: Sex Differences in Aggressive Content," *Journal of Projective Techniques and Personality Assessment*, 28 (1964), 219-226.

25. C. Brenneis, "Differences in Male and Female Styles in Manifest Dream Content," *Dissertation Abstracts* 28 (1968), 3056.

26. L. Larson and R. Knapp, "Sex Differences in Symbolic Conceptions of the Deity," *Journal of Projective Techniques and Personality Assessment* (1968, 1964), 303-306.

27. E. Maccoby, op. cit.

28. Charles Darwin, *The Expression of Emotions in Man and Animals* (London: John Murray), 1872.

29. F. Cosentino and A. Heilbrun, "Anxiety Correlates of Sex-Role Identity in College Students," *Psychological Reports* 14 (1964), 729-730.

30. E. Maccoby, op. cit.

31. E. Maccoby, op. cit.

32. V. Crandall, W. Katkowsky and A. Preston, "Motivational and Ability Determinants of Young Children's Intellectual Achievement Behaviors," *Child Development* 33 (1962), 642-661.

33. F. Rebelsky, W. Allinsmith and R. Grinder, "Sex Differences in Children's Use of Fantasy Confession and Their Relation to Temptation," *Child Development* 34 (1963), 955-962.

34. L. Siebert, *Superego Sex Differences,* op. cit.

35. L. Larson and R. Knapp, op. cit.

36. J. Binder, "The Relative Proneness to Shame or Guilt As a Dimension of Character Style," dissertation abstracts, University of Michigan, 1970.

37. G. Gleser, L. Gottschalk and K. Springer, "An Anxiety Scale Applicable to Verbal Samples," *Archives of General Psychiatry* 5 (1961), 593-605.

38. W. Ehrmann, *Premarital Dating Behavior* (New York: Holt, 1959).

PART IV

Alternate Routes to Madness

CHAPTER 15

A Head-Count of Mental Casualties by Sexes?

Do men and women fall mentally ill in equal numbers? If not, which sex is more often hit by mental illness? The answer to these questions varies with time (and place) at which rates of mental illness have been sampled in the population. At least, until 1950, the most reliable statistics showed that men were more often victims of mental illness than women.[1] In recent times, women have been joining the ranks of the mentally ill in increasing numbers,[2] paralleling an ever-increasing rate of mental illness for men. Phyllis Chesler has reported some recent statistical studies which found a higher count of mental illness for women than for men,[3] but these statistics may be misleading.

Just counting people of both sexes in mental hospitals or other psychiatric facilities is an inadequate method of assessing the proneness of men and women to mental disorders. Let me illustrate with a bit of history. It used to be believed during the nineteenth century that women were more prone to mental illness than men. This belief was based on the number of men and women patients residing in mental hospitals. When it was realized that women live longer than men—even in mental hospitals—so that the accumulation of women patients was greater, the fallacy in these statistics was discovered. The idea that women are more prone to mental illness than men could then be relegated to the status of an antifemale myth. The interpretation of statistical studies thus requires a number of elementary, common-sense precautions if these studies are to be valid and reliable indicators of genuine trends.

Even more important, however, a genuine trend for either sex to be ahead in frequency of mental illness must not be interpreted as a deficiency in the member of that sex so much as a reflection of a difference in the way society injures both sexes. If more men are "battle casualties" than women, it is because society requires that men be more often in battle. Studies, even accurate ones, which simply compare the rate of total mental illness in men and women, do not do justice to the salient fact that men and women fall mentally ill, not just in different numbers but in different ways.

I have made a particular study of the different kinds of mental illness to which men and women are prone.[4] All statistical (as well as observational) studies agree that women fall ill of depression ° and hysteria more often than men. The evidence shows that men fall ill of alcoholism, addictions, sexual perversions, obsessional neurosis, and schizophrenia more often than women. For all these categories, except schizophrenia, the evidence is unambiguous. In the case of schizophrenia, the evidence is clear that men are more often its victims especially between the ages of fifteen and thirty, when careers must be established.

Schizophrenia and psychotic depression are often considered "contrasting poles" in psychiatric literature. These two major psychoses differ from each other qualitatively in many important respects. They run different courses and follow different ecological patterns, as well as attacking the two sexes in different frequencies. Let's look very briefly at some of the differences.

As Solomon Snyder puts it, in his book, *Madness and the Brain*,[5]

° I am using the term "depression" as the overall term for at least three varieties described in the literature: manic-depression psychosis, in which periods of mania alternate with periods of depression; psychotic depression, that is, periodic depression (without mania) which is severe enough to require hospitalization; and neurotic depression, an experience familiar to us all, but which is so persistent in some individuals that they seek (usually) outpatient psychiatriac treatment for it.

when people think about out-and-out "madness," they are thinking about schizophrenia. In schizophrenia, there has been a shutdown of ordinary human feeling so that the person's behavior is totally incomprehensible to others, and therefore appears bizarre. (It took dedicated psychoanalysts, like Paul Federn, Harry Stack Sullivan, and Frieda Fromm-Reichmann to persist in treating schizophrenic patients long enough to discover the deeply buried feelings which had been turned off.) The depressive psychotic is, in contrast, still in emotional contact with his (or her) environment. The symptoms of depression are exaggerations of ordinary feelings, with which we are all familiar; the symptoms are all too human. "By contrast," writes Snyder, "even when he is hypermanic, the catatonic schizophrenic gives off the same aura of death-in-life as when he is stuporous."

Schizophrenia is thus a more serious disorder than psychotic depression, since it carries its victims "way out" into "madness." Schizophrenia is more serious illness also because it is often an unremitting, lifelong illness. Depression, in contrast, is well-known to run its course and eventually lift, even if it will sometime reappear. Schizophrenia is also a much more frequent illness than psychotic depression. It accounts for between 30 percent and 50 percent of the mentally ill. In contrast, psychotic depression accounts for a much smaller proportion—from about 5 percent to 10 percent of the total.[6]

Most important of all, schizophrenia and depression follow very different social ecologies.[7] Schizophrenia is strongly associated with poverty and social disorganization. The ecological picture of schizophrenia thus parallels the fact that men are directly involved in our exploitative society and therefore more directly subject to pressures which can dehumanize them. Depression is only slightly, if at all, associated with socioeconomic factors.[8, 9] The ecological picture of depression, which draws patients almost equally from all social classes, parallels the fact that women participate less directly than men in our exploitative society; therefore, their more frequent mental illness is less directly related to poverty and social disorganization.

Before we can go more deeply into the question of which mental illness afflicts which sex more often it is necessary to consider some essential questions about how statistics on mental illness are established. The following are some of the most obvious factors to be reckoned with in evaluating the reliability and validity of statistical counts:

(1) If it happened that there were more men than women living in a particular area, more men than women might be represented in a count of admissions to psychiatric facilities. Statistics on admissions to psychiatric facilities are therefore calculated per 100,000 of the population. Failure to calculate admissions to mental hospitals per 100,000 of the population was one of the errors which led to the nineteenth-century belief that women were more prone to mental illness than men. The same failure may account for Chesler's recent finding that women are more prone to mental illness than men.

(2) The same person is often admitted more than once to a psychiatric facility. One kind of count is the first time a person is admitted it is called a "first admission." Another count is "readmission," if that should happen. Still, a third kind of count is called "unduplicated admissions." This counts the same person only once, adding together his or her first admission and readmissions. Clearly, a high "unduplicated admissions" rate reflects chronic and severe mental illness.

(3) Statistics are often developed by simply counting the people who are in some kind of psychiatric facility. But such figures may themselves reflect the number of treatment facilities available. So, for example, statistics on mental illness in the South once showed fewer cases (per 100,000 of the population) in that region than in the rest of the country. But this reflected not a true picture of the South as a haven in which mental illness did not occur, but a relative lack of psychiatric facilities, particularly for blacks, who form a large proportion of the Southern population.[10] In addition, one cannot rely on statistics from areas where there are changes taking place in the number of psychiatric facilities and in social attitudes about using them. The statistics which have been gathered since 1910 (and earlier) from the New York state hospital facilities are particularly valuable, because they have been developed out of a relatively stable "hospital ecology," as well as over a long period of time.[11] We shall be making use of these reliable statistics in this and subsequent chapters.

(4) A count of hospital residents or of the number of people enrolled in an outpatient clinic at any one time can be misleading, even if the count is calculated per 100,000 of the population.

Hospitals and clinics vary in their criteria and rates of discharge. Also, residents are in varying degrees of "chronicity" or "acuteness" of illness. So statistics which count the number of residents in a psychiatric facility may be of little value in reflecting the true rate of mental illness for men and women (or for any other comparison, for that matter). First admissions and readmissions need to be counted as well, since they reflect illness acute enough to require hospitalization at the time.

(5) Psychiatric facilities differ in the class of population they serve. Private psychiatric facilities (both outpatient and inpatient) serve people who are better able to pay than those in state hospital facilities. On the whole, outpatient clinics serve people who are less severely disturbed than the people in hospitals. Psychiatric wards in general hospitals also probably carry a smaller proportion of the severely disturbed, since these psychiatric wards are usually regarded as temporary facilities. It follows that statistics on inpatients in state and other public institutions reflect mental illness among the sickest people and the lowest socioeconomic classes. As we shall see a bit later on, Chesler's statistics, which have shown more women than men in psychiatric facilities, have suffered from two defects: they have not always been calculated per 100,000 of the population, and they have come mainly from the better psychiatric facilities, rather than from state hospitals.

So far, we have been concerned with what might be called the mechanics of making an accurate count of the mentally ill, including the socioeconomic factors which have well-established connections with the rate of mental illness. Let's look more closely at the way mental illness is connected to social class before coming back to the different ways in which the two sexes fall mentally ill. As one very recent study of the "ecology of mental disorders" put it: "The old villain, poverty, emerges in our study once again, as a significant factor related to the prevalence of serious mental disorder," [11,12] Pioneering studies of the relation between social class and mental illness appeared in the 1930s.[13,14] Among the most famous was a classic study of the city of Chicago, by Faris and Dunham,[15] which demonstrated that the slums contributed the heaviest rates of mental illness. An ecological map of Chicago could be drawn which showed that the closer an area was to the slums, the higher the rate of mental illness of its occupants. Following the lead of Faris and Dunham, similarly designed and executed studies [16] yielded very similar results for St. Louis, Milwaukee, Omaha, Kansas City, Rockford, Peoria, Cleveland, and Providence. A still more recent study in Mannheim, Germany, also reported similar results! [17]

An interesting sidelight on the importance of being able to make proper interpretations of statistics, comes from the most recent study of mental illness in Chicago.[18] One finding of this study, by Levy and Rowitz, was that first admissions statistics which had been most highly correlated with poverty in the Faris and Dunham study no longer yielded the same results. First admission came almost equally from all areas of Chicago. But this finding, although a technical failure to replicate Faris and Dunham's findings was not an actual contradiction. Instead, the first admission statistics now represented the fact that psychiatric facilities were more numerous in all parts of the city. With more tolerant attitudes toward psychiatry and more psychiatric facilities in additional areas, the facilities were being more generally used. Faris and Dunham's essential finding, that mental illness is more widespread in areas of poverty and social disorganization was confirmed by the fact that unduplicated admissions, which represent the most chronic and severe cases, were clearly predominant in the Chicago slums.

As one might expect, the meaning of the relationship between poverty and mental illness is a question of controversy.[19] Everyone agrees that the existence of a relationship does not by itself prove a causal connection between poverty and mental illness. Some investigators, in fact, have argued that the slums attract those people who are less able, either for genetic or other reasons, to make it in the competitive world. This idea, sometimes called the "social drift theory," attributes the slums' contribution to a greater frequency of mental illness to the fact that the slums are a dumping ground for the disabled. Others argue that the slums provide an atmosphere of poverty and social disorganization in which human beings cannot flourish. Still others argue that both theories reflect some degree of truth.

The recent Chicago study has also shown that the relation between schizophrenia and social disorganization is particularly strong. "Unduplicated admissions" for schizophrenia representing the most chronic and severe cases, come from areas in Chicago where the population is poor, where there is a high percentage of substandard housing, high residential mobility, high unem-

ployment, high male delinquency rate, high rate of ille-
gitimate births, and a high percentage of welfare recipients.[20]
A positive correlation was obtained (+0.85 between readmission
for schizophrenia and income of under $3,000, while a high
negative correlation (-0.73) obtained between schizophrenia
readmissions and income over $10,000.

There was, in contrast, little connection between manic-
depressive psychosis and ecological pattern. Rates of admission
for this illness were about the same from all areas of Chicago. This
connects with the finding that manic-depressive psychosis is the
illness more likely to afflict women, while schizophrenia is the
illness more likely to afflict men. Moreover, the total admission
rates for males tended to follow the ecological pattern of
schizophrenia, while the rate for females did not vary with economic class.

One of the most important and famous studies of the connection
between socioeconomic factors and mental illness has been the
work of Hollingshead and Redlich.[21] In their classic study, *Social
Class and Mental Illness,* they found that the poorest segments of
the population were overrepresented in state mental hospitals.
They made use of Hollingshead's *Index of Social Position,* a system
for describing socioeconomic class which combines area of residence, occupation, and education into a single measure by which
a person is assigned a class rating. Since its development, the
Hollingshead Index is a widely used research tool. Hollingshead
and Redlich found, also, that the diagnosis conferred upon a
patient is in part a function of the distance in social class between
the conferrer and the conferee. The more serious diagnosis,
schizophrenia, is more likely to be conferred upon someone poor
and black. They also found that depression and psychoneurosis,
the less serious mental disorders, were less strongly associated
with social class. If anything, these diagnoses came from more
affluent segments of society.

We come back, now, to the question whether more men or
women succumb to mental illness. Within the same hospital
ecology, and with precautions to take account of the ratio to
population, more men than women fall victim to mental disorder.
The following is a table prepared by Malzberg for the 1959 edition
of the *American Handbook of Psychiatry.*[22] This table shows the
greater frequency of mental illness among men than women over
a period of forty years from 1910 to 1950.

Table 1
FIRST ADMISSIONS TO NEW YORK STATE HOSPITALS
1910-50 PER 100,000 POPULATION °
° (Adapted from B. Malzberg.)

Fiscal Year	Males	Females	Total
1910	9.7	3.0	6.4
1912	9.4	3.0	6.2
1914	7.2	2.4	4.8
1916	6.7	2.4	4.6
1918	5.9	2.1	4.0
1920	3.0	0.8	1.9
1922	3.6	0.7	2.2
1924	5.3	1.3	3.3
1926	6.6	1.7	4.1
1928	7.4	1.5	4.4
1930	7.4	1.4	4.4
1932	8.1	2.0	5.1
1934	9.9	2.4	6.2
1936	10.2	2.7	6.4
1938	10.9	2.3	6.6
1940	11.3	2.4	6.8
1942	11.4	2.7	6.9
1944	8.0	2.4	5.1
1946	8.3	2.4	5.3
1948	10.0	3.1	6.4
1950	11.0	3.2	7.0

°The rates are based upon the average annual number of first admissions during three years; that is, the rate for 1910 is the average for 1909–11, inclusive.

The recent Chicago study also showed a greater frequency of mental illness in men than in women.[23] A brief glance at the figures derived from one of Chicago's worst areas, tells the story dramatically. In this area, the "unduplicated admissions" rate per 100,000 of the population was 6115.6 for men and 2561.2 for women. It is worth noting, in passing, that the greater vulnerability of men to mental illness parallels their greater vulnerability to physical diseases [24] as well as their more direct participation in the psychological stresses of an exploitative environment.

Phyllis Chesler has recently presented some statistics which suggest that women's rate of mental illness is increasing.[25] She also presents figures which show that more women than men fall ill of mental disorder, interpreting this as a reflection of the oppression of women by men. A careful examination of the tables present in *Women and Madness* suggests that women are in greater numbers when the rate is not calculated per 100,000 of the population. They are also in greater numbers (still not per 100,000) in general hospitals, outpatient clinics, and private treatment facilities. These are, as we indicated earlier, psychiatric facilities which cater to the more affluent and less disturbed patients. Chesler's own tables show that in state and county hospitals, the ratio of men to women is either about equal (from 1960 to 1966) or that men are more numerous than women (after 1966) [26]. Since the figures which show more women than men are derived from the "better" psychiatric facilities, they may reflect the fact that at this economic level more women than men can afford to be psychiatric patients. Chesler acknowledges that women are "underrepresented in state hospitals." She also tells us that they are concentrated more in outpatient clinics and private facilities, but she does not connect this fact with the higher economic base and the less disturbed population who are in these facilities. Her figures showing more women than men in psychiatric treatment may not represent a true difference but only a difference at higher economic levels and in less serious disturbances. This kind of finding in turn jibes with Hollingshead and Redlich's [27] that less severe mental illnesses come from both higher and lower income groups.

This is not to disagree with Chesler that women are oppressed, and by men, only with the interpretation of the figures on mental illness which she presents in support of that view. As I have indicated earlier, the most significant figures on mental illness are not those showing the gross total difference between the sexes, but rather the difference in the characteristic type of mental disorders to which each sex is prone.

One fascinating piece of evidence presented by Chesler shows that women *feel* more disturbed than men. The following table, adapted from *Women and Madness*, compares the answers by the two sexes to a questionnaire about their experiences. The survey was conducted in 1960-62 on a probability sample of 7,710 persons selected to represent the 111 million (noninstitutionalized) adults in the United States, and between the ages of nineteen and seventy-nine years. The symptom rates shown are projected percentages for the total population. These figures represent self-reports of symptoms, not actual admissions to a psychiatric facility.

It will be seen that more women than men reported symptoms of nervous breakdowns, impending nervous breakdowns, nervousness, inertia, insomnia, trembling hands, nightmares, perspiring hands, fainting, headaches, and heart palpitations. As we shall see in Chapters 16 and 17, these are the symptoms which characterize both depression and hysteria, two illnesses to which women are more prone than men.

Table 2
SYMPTOM RATES BY SEX
° (Adapted from P. Chesler, *Women and Madness*.)

Symptom and Sex	Total, 18-79 Years
Nervous Breakdowns:	
Male	3.2
Female	6.4
Impending Nervous Breakdowns:	
Male	7.7
Female	17.5
Nervousness:	
Male	45.1
Female	70.6
Inertia:	
Male	16.8
Female	32.5
Insomnia:	
Male	23.5
Female	40.4
Trembling Hands:	
Male	7.9
Female	10.9
Nightmares:	
Male	7.6
Female	12.4

Table 2
SYMPTOM RATES BY SEX
° (Adapted from P. Chesler, *Women and Madness.*)

Symptom and Sex	Total, 18-79 Years
Perspiring Hands:	
Male	17.0
Female	21.4
Fainting:	
Male	16.9
Female	29.1
Headaches:	
Male	13.7
Female	27.8
Dizziness:	
Male	7.1
Female	10.9
Heart Palpitations:	
Male	3.7
Female	5.8

The symptoms in this table are all ordinary, familiar experiences, which normal as well as psychotic persons have. Men are less likely than women to complain of these (or any) symptoms. In fact, one of Hollingshead and Redlich's findings [28] was that even at upper-class levels, schizophrenic men were not *self*-referred to mental institutions, but brought there by family or friends. As we shall see in Chapters 18 and 19, men are more likely to have thought disorders which carry them into abnormal, bizarre distortions of the world and of themselves.

References

1. B. Malzberg, "Important Statistical Data about Mental Illness," ed. S. Arieti, *American Handbook of Psychiatry* (New York: Basic Books, 1959), pp. 161-174.

2. P. Chesler, *Women and Madness* (New York: Doubleday, 1972).

3. Ibid.

4. Helen B. Lewis, Sex Differences in Superego Style: Psychiatric Implications, unpublished manuscript.

5. S. Snyder, *Madness and the Brain* (New York: McGraw-Hill, 1974), p. 128.

6. B. Malzberg, op. cit.

7. L. Levy and L. Rowitz, *The Ecology of Mental Disorder* (New York: Behavioral Publications, 1973).

8. Ibid.

9. A. Hollingshead and F. Redlich, *Social Class and Mental Illness* (New York: Wiley, 1958).

10. B. Malzberg, op. cit.

11. B. Malzberg, op. cit.

12. L. Levy and L. Rowitz, op. cit., p. 155.

13. C. Landis and J. Page, *Modern Society and Mental Disease* (New York: Farrar & Rinehart, 1938).

14. R. E. L. Faris and H. W. Dunham, *Mental Disorder in Urban Areas* (New York: Hafner, 1960).

15. Ibid.

16. Ibid.

17. Ibid.

18. Ibid.

19. B. P. Dohrenwend and B. S. Dohrenwend, *Social Status and Psychological Disorder: A Causal Inquiry* (New York: Wiley, 1969).

20. L. Levy and L. Rowitz, op. cit., pp. 53-54.

21. A. Hollingshead and F. Redlich, op. cit.

22. B. Malzberg, op. cit.

23. L. Levy and L. Rowitz, op. cit.

24. D. C. Taylor and C. Ounsted, "The Nature of Gender Differences Explored Through Ontogenetic Analyses of Sex Ratios in Disease," eds. R. Ounsted and D. C. Taylor, *Gender Differences: Their Ontogeny and Significance* (Baltimore, Md.: Williams and Wilkins, 1972).

25. P. Chesler, op. cit.

26. P. Chesler, op. cit., pp. 42-43.

27. A Hollingshead and F. Redlich, op. cit.

28. Ibid.

CHAPTER 16

Madness in Women: Depression

To fall ill of depression is more often women's lot than men's. Depression in everyday life is, as everyone knows, a temporary experience which can range from mild dejection to profound despair. Depression becomes an illness when the person cannot throw off a state of deep sadness which paralyzes the self. Even then, the symptoms of depression are understandable to the lay person. As one expert puts it: "Affective disorders . . . strike the student of psychiatry for the facility with which their clinical concepts are grasped even by the beginner." [1]

The only other major mental illness which claims more women than men is hysteria. "Hysteria" is a more recondite label than "depression," but its symptoms are equally mundane. In one kind, called "conversion hysteria," the person is afflicted with physical symptoms with no discernible organic base. The other kind of hysteria involves massive anxiety, sometimes to the point of "fugue" or amnesia. In other instances, the anxiety takes a specific form and the person is phobic about some particular thing: for example, snakes, heights, airplane travel, and so forth. Such cases are given the name, "anxiety hysteria," or "phobia." In other cases, a massive anxiety occurs "for no reason," and the person who has once experienced it dreads a recurrence.

In this chapter we shall be concerned mainly with women's proneness to depression. Discussion of women's proneness to hysteria is being postponed to Chapter 17. But before concentrating on depression, it is useful to consider what depression and hysteria have in common besides claiming more women than men as victims. For one thing, symptoms of depression and hysteria often occur together. The experience of unutterable sadness feels literally like a weight on one's insides, so depressed patients often worry that something is wrong with them physically. Individuals plagued with unaccountable ("hysterical") pain or body symptoms tend to be depressed because of their inability to shake their symptoms. There are thus few cases of depression without increased physical awareness of the self, or of hysteria without some depression because the anxiety is so debilitating.

The close link between depression and body symptoms is well-known. One authority describes for us how easy it is to be led astray by the depressive patient whose complaints are often about "physical pain, a feeling of discomfort, digestive difficulties, lack of appetite and insomnia . . . [which seem like] simple psychosomatic dysfunctions." [2] The link between hysteria and depression is less well known. A psychiatric stereotype about hystericals is that they are *not* depressed, but rather show a *"la belle indifférence"* to their illness. Hystericals are often described as dramatic, exhibitionistic, narcissistic, and seductive. As we shall see in Chapter 17, these stereotypes about hystericals were developed by male psychiatrists who have had a particularly hard time understanding women. Hystericals do suffer depression over their physical symptoms or their uncontrollable anxiety.

In both depression and hysteria, a plague has descended upon the experience of the *self*, literally including the body. The self dominates the patient's awareness, with a resulting magnification of body sensations. It is interesting that depression and hysteria do not involve dramatic or bizarre disturbances of sexual identity. The symptoms in depression and hysteria are exaggerations of ordinary feelings: sadness, ache or pain, or anxiety (fear) are all everyday experiences. In this respect, women's more frequent mental illnesses are very different from the sexual perversions,

obsessional neurosis, and schizophrenia—men's more frequent illnesses. These latter illnesses sometimes involve elaborate transformations of the self, and bizarre ideas of transforming the world.
Underlying this bizarreness is a profound loss of emotional connection to other people. Women's illnesses are not bizarre, only an
exaggeration of ordinary feelings. Women's more frequent mental
illnesses are cast in common human terms, perhaps because
women have not given up their affectionateness, only devalued it.
Paradoxically, women, who are trained to be "selfless"—to be
more concerned with others than with themselves—fall victim to
mental illness in which the malfunctioning *self* takes over their
lives.

Although the self is carrying this burden of bad experience, it is
also clear that both depressives and hystericals are very much and
very openly involved with significant other people. Often the
patient is accompanied to the doctor by a devoted husband, parent, or child. Often something has gone wrong with a close relationship and the depressive or hysterical patient is trying to cope
with the resulting disappointment. Symptoms arise which could
have the effect of disturbing the significant other's well-being. For
this the patient feels guilty. The observer (and often the patient)
cannot escape the idea that the symptoms are "put on" to plague
the other person. It is easy for an observer (and sometimes even for
the patient) to see that the plague which has descended upon the
self is some kind of protest against the self's close involvement
with an "important" other person. So depressive and hysterical
patients, while they are coping with some awful experience being
borne by the *self*, are also defending themselves against the fact
that their symptoms are transparently "other-connected."

Of course, men also fall ill of depression and the hysterias. But as
we shall see in this and subsequent chapters, considering why
women are more frequently afflicted in these ways helps to illuminate one kind of insoluble conflict between affectionateness
and exploitative values. Women are not pushed by cultural expectations to give up their affectionateness. On the contrary, as
childbearers, they are expected to cultivate it only to discover that
affectionateness is actually devalued by our society, however
much it is hypocritically praised. Women thus become ashamed
of their own loving feelings, which actually do not count for much

in the marketplace. And, by a process which is not altogether clear, the chronic state of shame is transformed into depressive illness or into one of the hysterias.

The statistics which tell the story of women's greater proneness to depression and the hysterias are themselves fascinating. For one thing they come from many different sources; sometimes they were entirely unexpected by the researchers themselves. For another thing, the statistics all speak the same answer. Usually, when one is trying to evaluate the evidence on a particular point, some studies give one answer, while others say the opposite. It becomes a hard job to evaluate whether the evidence says yes when on the other hand it is saying no. But in the case of women suffering from depression and the hysterias more often than men, all the statistics say yes. Studies which say that women are more "people-oriented" than men are also practically unanimous, as are the studies which say that men are more aggressive than women (see Chapter 14). Women's greater proneness to depression and the hysterias has a great deal to do with their greater degree of people-orientation and their lesser aggressiveness as well as with their greater shame-proneness.

Let's turn now to depressive illness and let's look first at the statistics on its frequency in men and women. One authority has estimated that about 70 percent of patients with manic-depressive psychosis are women.[3]

More precise evidence comes from statistics on "first admissions to state hospitals." As we saw in Chapter 15, these fiqures apply more to poor people who cannot afford private hospitals or private individual treatment. They apply to quite sick people since people with less severe symptoms of depression can usually stay out of hospitals. The statistics show that, from 1910 on, year by year, women were at least twice as often afflicted with depression as men.[4,5]

The reader will note that there has been a decline in the diagnosis of manic-depressive psychosis over the years. This decline is not understood: A guess is that it reflects an increasing tendency in recent years to diagnose schizophrenia in cases of severe mental disturbance.

Evidence that women are more often depressed than men comes not only from statistics on first admissions to state hospitals, but from private, middle-class hospitals as well.[6,7] Middle-class

Table 1
FIRST ADMISSIONS TO NEW YORK STATE HOSPITALS
1910-50 PER 100,000 POPULATION
FOR MANIC-DEPRESSIVE PSYCHOSIS°
°(Adapted from B. Malzberg.)

Year	Men	Women	Total
1910	4.5	7.4	6.0
1912	5.7	8.6	7.1
1914	5.7	8.4	7.0
1916	5.8	9.9	7.8
1918	6.6	12.0	9.3
1920	6.4	12.1	9.2
1922	6.8	12.1	9.4
1924	6.7	11.8	9.2
1926	6.7	11.6	9.2
1928	7.1	12.3	9.7
1930	7.4	11.7	9.5
1932	8.3	12.4	10.4
1934	7.6	12.2	9.9
1936	5.8	10.4	8.2
1938	5.0	9.8	7.4
1940	4.4	8.2	6.3
1942	3.7	6.8	5.3
1944	2.7	7.0	4.9
1946	2.6	6.0	4.4
1948	2.4	4.3	3.3
1950	1.9	3.1	2.5

° Rates are based on the average annual number of first admissions during three years; that is, the rate for 1910 is the average for 1909–11, inclusive.

women, as well as poor women, are more prone to depression than men. In fact, women's greater tendency to depression is so pervasive that they are more often depressed whatever the official diagnosis with which they are admitted to a mental hospital. Not only among patients officially diagnosed as depressed, but among all patients in mental hospitals, whatever the diagnosis, the women are more depressed than the men.[8,9,10]

Not only in hospitals, but among less sick patients in outpatient clinics as well, women come to psychiatry for depression more often than men. Women are more depressed than men in both rural and urban areas. A study of 400 new cases seen between 1963 and 1967 in an outpatient clinic in rural England showed that women were more often depressed than men.[11] A study of more than 2,000 patients who applied for treatment to a midtown New York mental health center also showed that women patients came for depression more often than men patients.[12]

When a finding is unexpected because it comes as an incidental result of looking into some other problem, it is even more dramatic and to some extent more persuasive because it cannot be the product of the investigators' unconscious bias in favor of their own hypothesis. One investigator conducted a follow-up study of 500 juvenile delinquents who grew to adulthood. She came upon the finding that depression was the more frequent diagnosis for the women who had been juvenile delinquents than for the men who had. She also found that depression occurred more often in women than in men among the "normals," that is nondelinquent cases she had assembled as her "controls." [13]

A very recent dissertation at Yale asked the question whether the depressive experience is different for blacks and whites. In a population of "normal" residents of New Haven, with socioeconomic factors controlled, there were no significant differences between blacks and whites in their report of depressive experience. Across both blacks and whites, however, the women, as usual, were more depressed than the men.[14] Thus, whether the question is studied among the poor or middle-class, in hospitals, outpatient clinics or among "normals," in cities or in rural areas, women are more prone to depression than men.

Among depressed men and women, the women report that they *feel* worse than the men.[15] Another study observed the frequency of episodes of actual crying among hospitalized depressed patients. About one-third of the women patients cried; *none* of the men patients was ever seen to cry.[16] Even when their feelings have got so out of hand as to warrant hospitalization for depression, men still have less overt feeling than women! Women are thus not only more often depressed than men but more deeply depressed.

These findings have often been interpreted to be the results of some hormonal factors which are different for women than they are for men. Women's tendency to go into a depression at menopause is cited as an example of the hormonal factor. The relatively good success which psychiatry has recently had in treating depression with mood-elevating and mood-stabilizing drugs is cited as further evidence of a chemical factor. Many women (and others) who hear this factor mentioned are likely to bristle because it is often cited in an effort to deny the importance of psychological conflicts. The idea is that women are helpless victims of their hereditary hormones. But if we disregard this false quarrel betweeen heredity and internalized social forces, there may indeed be a hormonal factor in women's falling ill of depression. This hormonal factor would only add an extra factor to an already existing set of psychological conflicts.

Let's look for a moment at what psychological effects hormones are known to have. Estrogen, the hormone females have more of than men is, among other things, a "gentling" secretion. Estrogen fosters maternal behavior, that is, caring for another life, as we saw in Chapter 2. Androgen, the hormone males have more of, is an "activity-inducing" secretion. Depression (and the hysterias) are mental illnesses which more often afflict the less aggressive people, women, who are "gentled" not only by their hormones but by cultural expectations which they absorb at their mother's breast.

Now that we have looked at some statistics on depression in men and women, let's look at what depression is like as an experience. Depression is an experiential state like the grief or sadness which ordinarily accompany bereavement. There is a loss of interest in the world, a sense of dullness about the self, and a feeling as if there were an intolerable "weight" on the self. But depression is unlike real bereavement because there has not been any visible or tangible loss. There is no good reason in reality why the patient should be feeling as if someone he or she loved had died. No one knows this better than the patient, but the knowledge is useless against the weight of depressed feeling which descends upon the self. When the state is so overwhelming that the patient cannot manage to hold on to a wish for life, we call it psychotic depression and suggest hospitalization. But even when depression is acute, we understand the quality if not the intensity of suffering.

One of the most faithful investigators of depressive illness, Dr. Aaron Beck, has developed a Depression Inventory, a questionnaire which tries to measure the state.[17] The topics covered under the headings of the questionnaire give us a vivid picture of what assorted miseries are assembled to plague the self of a patient in depression. Here is a list of the headings and a brief sample of the statements under one heading. The other headings also had five appropriate statements under each.

A. Sadness

I do not feel sad.
I feel blue or sad.
I am blue or sad all the time and I can't snap out of it.
I am so sad or unhappy that it is quite painful.
I am so sad or unhappy that I can't stand it.

B. Pessimism
C. Sense of Failure
D. Dissatisfaction
E. Guilt
F. Expectation of Punishment
G. Self-Dislike
H. Self-Accusations
I. Suicidal Ideas
J. Crying
K. Irritability
L. Social Withdrawal
M. Indecisiveness
N. Body-Image Change
O. Work Retardation
P. Insomnia
Q. Fatiguability
R. Loss of Appetite
S. Weight Loss
T. Body Worries
U. Loss of Libido (Sex Interest)

These are twenty-one assorted ways of being miserable, readily understandable to us all, which descend much more frequently on women than on men. And in a comparable group of men and women patients, women get a higher score on Beck's Depression Inventory.[18]

What is hard for the observer of depression to take is that there is no visible reason for it and that the depressed state does not seem to go away. Depressive people are monotonous to us in their misery (as well as to themselves). They evoke our scorn for their endless suffering and thus put us into a state of guilt toward them—which in turn makes us tend to be impatient with them. So we suppress as long as we can the impulse to tell them to "snap out of it," or "stop pitying themselves," and to "get interested in *something.*" The depressive patient of course agrees with us, because he or she also sees no reason to be depressed and would desperately like to get interested in something. So the depressive patient is all the more ashamed of failure to "straighten up and fly right," and becomes even more depressed and more ashamed of being depressed, in a vicious cycle.

Before they fall ill, depressed patients are generally affectionate, warm-hearted people who have little difficulty in being close to people. If anything, they tend to be overinvolved with other people rather than detached from them. Above all, their feelings are easily evoked, so that, although they may be rather shy of initiating relationships, once the initial barrier is overcome, it is easy for them to form close friendships. Depressive people do little to give offense to others; correspondingly, they are relatively unaccustomed to take up arms when they are put down. Depressive people are noted for their lack of aggressivity. One study, for example, showed that a group of paranoid women projected more hostility than a comparable group of depressed women.[19] Another study showed that depressive women patients are much less hostile verbally than non-depressed "controls." [20]

When they fall ill, depressed patients have no idea what has made such a change in their customary well-being. That they have fallen into a state of unremitting sadness as if they had suffered some profound loss makes sense to them descriptively. But who or what has been lost? Little children often deal with the loss of a beloved person by yelling and screaming about it sometimes for days on end. Only after they become aware that their rage is ineffectual do they settle into a depressed mood, which also expresses their helplessness. Their rage is directed exactly against the person who is beloved and who has deserted them. Very often these children begin to behave as if they were somehow defective or unworthy.[21] They are no longer enraged, or even grieving, but rather they seem easily made ashamed of themselves. Depressed patients are in a state of chronic grief and are also easily humiliated, as if they were bereaved children. But why should they more often be women than men?

The theory has been put forward that depressed patients may actually have suffered the childhood loss of a parent and are still, because of their emotional scars, subject to a renewal of their childhood grief in adulthood. Ever since Freud's fundamental discovery that much of mental illness is of emotional origin and based in childhood experience, it has been taken for granted that such a profound emotional upheaval as losing a parent in childhood would increase the chances of later mental illness. But have women depressives actually suffered more often from childhood bereavement than other kinds of psychiatric patients? Or than other adults from the same general environment who do not become ill? Or than men?

The answer to these questions requires putting together the results of several studies. In general, psychiatric patients (of all kinds) have suffered more often from bereavement in childhood than ordinary individuals living in the same region who do not fall ill.[22] And women psychiatric patients (all diagnoses) have suffered childhood bereavement even more often than men.[23] This same study showed that there were more women psychiatric patients who had lost their mothers and been left with younger siblings to take care of than there were men patients in the same circumstance. And, in fact, there is some evidence that *depressed* women are more likely to have suffered from being orphaned before adulthood than depressed men.[24] Losing a parent in childhood does make women more vulnerable to later illness than men. Depressives who seem to be mourning a loss may actually be reliving a childhood bereavement—and the chances that this is so are even greater for women than for men.

The most important dynamics of the depressive illness thus come from an internalized conflict resulting from closeness to other people. Women are even more vulnerable to bereavement in the course of growing up than men. Their greater vulnerability to bereavement fits with the fact that they have a self which attaches itself to mother during infancy earlier than boy infants (Chapter 6). But women are scorned, and scorn themselves, for this emotional closeness which makes them emotionally dependent.

Insight into the dynamics of depression becomes clearer if we go with a therapist through some of the steps in treating a depressed patient. Depressed patients when we first meet them are obviously very dependent on the people around them for support. This "dependency" of depressed patients is not just a widespread clinical observation. In fact, depressed patients are more likely than other psychiatric patients to be field-dependent perceivers [25] (see Chapter 7). And field-dependent patients are likely to be shame prone.[26] Depressed patients are in a chronic state of shame proneness, if only because they are depressed and helpless to get out of it. But although they are in a humiliated state—a state, incidentally, usually accompanied by quick fury—they are not at all *conscious* of being angry at anyone. Of course, they are angry at their own helplessness, but what sense is there in being angry at anyone for that? Of course, they are envious of the close persons who are not depressed, but what justice is there in hating them? Especially when they are just the people most needed and most helpful?

One of the first discoveries to be made by these patients in therapy is that their envy of the important "other" people in their lives who are "healthy" is perfectly natural, in fact, an inescapable feeling. And the humiliated fury—the hatred—which is the inevitable accompaniment of envy, is also inescapable. At the same time, however, humiliated fury—shame fury—is an unacceptable, in fact, a demeaning state. To hate someone you need and love, not only involves you in a profound disloyalty, but it is a state of fury allowable only to helpless children, not to self-sufficient adults. Humiliated fury is a feeling trap; it feeds upon itself because it is such an unacceptable and "illogical" feeling that it cannot be expressed.

The release of these feelings within the confines of therapy sessions is very relieving. Release usually comes with the understanding that the person who is in a humiliated fury is an inevitable "loser" compared to the "calm," unhumiliated therapist. This puts some distance between the state of humiliated fury and the sufferer. The solution to a depressive state, however, is not just the freedom to feel and express humiliated fury without shame. Some understanding is also needed that proneness to humiliated fury itself does not occur without one's having embraced a very high standard of affectionateness and closeness to others: a most oppressive ego-ideal.

This ego ideal of affectionateness and closeness not only makes it intolerable to hate and envy others, but it makes it difficult always to keep the internal image of the self distinct from the image of the other. To love someone deeply means that he or she becomes a "part" of yourself, as we all know when we actually suffer bereavement. It takes some time and is the work of mourning during actual bereavement to divest oneself of a lost person, to stop feeling lost without his (or her) presence. In neurotic or psychotic depression, the person needs to stop feeling lost without the important (living) person with whom he or she is "overinvolved," and on whom the ego-ideal has been projected.

Women in our society are trained to devote their lives to others. The biological and cultural expectation that they will be mothers makes it appear natural that they should spend their lives devoted to others—husband and children. But our society also scorns people who are not self-sufficient and independent of others. Women thus learn early that they should be ashamed of the very set of qualities which are particularly theirs. Ironically, at the same time, they are constantly threatened by the prospect that if they are not affectionate enough and as close and loving to others as they ought to be, they will have failed in their own and others' eyes. They are ashamed of themselves if they are close to others and guilty and ashamed of themselves if they are not. Within this profound conflict, the chances for throttled humiliated fury are great. Any disturbance in their relationship to others—either the cooling of husband's ardor in marriage, or the failure to get a husband, or the arrival of a new baby which seems to demand more nurturance than can be given, or the departure of a child who was once so close—any of these circumstances in a woman's life can throw her into a state of unconscious fury at the way her self has been torn. But at whom is she furious—herself or the beloved, admired other with whom she is so close? This is the same confusion she faced when first she experienced rivalrous hatred of her mother. Then, also, it was hard to separate the hatred of herself from the hatred of her first caretaker, in emulation of whom her self had been developed. In adulthood, humiliated fury is deflected by women from the "other," who is its "unjust" target, back upon the self. The resulting experience is depression.

Patients can say it in their own words better than the observer. Here is the way one attractive young woman depressive put it.[27]

She is talking about herself and her mother in connection with her own engagement to be married:

> **P:** . . . As a child . . . I—we were very affectionate; we were very close. We were just about inseparable. But as I got older and I started dating . . . well, suddenly so much dissension and disagreement and not getting along. . . . She doesn't let me feel optimistic in any way . . . She has no faith in me, and she has no faith in my boyfriend. And she doesn't know how I feel . . . about constantly ridiculing and criticizing him. Even if she feels that it's true and that she's justified, I don't feel she should do it. Because if I love him, I feel she should take it into consideration and try to give me more confidence in myself and him. She doesn't. No confidence. Constantly criticizing and doom doom doom. And I start to believe it . . . because I hear it all the time. . . . And then if my boyfriend happens to go down in the dumps—oh boy, I go right with him. I mean I need him; he's my morale . . . he's gotta be there to tell me that things will be all right and that we will have money and that we will be happy. . . . Because when I'm with the family—I might just lay down and die. . . .
>
> **T:** You take on your mother's . . . opinion?
>
> **P:** Yeah. I can't help it. I try to fight against—when I'm with them you know I'll fight down to the end, and yet when I leave . . . I get so depressed. I'm so down in the dumps. . . . And I feel inside of me, a kind of sickness comes over me, and they always do this to me . . .

The patient, whose wish is to be admired and praised for having an admirable boy friend, feels hurt by her mother's refusal of praise. She cannot be as loving to either her mother or her boyfriend as her ego-ideal demands. She "tries to fight"—she's angry—but it is shame-fury, that is, anger at not being admired. Shame fury easily boomerangs on the self. She is so close to her mother that hatred of mother feels like hatred of herself, like a "kind of sickness" that is "inside" of her: depression.

Pauline Bart has made a special study of depression in middle-aged women.[28] She was particularly interested in pursuing the question of *why* middle age is a problem for some women, and not for others: "Why is it that the woman whose son has been launched says: 'I don't feel as if I've lost a son; I feel as if I've gained a dentist,' while another thinks [it was] 'the worst thing that ever happened to her.' " [29] Bart hypothesized that middle-class Jewish women, whose tradition dictates a heavy emotional investment in their families, would be more prone to depression than other ethnic groups.

As part of her investigation, she studied the records of 533 women between the ages of forty and fifty-nine who had had no previous record of hospitalization but were now "first admissions" to psychiatric facilities. She compared the women diagnosed "depressed" with women who had other functional (nonorganic) diagnoses. Bart exercised particular care to overcome diagnostic biases: She obtained her records from five different hospitals and used interviews, projective tests, and pre-tested, reliable coding systems for the evaluation of psychological variables.

She found, as hypothesized, that Jewish women were more often depressed than women from other ethnic groups. As she puts it: "Since in the traditional Jewish family, the most important tie is between the mother and her children . . . the higher rate of depression among Jewish women in middle age when their children leave is not surprising." [30]

Here is a table from Bart's study which shows her findings:

Table 2
RELATIONSHIP BETWEEN ETHNICITY AND DEPRESSION
IN WOMEN°
° (Adapted from P. Bart)

Ethnicity	Percent Depressed	Total N (Base)
Jewish women	84	122
Non-Jewish women	47	383

As Bart herself puts her findings: "You don't have to be Jewish to be a Jewish mother, but it helps." [31] Bart remarks that "it is easy to make fun of these women, to ridicule their pride in their children." [32]

Why are these mothers so often ridiculed (and hated) by their children? "Jewish mothers" of whatever ethnic background are champion inducers of guilt, especially in their children. It is when these women grow depressed that we see how deeply they are caught in a conflict between the affectionateness which their heritage has inculcated in them and the scorn with which the culture treats emotional closeness or "dependency."

The story of Virginia Woolf's mental illness is a classic example of depression in women.[33] Although she was gently reared, and was a most gifted and beautiful woman, Woolf repeatedly fell into depressions so severe she had to be hospitalized. She finally took her life when she was faced with another depressive episode. It was observed that she was most vulnerable to depression whenever she had finished a piece of creative work and was in suspense about its critical reception, but this hardly seemed a sufficient explanation for her depressive episodes. Ironically, although she and her husband were the publishers of Freud's work in English translation, psychoanalytically-oriented treatment was never tried. Yet all the main psychological ingredients we have been talking about were present in her life story.

There had been an early bereavement in the loss of her mother. There was a most beloved sister with whom unsuccessful rivalry was a chronic source of shame and guilt. Another, much loved, brother died suddenly of an acute illness. Later on there was a devoted, sensible, respected husband, all goodness to her, so that hatred of him was unthinkable. And this personal history was taking place in an era when the inferiority of women was a taken-for-granted fact of life.

Virginia adored her gentle, affectionate, yielding mother, who died when Virginia was thirteen. She admired and feared her demanding, ill-tempered, "important" father, a noted scholar. She and her sister saw their brothers go off to Cambridge University to study, while the sisters were expected only to marry "well." If they wanted to be intellectuals, they had to study on their own, unlike their brothers who "belonged" as intellectuals.

To compound the injustice, Virginia's half-brother, more than twelve years older than she, had been accustomed to playing with her genitals from the time she was six years old. This was a guilty secret for which *she* was so ashamed she could tell no one for many years after she reached adulthood. For reasons she herself could not understand and did not connect with her shameful secret, "normal" young men of her own near-aristocratic class frightened her, or else evoked her scorn, so that her twenties were spent in dreadful social shyness.

She was briefly engaged to be married to Lytton Strachey, already an established literary figure, with whom she was in love. But although he broke the engagement because he was a homosexual *she* suffered from the rejection. When, at last, she married Leonard Woolf, "a penniless Jew," to use her phrase, she admired, respected, and loved him—but *not* sexually (a turnabout of what she had experienced from Lytton). This is how she wrote to Leonard about her feelings before agreeing to marry him; it is clear that she was profoundly guilty and ashamed of herself in marrying him. "The obvious advantages of marriage stand in my way. I say to myself, anyhow, you'll be quite happy with him and he will give you companionship; children and a busy life. Then I say, by God I will not look upon marriage as a profession. . . . Then, of course, I feel angry at the strength of your desire. Possibly your being a Jew comes in at this point. You seem so foreign. And then I am fearfully unstable. I pass from hot to cold in an instant, without any reason. . . . When you kissed me the other day I felt no more than a rock. And yet your caring for me as much as you do almost overwhelms me. It is so real and so strange. Why should you?" [34]

She was ashamed of herself for her lack of sexual response and of him for being Jewish, and she was guilty for wanting all the "advantages of marriage." Shortly after she married, she had a severe episode. Leonard remained devoted to her—they were a "devoted couple." He kept a "laconic daily record" [35] of her psychic states for the rest of their lives together. The letters "v.f.w." meant that Virginia was fairly well; "v.sl.h." meant that she had had a slight headache; "f.g.n." meant a fairly good night; "b.n." meant a bad night.

What a conflict is evoked by such devotion from another person! On the one hand, it is sweet to be so well-loved. On the other hand, what a humiliation it is to have the daily variations in one's psychic state so minutely inspected. And how guilt-making it is to resent being so tenderly monitored.

On her side, Virginia was very dependent on Leonard for "all practical matters and all judgments requiring calculation and good sense." [36] Her diary makes clear how much she feared

Leonard's disapproval. And how completely dependent upon him she felt, hating herself (and him) unconsciously all the time. Here is how she writes about it in her diary:[37]

> I could not stay at 46 (Gordon Square) last night, because L. on the telephone expressed displeasure ... and so my self-reliance being sapped, I had no courage to venture against his will. Then I react. Of course, it's a difficult question. For undoubtedly I get headaches or the jump in the heart, and then this spoils *his* [italics mine] pleasure and if one lives with a person, has one the right. And so it goes on.

Clearly, Virginia connected her headaches and anxiety ("jump in the heart") to her own reaction to Leonard's displeasure. Characteristically she was ashamed of herself for "not having the courage to venture against his will." But his displeasure must also have evoked humiliated fury—since it was presumably based on the need for Virginia to lead a quiet life in order to avoid falling ill. And she was guilty for how her symptoms affected him.

Here is another excerpt from her diary which shows also how ashamed she was of her childlessness:[38]

> Let me have the confessional. ... Years and years ago, after the Lytton affair, I said to myself, walking up the hill at Bayreuth, never pretend that the things you haven't got are not worth having; good advice, I think. ... Never pretend that children, for instance, can be replaced by other things ... one must like things for themselves; or rather rid them of their bearing on one's personal life. ... Now this is very hard for a young woman to do. And now married to L., I never *have* to make the effort. ... Perhaps I have been cowardly and self-indulgent. And does some of that discontent come from that feeling?

Virginia thus glimpsed that it is very hard for a woman to rid husband and children of "their bearing on one's personal life"; that is, to free herself of her closeness to others. She herself scorned her own closeness to Leonard as "self-indulgent and cowardly."

Her ideal image of a woman was of someone "free" of binding emotional ties. She was in love for years with someone who represented her ideal—the unfettered, courageous aristocrat, Vita Sackville-West, a woman apparently able to tolerate her husband's homosexual affairs and to please herself in her own bisexual affairs.

Here is another excerpt from Virginia's diary [39] which tells how she adored Vita for being the "real woman" Virginia never felt she was. Virginia is aware that her own feelings are "very mixed." But the extent of her envious hatred of "pink-glowing, grape-clustered, pearl-hung" Vita is apparent only to us, not to Virginia. Instead, in her adoration of Vita, Virginia feels only conscious gratitude (and guilt) for the "maternal protection" lavished on her—which she hates herself for always wanting.

> Vita—or three days at Long Barn. . . . I like her and being with her and the splendor—she shines in the grocer's shop in Sevenoaks with a candle-lit radiance, stalking on legs like beech trees, pink-glowing, grape-clustered, pearl-hung. . . . What is the effect of all this on me? Very mixed. There is her maturity and full-breastedness; her being so much in full sail on the high tides, where I am coasting down backwaters; her capacity I mean to take the floor in any company, to represent her country, to visit Chatsworth, to control silver, servants, chow dogs, her motherhood (but she is a little cold and off-hand with her boys), her being in short (what I have never been) a real woman. Then there is some voluptuousness about her; the grapes are ripe; and not reflective. No. In brain and insight she is not so highly organized as I am. But then she is aware of this and so lavishes on me the maternal protection which, for some reason, I have always most wished from everyone.

Virginia's scorn of her husband, and her unconscious hatred of him had no room for expression in her life, except in a transformed version; in "headaches," "heart-jumps," and "discontent." Behind the unconscious hatred of Leonard was the broader context of women's inferior position in the world contributing its share of humiliated fury. And so her symptoms descended upon her after the completion of a piece of her own independent work, her only acceptable avenue of self-expression. When she waited for the world's reactions, she despised herself for her helpless dependency on other people's good opinion. She was in a state of throttled shame-fury not only at Leonard, but at all her internalized "judges." Her hatred descended not on them, however, but on herself in the form of depression.

References

1. S. Arieti, "Affective Disorders" ed. S. Arieti, *American Handbook of Psychiatry*, 2d Ed. (New York: Basic Books, 1974), p. 449.

2. Ibid., p. 456.

3. Ibid.

4. B. Malzberg, *Social and Biological Aspects of Mental Disease* (Utica, N.Y.: State Hospitals Press, 1940).

5. B. Malzberg, "Important Statistical Data about Mental Illness," ed. S. Arieti, *American Handbook of Psychiatry* (New York: Basic Books, 1959).

6. S. Tarnower and M. Humphries, "Depression: A Recurring Genetic Illness more Common Among Females," *Diseases of the Nervous System* 30 (1969), 601-604.

7. P. Chesler, *Women and Madness* (New York: Doubleday, 1972), p. 43.

8. E. Zigler and L. Phillips, "Social Effectiveness and Symptomatic Behaviors," *Journal of Abnormal and Social Psychology* 61 (1960), 231-238.

9. A. Beck, *Depression: Clinical, Experimental and Theoretical Aspects* (New York: Harper & Row, 1967).

10. P. Blaser, D. Löw and A. Schäublin, "Die Messung der Depressionsstyle mit einem Fragebogen," *Psychiatrica Clinica* 1 (1968), 299-319.

11. N. Mitchell-Heggs, "Aspects of Natural History and Clinical Presentation of Depression," *Proceedings of the Royal Society of Medicine* 64 (1971), 1174.

12. Personal communication from Jeanne Safer, Postgraduate Center for Mental Health, New York City.

13. L. Robins, *Deviant Children Grow Up* (Baltimore, Md.: Williams and Wilkins, 1966).

14. Personal communication from Robert Steele.

15. V. Sedivec, "Manic Phases of Manic-Melancholy and Its Forms During the Course of Illness," *Czekoslovanska Psychiatrica* 65 (1969), 85-91 (abstract).

16. D. Davis, J. Lamberti and Z. Ajans, "Crying in Depression," *British Journal of Psychiatry* 115 (1969), 597-598.

17. A. Beck, *Depression,* op. cit.

18. A. Beck, *Depression,* op. cit.

19. T. M. Caine, "The Expression of Hostility and Guilt in Melancholic and Paranoid Women," *Journal of Consulting Psychology* 24 (1960), 18-22.

20. A. Friedman, "Hostility Factors and Clinical Improvement in Depressed Patients," *Archives of General Psychiatry* 23 (1970).

21. J. Bowlby, *Attachment and Loss,* vol. 1 (New York: Basic Books, 1969).

22. C. M. Dennehy, "Childhood Bereavement and Psychiatric Illness," *British Journal of Psychiatry* 112 (1966), 1049-1069.

23. J. Birtchnell, "Case-register Study of Bereavement," *Proceedings of the Royal Society of Medicine* 64 (1971), 279-282.

24. A. Beck, *Depression,* op. cit.

25. H. B. Lewis, *Shame and Guilt in Neurosis* (New York: International Universities Press, 1971).

26. Ibid.

27. Ibid.

28. P. Bart, "Depression in Middle-aged Women," eds. V. Gornick and B. Moran, *Woman in Sexist Society* (New York: New American Library, 1971).

29. Ibid., p. 167.

30. Ibid., p. 178.

31. Ibid., p. 176.

32. Ibid.

33. Quentin Bell, *Virginia Woolf: A Biography,* vol. 1 (New York: Harcourt Brace Jovanovich, 1972), p. 185.

34. Ibid., vol. II, p. 94.

35. Ibid., vol. 2, p. 89.

36. Ibid., vol. 2, p. 89.

37. Ibid.

38. Ibid.

39. Ibid.

CHAPTER 17

Madness in Women: The Hysterias

"Hysteria," writes an authority on the subject, "is a term loosely applied to a wide variety of sensory, motor, and psychic disturbances which may appear in the absence of any known organic pathology." [1] I have chosen to speak of the "hysterias" precisely because the range of symptoms covered is so broad. In the hysterias there can be body dysfunction or a dissociated state of consciousness, such as "fugue," amnesia, or some acute, unbearable, irrational anxiety. When there is a body dysfunction without known organic base, the patient is diagnosed as having "conversion hysteria." The assumption is that an underlying emotional conflict which threatens anxiety has been "converted" into a physical symptom. These range in severity from ordinary pains and aches to paralyses, convulsions, or even blindness.

Dissociated states of consciousness are another kind of flight from anxiety, and they are given the following diagnosis: hysteria, dissociated state. These are the most dramatic of the hysterias, as, for example, the patient described so vividly in *The Three Faces of Eve*.[2] These cases are relatively rare—too rare for statistics. The general impression is they occur more often among women, except when there are men on the battlefield.

251

When there is strong, conscious anxiety about encountering some specific event, the patient is said to have "anxiety hysteria," (Freud's term) for which the more usual term now is phobia. Anxiety hysteria also refers to cases of sudden, acute anxiety states which come unexpectedly "out of the blue," and for no apparent reason. In cases where there is more generalized, pervasive anxiety, without specific content, the patient is said to be suffering from anxiety neurosis, a category in-between hysteria and obsessional neurosis. The hysterias thus cover physical conversions, dissociated states, phobias, and other acute anxiety states. Although the overt anxiety states and phobias are often sharply distinguished diagnostically from hysteria, I prefer to classify them with the other hysterias, not only because anxiety is so prominent, but because their dynamics involve the other-connected superego mode, shame.

Why hysterical symptoms should be to the fore of some people's experience, while depression is to the fore in others' is a puzzling question. There is some specific connection between forbidden sexual excitement and hysterical symptoms. Depressive patients seem to have no interest at all in sex, at least while they are depressed, unlike hysterical patients whose struggles against forbidden sexuality are often pathetically clear to an observer, as well as to themselves.

Hysterical symptoms were the symptoms which first aroused the attention of psychiatrists during the nineteenth century. The history of the hysterias is, in fact, a reminder that the era when people were treated as if possessed of the devil was not so long ago. The crazy people who showed hysterical symptoms were mostly women. Aldous Huxley's *The Devils of Loudon* is a magnificent reconstruction of the terrible suffering of hysterical women accused as witches and the terrible fate of the priest who had trifled with them sexually.[3] A very recent study of the persecution of witches during the fifteenth to the seventeenth centuries tells us, furthermore, that the fantasy of a clandestine society of women practicing "wholly abominable" rites originated not in the minds of the poor and unlettered, but with the learned and those in authority: "monks, bishops and popes, great nobles, orthodox theologians and inquisitors and magistrates." Needless to say, these authorities were all men.[4]

The early modern psychiatrists, who were the enlightened

French, approached hysterical symptoms as if they sprang from natural causes instead of the machinations of witchcraft. They had made the discovery that they could make the symptoms at least temporarily disappear by putting the patients into an hypnotic trance. The fact that the symptoms were so malleable led some psychiatrists (who were, of course, all men) to believe that the symptoms were "put on" (an attitude still with us today). Others accepted that the symptoms were not under voluntary control, but hypothesized that they were the result of some kind of failure in the level of brain functioning.[5]

Because so many of the patients suffering from hysteria were women, it was also supposed that their symptoms had something to do with the functioning of the uterus, and accordingly the term "hysteria" was derived from the Greek word for the uterus, *hysteron*. "Hysteria" thus reflects a tradition of observations about the connection between mental illness and frustrated sexuality going back to ancient Greece. Plato, for example, writes about the "lust for generation" as a cause of mental illness. He writes:

> In the male the genitals are mutinous and self-willed, and, like a beast deaf to the voice of reason, attempt to have all their will because of their frenzied passion; while in women what is called the matrix or womb, a living creature within them longing for childbearing, when remaining unfruitful long beyond its proper time, becomes discontented and, wandering about through the body, closes up the passages of the breath, and obstructs respiration, thus provoking extreme disorientation, and all sorts of other diseases.[6]

Plato is here clearly describing the symptoms of anxiety, which ancient theories linked to frustrated sexuality.

In more modern times, it was the French psychiatrist, Charcot, Freud's teacher, who believed that hysterical symptoms have something to do with women's unfulfilled and deeply forbidden sexual desires. It took Freud's courage, however, to say that openly and by saying it, to put forward the basic assumption that hysteria as well as other mental illness is of emotional origin.

Most often the body dysfunction in conversion hysteria is not so extreme as a seizure, blindness or paralysis. Rather there is some plaguing pain or discomfort in some (vaguely localized) part of the body. The pain does not correspond to the pattern it ought to take if it followed the anatomy of the nervous system. It is not totally incapacitating but is nevertheless a decided interference with the patient's ability to follow normal activities mostly because, as it appears to the observer, she is so preoccupied with her symptoms. The patient is also likely to be quite depressed at having such a puzzling symptom. Confronted with a "sad sack" patient, who is emotionally involved in a set of peculiar physical symptoms which need not incapacitate her but do, the physician-observer is likely to develop the angry suspicion that he is the victim of a "put-on." As one medical authority, speaking gently, put it, ". . . the term 'hysterical' is often used as a defamatory colloquialism and . . . this usage is to a varying extent carried over into the medical sphere." [7]

In recent years, the knowledge that physical illness often accompanies times of emotional stress has made the term "psycho-somatic illness" a household word. This term is used to cover not only physical illnesses with a possible emotional component, like asthma or ulcers, but hypochondriacal symptoms, and any illness which physicians cannot diagnose. Thus the understanding of hysteria, which increased our knowledge of a close tie between emotional stress and physical illness has, paradoxically, tended to obscure the fact that hysterical symptoms need to be taken seriously and that they require therapy.

It also sometimes happens that today's patients have to insist on a thorough physical examination because their illness, if at all mysterious, is all too easy to diagnose as "psychosomatic." And this diagnosis, although an elegant term, is often used hypo-critically, as a fancy way of saying that the patient is faking. It is a diagnosis which carries with it a powerful threat of "put-down." And since hysterical symptoms more often afflict women than men, women are more often caught in this bind. On the one hand, they have a physical symptom which is worrisome and debilitating; on the other hand, it threatens them with the mortification of being thought a fake. As to the latter possibility, the women themselves are not always sure.

There is an amusing instance of sexism in the history of the way hysteria has figured in psychoanalytic theory. This example of sexism has to do with the concept that different mental illnesses represent fixations at different levels of infantile sexuality. An important part of Freud's theory was the idea that sexual life begins in infancy and develops on different levels as the person matures. So, early in life when nursing at its mother's breast is most important, infantile sexuality is at the oral level; later on, when toilet training is to the fore, sexuality is anal, and still later, when children identify their own sexual organs, sexuality is more specifically sexual or "phallic." The earlier the level of infantile sexuality at which the mentally ill person is fixated in his mental illness—oral, and, or "phallic"—the more "regressed" or severely ill he or she is thought to be.

It was clear early on that hysterical mental illness has a strong overt phallic sexual component in its dynamics. On this basis, then, it represents a later level of personal development than obsessional neurosis, which is clearly "anal" in its dynamics. But somehow, the statement that women's more frequent mental illness is at a "higher level" than men's is hardly to be found in psychoanalytic literature. This in spite of the fact that obsessional neurosis is a more stubborn illness than hysteria, which often disappears for long periods of time. On the contrary, hysteria is said to reflect an orally regressed personality.[8]

The way the concept of hysterical personality has been used in psychiatry is another instance of sexism. One subcategory of hysteria in the official American Psychiatric Association nomenclature is called "hysterical personality, histrionic style." Such personalities are, in the words of a pair of experts, "vain, egocentric individuals, displaying labile and excitable but shallow affectivity. Their attention-seeking and histrionic behavior may encompass lying and pseudolgia phantastica. They are conscious of sex and appear provocative. . . . Histrionic character features occur frequently . . . among women. They are considered feminine by our societal standards. . . .[9]

The reader can surely discern the heavy disapproval between the lines of this psychiatric personality description. And indeed, such malformed characters do occur among women (as well as men). The point is that if such people come to psychiatrists for help in reforming their characters, then the psychiatric description ought at least to allow points for self-awareness. If not, and, as is more likely, they come for conversion hysteria, or some other painful symptoms, then the defamatory personality description hardly augurs a sympathetic listener in the psychiatrist.

Amusingly enough, one study of conversion hystericals demonstrated that their symptoms did *not* occur within the context of an hysterical personality.[10] Careful examination of case material suggested that conversion hysteria occurred in a variety of personalities, a finding which ran contrary to Wilhelm Reich's (and other post-Freudians') view that hysterical symptoms were reflections of hysterical personality.[11] (Freud himself was careful not to confuse hysterical personality with hysterical symptom.[12]) Another careful study of hysterical personalities in psychoanalysis failed to observe the "provocative, seductive, exhibitionistic" behavior commonly ascribed to these patients.[13] A sensible solution might have been to drop the category of hysterical personality at least from the official American Psychiatric Association list. Instead, the diagnosis of hysterical personality continues to be "promiscuously used." [14] The myth of Eve's wickedness dies hard, especially in male-dominated psychiatry.

An important study by Pauline Bart [15] tells us, further, that it is poor and ignorant women who are more likely to be diagnosed hysterical more often than their more affluent sisters. Hollingshead and Redlich [16] had observed that hysteria occurs more often in the lowest social class; the poor expect "pills and needles" as their treatment. Following up on this observation by Hollingshead and Redlich, Bart studied women between the ages of forty and fifty-nine who were admitted to the *neurological* service of UCLA Neuropsychiatric Institute, and who emerged with a psychiatric diagnosis, usually hysteria. These women tended to come from poor, rural areas where, as Bart puts it, they did not have available the "psychiatric vocabulary of discomfort." They experienced themselves as physically ill—their vocabulary of psychic distress. A comparable group of women who entered the psychiatric service, that is, volunteering psychiatric reasons for their distress, were of higher social status and urban residents.

Bart's results remind us that, in the nineteenth century, sexual mores were cruelly restrictive against women of all classes, so that even the most cultivated and educated women were liable to hysteria. In modern times, sexual enlightenment is more widespread; hysteria has become the lot of poor, uneducated women. As we saw in Chapter 9, these women have the least sexual pleasure.

Bart's study also makes it easier to understand how conversion hystericals originally came to be thought of as displaying *"la belle indifférence"* to their own sufferings. In the absence of a "psychiatric vocabulary," women patients in the last century naively described physical symptoms without the slightest awareness of their symbolic meaning. Even though a "spasm" might perfectly describe motions suggestive of intercourse, the women were not aware of what they were "saying." Even though Janet, who first used the term, *"la belle indifférence,"* specifically described it as a façade covering profound anxiety, this part of Janet's description tended to be lost. A sexist climate in psychiatry transmuted *"la belle indifférence"* into a sign that the women really did not suffer.

Hysteria, women's more frequent illness, is an inarticulate body language in which women protest their emotional distress. More direct expression of their protest would involve them in too much anxiety. Because their symptoms are so "primitive" and so transparently emotional in origin, women patients are likely to evoke the scorn of their more intellectual, articulate (male) psychiatrists. "It is remarkable" says one authority, "with what contempt these (hysterical) symptoms may be treated by some physicians. . . ." [17]

It is instructive to note, in this connection, that obsessional neurosis is a much more solidly defined and well-understood illness, in contrast to hysteria. It has been suggested that "intellectualized, scientific, methodologically bound investigators have been more at ease in the study of patients characterized by rigid, intellectual and definitive ego maneuvers, namely obsessionals." [18] To which we might add that *male* psychiatrists may find it easier to understand patients more like themselves. In Chapter 20, we shall see in detail how "repulsive" a hysterical patient can be to her male therapist.

Now let's briefly look at the statistics on the hysterias. At a general hospital in Wisconsin during 1963 about 1 percent of the patients were discharged with a diagnosis of conversion hysteria. This is the diagnosis which is given when no organic basis can be found for the patient's complaints. Within this group of patients there were four women for every one man.[19] In an outpatient clinic in New York, a survey showed women diagnosed as "hysterical" significantly more often than men.[20] Not only in our own country, but in a recent study in India, a preponderance of women was found among those patients diagnosed as hysterical.[21]

Another kind of evidence which makes the same point comes

from making a comparison between the number of "medical symptoms" and the number of actual physical illnesses. If more "medical symptoms" are complained of by patients than there are physical illnesses diagnosed, the difference represents "conversion symptoms." In two separate studies done in general hospitals, women reported more "medical symptoms" than men, although the two sexes were equal in the number of physical illnesses.[22,23] The inference drawn by the researchers is that the greater number of complaints by women represents a greater frequency of conversion hysteria. In another study, the number of "medical symptoms" was compared to the number of "psychiatric symptoms" reported by the two sexes.[24] In general, the number of psychiatric symptoms varies in the same way as the number of "medical symptoms." When people are complaining of pains and aches they are also likely to be complaining of anxiety or worry or depression. But in this study, women did *not* report more psychiatric symptoms than men, only more *medical* symptoms. Again, the researchers drew the inference that the women were reporting more conversion-hysterical symptoms.

With respect to anxiety hysteria, the evidence is also that women are more prone to it than men. A recent study done at a famous mental hospital in New York (Hillside) found that anxiety attacks were the reason why 4 percent of the patients had been admitted. These anxiety attacks were so terrifying that the patients had become afraid to leave their homes for fear of a recurrence. And there was a decided preponderance of women among these terrified patients.[25]

One investigator, reporting from England, tells us that two-thirds of agoraphobic patients seen by psychiatrists are women.[26] An epidemiological study done in the United States also showed that women suffer from anxiety states about twice as often as men.[27] These figures coincide with the findings we saw in Chapter 15 which showed women reporting more symptoms of nervousness, nightmares, and other anxiety experiences than men. Among "normal" people, women also report more anxiety than men.[28]

Let's look more closely now at the person's experience in hysteria. First, let's study a description [29] of an acute anxiety attack, one that occurred "out of the blue," with the patient completely unaware of any "reason" for anxiety.

All at once, without any warning, I felt something start up in me. It was as if a sudden, slight impulsion had hit my upper chest and head. I was momentarily thrown off balance and felt I was swaying to the left (although I am sure my body did not really move) and I experienced a mild fullness in my throat. . . . My heart began to race, I broke into a sweat, especially across my forehead, around my eyes and upper lips, and felt flushed in the face and a fullness in the front of my head that seemed to be almost an inner confusion. Central to this was a feeling of what I would almost call panic, which seemed to fill my whole awareness. . . . I find it almost impossible to describe in words. It was a kind of dire apprehension of I know not what.

This is the kind of anxiety state which patients dread reexperiencing and which can make them so fearful they become housebound. It is the state which had preceded hospitalization of the Hillside patients who became agoraphobic, and who were, it will be remembered, predominantly women.

Let's look also at a dramatic case of conversion hysteria, one in which the patient has a seizure or "fit." The patient is a nineteen-year-old girl.

The fits occurred about 6:30 P.M. every evening when she was listening to the radio. The attacks had commenced following the dissolution of a love affair. The young man . . . had regularly appeared at the house at this time and had listened with her. The fit was preceded by a painful sensation on the right side of her body. Here she had formerly experienced pleasurable sensation, for her boyfriend had sat closely at her side.[30]

Let's look next at one of Breuer and Freud's first cases of conversion hysteria to see how they understood the dynamics. Anna O., one of these first cases, recovered and went on to become one of the founders of the social work movement in Austria. Her real name was Bertha Papperheim, and she was a friend of Freud's wife.[31]

Anna O. had a "private theater" of sexual fantasy life.[32] A private theater of sexual fantasy life is something which all human beings can empathize. It is a state in which we imagine ourselves talking to, responding to, making love to, or quarreling with important other people. Sometimes we impress them, sometimes we horrify or shock them, sometimes we make them suffer, sometimes we rescue them from danger, and sometimes they weep for us as we lie dead. There can be many people in the cast of characters, and many different scenes, limited only by the creativity of our imaginations. Often masturbation accompanies fantasying in a private theater and the scenes end abruptly with orgasm. The self is in a very complicated situation during a private theater session—it is in many people's shoes, so to speak, experiencing vicarious statisfactions and miseries while at the same time experiencing its own body gratification to the point of orgasm.

Such private theaters are gratifying experiences as long as they remain private. To tell about them, except in abstract or general terms, is something most people find embarrassing, especially when it comes to specific details of fantasy exploits. It is a measure of closeness and intimacy when one tells these precious moments to other people, with the implicit trust that one will not be ridiculed or shamed. It is only in deepest intimacy that one person will match another's openness with equally shameful confessions. Private theaters of fantasy are particularly shame-evoking because, as noted, they often accompany masturbation. In these enlightened times it is often easy to say that one masturbates or has done so, but it is still hard to reveal the imaginary exploits that went along with masturbation. The reason is at once simple and yet puzzling: The exploits all have as their theme a longing to be loved and admired. Exposing the details exposes the self to a very painful state: The shame of longing to be loved. Why this should be such a painful experience for adult human beings is puzzling, until we remember that Western culture particularly values self-sufficiency and independence. It scorns needing to be loved. In this context, the self caught up in a fantasy state of vicarious experience and in danger of "losing" itself, that is, losing its identity, suddenly switches from pleasure to pain. It experiences the shame of others' disapproval as a painful reminder of its own separate identity.

Freud's first insight into mental illness was his realization that hysterical symptoms are the products of unconscious conflicts. He was able to unravel the salient sexual experiences which had been kept unconscious by guilt and shame. "Strangulated affect," as he called it, was released and the symptoms relieved. The conflicts were over sexual longings—longings to be loved, of which the women patients were dreadfully ashamed. Anna O., for example, described her private fantasy theater with tremendous shame—only after an atmosphere of acceptance of all her "free associations" had been established. Her fantasy life had been shamefully active indeed during the time she had accepted the obligation of nursing her beloved father, who was dying. She told of once "seeing her own pale face in the mirror during her father's illness," after being in such a forbidden fantasy state. Freud was able to trace this moment as the start of Anna's terrifying hallucination of a death's head, one of the symptoms which developed after her father's death. It was as if Anna had transformed the image of herself *alive*, looking at herself in the mirror, into a terrifying (guilty) image of her father, *dead*. We can guess that herself *alive* was the equivalent of herself aroused; the dreadful image of her father's *dead* face represents her agony of shame and guilt over her own forbidden sexual desires.

Lucy R., an English governess in a Viennese widower's household, was another of Freud's hysterical patients. She suffered from chronic nose and throat symptoms, and from experiences of smelling cigar smoke which she thought were hallucinatory. She was also quite depressed. Freud offered her the interpretation that these symptoms resulted from her being in love with her employer. He suggested that she had had the secret hope of marrying him. Lucy answered in her usual "laconic" fashion: "Yes, I think that's true." When Freud asked her why she hadn't told him this before, she said: "I didn't know, or rather I didn't want to know. I wanted to drive it out of my head and not think of it again. I believe latterly I have succeeded. . . ." "Were you ashamed of loving a man?" Freud asked. "No," came the answer from Lucy, "I'm not unreasonably prudish. We are not responsible for our feelings. But," she went on, "it was so distressing to me because he is my employer and I am in service and live in his house. I don't feel the same independence toward him that I could toward anyone else. I am a poor girl and he is a rich man. People would laugh at me if they had any idea of it."

So Lucy tells us explicitly that she was not "responsible" for, that is, not *guilty* of her sexual thoughts or feelings and that she was not "unreasonably prudish." In her own good judgment, therefore, she ought to have been able to put the feelings she had out of her head. And she thought she had succeeded in forcing her feelings underground. But there came instead a chronic running nose and cough and the cigar smell and an awful feeling of depression. In some way that still is not exactly clear, the feelings she had were converted into physical sensations which gave her no rest. Lucy R. is a classic case of conversion hysteria.

That she was ashamed of her unrequited love, even though she didn't think she ought to be, is a perfect description of her conflict. That she had no "good reason" to feel humiliated fury toward her employer is also the force which would automatically throttle her humiliated fury at her unrequited love. What was left in her experience was depression and a running nose—as if she had been crying. And—you've guessed it—the smell of cigar smoke which, although she was not aware of it, was a symbol of the man she loved. Women are all too frequently ashamed of themselves if they are in a fury, if, that is, they are *not* loving enough, and at the same time ashamed of themselves if they *are* in love.

This profound conflict is all the more difficult to grasp because it is not "rational," and because the person is so deeply involved in loving. Hysterical patients are said to have "love-craving" characters,[33] or "erotic" personalities.[34] This is pretty much what women are trained to expect themselves to be. When they fall ill of it, especially from disappointments in loving, they themselves do not feel entitled to anger, because their "demands" were "inappropriate" in their own eyes. Their humiliated fury is repressed and transformed into the body language of self-hatred.

Since it is repressed humiliated fury which is causing the trouble, the answer often held out to women patients is that they should become more aggressive. The implication is that if they did, they would be less terrified, less afflicted with body symptoms, and less depressed. There is a kind of easy rightness about this answer since the observer senses what a price women patients pay for their affectionateness. Patients are often urged to cultivate anger during therapy—sometimes they even "put it on" in the vain hope that they will experience a catharsis. Usually, the only result is that they feel even more defeated because they are too "chicken" to be properly angry.

Another answer often held out to depressed and hysterical patients is to "get interested in something," some cause larger than themselves. This is excellent advice, except that detaching the self from its closeness to others, and attaching it to more important causes is not so easily done. Depression and hysteria are not so easily treated. They are not "put on," or a result of self-indulgence. In short, they are not so easily exhorted away. That was the way exhortations used to be made to witches to dispossess themselves of the devil.

Taking on men's role as exploiters, adopting their pattern and level of aggression is also not the answer. The conflict which produces depressive and hysterical symptoms, like the conflict which produces obsessional neurosis and schizophrenia, is unconscious. Women's symptoms originate in and reflect a profound contradiction between their natural affectionateness which has also become an ego-ideal, and the internalized cultural scorn of it as weakness.

References

1. W. Abse, "Hysterical Conversions and Dissociative Syndromes and the Hysterical Character," ed. S. Arieti, *American Handbook of Psychiatry*, 2d ed. (New York: Basic Books, 1974), p. 155.

2. H. Thigpen and H. M. Cleckley, *The Three Faces of Eve* (New York: McGraw-Hill, 1957).

3. A. Huxley, *The Devils of Loudon*, (New York: Harper and Row, 1971).

4. Norman Cohn, *Europe's Inner Demons: An Enquiry Inspired by the Great Witch-Hunt* (New York: Basic Books, 1975).

5. P. Janet, *The Major Symptoms of Hysteria*, 2d ed. (New York: Macmillan and Company, 1920).

6. Plato, *Timaeus* 91 B. C. (tr. by N. Lewis).

7. W. Abse, op. cit., p. 106.

8. J. Marmor, "Orality in the Hysterical Personality," *Journal of the American Psychoanalytic Association* 1 (1954), 656-671.

9. E. B. Brody and L. S. Sata, "Personality Disorders. I Trait and Patterns Disturbances." *Comprehensive Textbook of Psychiatry* (Baltimore: Williams and Wilkins, 1967), Chap. 25.

10. P. Chodoff and H. Lyons, "Hysteria, The Hysterical Personality and 'Hysterical Conversion.'" *American Journal of Psychiatry*, 114 (1958), 734.

11. W. Reich, *Character Analysis*, (New York, Farrar, Straus and Giroux, 1972).

12. S. Freud, *On Libidinal Types*, Standard Edition, Vol. 21

13. B. Easser and S. Lesser, "Hysterical Personality: A Re-evaluation," *Psychoanalytic Quarterly* 34 (1965), 390-405.

14. Ibid.

15. P. Bart, "Social Structure and the Vocabularies of Discomfort: What Happened to Female Hysteria?" *Journal of Health and Social Behavior* 9 (1968), 188-193.

16. P. Janet, op. cit.

17. W. Abse, op. cit., p. 174.

18. B. Easser and S. Lesser, op. cit., p. 391.

19. C. Lewis and M. Berman, "Studies of Conversion Hysteria," *Archives of General Psychiatry* 13 (1965), 275-282.

20. Personal communication from Jeanne Safer, Postgraduate Center for Mental Health, New York.

21. K. C. Dube, "Mental Disorders in Agra," *Social Psychiatry* 3 (1968), 139-143.

22. K. Brodman, A. Erdman, I. Lorge and H. Wolff, "The Cornell Medical Index-Health Questionnaire VI. The Relation of Patients' Complaints to Age, Sex, Race and Education," *Journal of Gerontology* 8 (1953), 339-342.

23. L. Phillips and B. Segal, "Sexual Status and Psychiatric Symptoms," *American Sociological Review* 34 (1969), 58-72.

24. R. Matarazzo, J. Matarazzo and G. Saslow, "The Relationship Between Medical and Psychiatric Symptoms," *Journal of Abnormal and Social Psychology* 62 (1961), 55-61.

25. J. Mendel and D. Klein, "Anxiety Attacks with Subsequent Agoraphobia," *Comprehensive Psychiatry* 10 (1969), 190-195.

26. I. M. Marks, *Fears and Phobias* (London: Heinemann Medical Co., 1969).

27. D. C. Leighton, J. S. Harding, D. B. Macklin, A. M. MacMillan and A. Leighton, *The Character of Danger* (New York: Basic Books, 1963).

28. E. Maccoby and C. Jacklin, *The Psychology of Sex Differences* (Stanford, Calif.: Stanford University Press, 1974).

29. J. Nemiah, "Anxiety: Signal, Symptom and Syndrome," ed. S. Arieti, *American Handbook of Psychiatry*, 2d ed. (New York: Basic Books, 1974), pp. 91-109.

30. W. Abse, op. cit., p. 166.

31. O. Mannoni, *Freud* (New York: Random House, 1971).

32. See the accounts of Freud's cases in H. B. Lewis, *Shame and Guilt in Neurosis* (New York: International Universities Press, 1971), Chap. 12.

33. O. Fitzgerald, "Love Deprivation and the Hysterical Personality," *Journal of Mental Science* 94 (1948), 701.

34. S. Freud, op. cit.

CHAPTER 18

Madness in Men: Alcoholism, Drug Addiction, Sexual Deviations, and Obsessional Neurosis

The mental illnesses to which men are more prone involve them in strange, sometimes radical transformations of themselves or the world. This is in contrast to the relatively mundane or ordinary symptoms of depression and the hysterias. Women's illnesses are exaggerations of everyday emotional experiences rather than bizarre visions and transformations of the world.

Let's look at the list of mental disorders which claim more men than women: alcoholism; drug addiction; homosexuality; other deviant sexual compulsions, such as transvestism, fetishism, sadism, masochism, exhibitionism, voyeurism, child-molesting, and rape; obsessional neurosis and schizophrenia. Schizophrenia needs a chapter by itself. Let's first look at what all these varied afflictions have in common besides claiming more men than women as victims.

In the first place, all these disorders transport the patient into a world of strange experiences. In the addictions and the sexual deviations, forbidden acts become compulsions which the patient *must* perform; in obsessional neurosis, "crazy" thoughts invade his thinking and command him to *do* something he knows he shouldn't do; in schizophrenia, delusions and hallucinations invade and transform his experience of the real world also with strange visions and commands. In all these bizarre symptoms, excluding schizophrenia, the observer senses an element which looks like free choice but is actually the opposite. An alcoholic or an addict seems to be choosing to ingest the drug which will take him into a strange world; sexual deviants seem to be choosing a forbidden form of sexual gratification. Actually, addicts and sex deviants are unable *not* to yield to their impulses which have become compulsions. Obsessional neurotics are clearly at the mercy of their own "crazy" thoughts, which will not stop bugging them with internal commands. Schizophrenics are similarly driven by an internal system of thoughts. But these have lost their usual connection to feelings and are comprehensible only to the patients. "Crazy" thoughts often drive the patient into some kind of aggressive *action*, for which the patient, were he in his "right mind," would feel terribly guilty. As we saw in Chapter 13, undischarged guilt is a trigger which sets off uncontrollable, obsessive ideation. When we hear an obsessional neurotic tell us that he can't stop thinking he ought to kill someone he loves, or when we see a schizophrenic who thinks he is the Messiah with a special mission which commands him to change the world, we shudder not only at the implied aggression, but at how bizarre the patient's conscience has become.

Women's madness is somehow connected with their being ashamed of *themselves.* It makes us impatient with them for exaggerating ordinary sadness, aches, and fears. We feel pity or scorn for how passive their symptoms have made women patients become. Men's madness, in contrast, frightens us because it often threatens us with danger from actions which might go out of control. These aggressive actions have an underlying theme of attempts to change or control the world in order to "improve" it. And, as we shall see later on in this chapter, this "improvement" turns out, ironically, to be a highly elaborated symbolic, "crazy" way of making it easier for men to be more loving and less aggressive.

Men are expected to "get over" their childhood affectionateness and their "childish" craving for affection. They are expected to become aggressive and competitive, especially in earning a livelihood. But our exploitative society also hypocritically disavows aggressive behavior, presenting men with moral dilemmas about just how aggressive they ought to be. So after renouncing their own intrinsically affectionate natures and cultivating aggression, men must make still another adaptive compromise with their cultivated aggressions. No wonder their mental illness is more bizarre than women's, and no wonder it so often seems to present them with an insoluble dilemma of guilt. No wonder they often try to solve the dilemma by turning off their feelings altogether.

In adult psychiatric wards, whatever the official diagnosis, the scene more often involves men's aggression toward others and women's collapse of the self. In one study, for example, the symptoms of men and women patients in the same psychiatric hospital were compared. Men patients showed more assaultive, sexually deviant behavior. Women patients were self-depreciatory and depressed.[1]

One trouble with these descriptions of sex differences in psychiatric patterns is that they correspond to stereotypes about how men and women generally behave. Observers who know the sex of the patient may be operating with an unconscious bias which makes them perceive men and women patients in stereotyped ways. One study attempted to get around this problem by asking judges to review case records of patients without any knowledge of whether the patient was a man or a woman. The ninety-two patients studied were all being admitted to an upstate New York psychiatric hospital. They ranged in age from twenty to thirty-five years. Five judges (all experienced clinicians) were asked to decide only whether the symptoms picture was "behavioral," meaning that the symptoms invoked overt actions, or "ideational," meaning that the symptoms involved only talk. Among the fifty-six men patients, the symptom pictures overwhelmingly involved action; the thirty-six women patients were just talking about their feelings.[2] Men *do* something in their illnesses; women collapse into their feelings. Both sexes thus caricature society's expectation of them in their ways of becoming mentally ill.

The way society's different expectations for men and women govern their psychiatric symptoms can be seen early in childhood, when the difference between the sexes in psychiatric patterns actually begins. One study of emotional symptoms among a large group of English school children from two to seven years of age showed that one in five children was showing disturbances. Within the group of disturbed children, boys showed more cruelty, obstinacy, and restlessness than girls.[3] Another study of children referred for psychiatric treatment showed not only that boys were referred more often than girls, but that boys were referred more often for hyperactivity and aggression. Girls were referred more often for being too frightened and shy.[4]

Let's turn now to statistics on the various diagnostic categories. The evidence on alcoholism, drug addiction, and the sexual deviations is ample and clear, mainly because the addictions and sexual deviations often drive their victims into acts which bring them into conflict with society and the law. Thus, statistics are available from our jails as well as from hospitals and clinics. Most of the people in jail for alcohol, drugs, or sex-related offenses are men. The statistics on obsessional neurosis are equally clear although the number of studies is sparse. (The reasons for this failure to pay attention to obsessional neurosis are themselves interesting, and we shall return to them shortly.) The statistics on men's greater proneness to schizophrenia are the most ambiguous, although, on balance, the evidence is that schizophrenia claims more men as victims than women.

Let's look at alcoholism first. The ratio of alcoholic men to women in the United States was estimated as five to one, in a study published in 1958.[5] Since then, the ratio of men to women has been decreasing, because the number of women alcoholics has been increasing.[6] Although the disproportion is no longer so great, there are still many more men than women alcoholics today.[7]

Findings reported to a 1972 National Institutes of Health conference on alcoholism suggest that men and women have very different reasons for becoming alcoholic.[8] David McClelland reported that men who are problem drinkers are obsessed by a need for personal power. McClelland reported, furthermore, that men drink more than women in all known societies, and he suggested that it is "proving themselves as men which gets them into these power conflicts." Sharon Wilsnack, reporting to the same conference, suggested that the primary gratification for women drinkers is an enhanced feeling of womanliness. "Many alcoholic women want to be good wives and mothers and they are concerned about their failure to perform these roles adequately."

Alcoholic men tend to be field-dependent perceivers.[9] As we saw in preceding chapters, field-dependent perceivers tend to be people who are less sure of themselves in general; they are also likely to be shame prone. This evidence, taken together with male alcoholics' need for power, suggests that they are drowning their shame of failure of power in drink. Women alcoholics, similarly, are drowning their shame of their failure of womanliness. Both sexes are coping with unrealistic although very different ego-ideals.

When it comes to drug addictions, there are also more men drug addicts than women.[10] The history of hard drug abuse in this country offers us an instructive sidelight on the social forces which contribute to this addictive proneness on the part of men. As we are now repeatedly reminded, hard drug use was quite legal in this country during the nineteenth century. During this period in our history, drugs were routinely used as painkillers or simply for pleasure.[11] Hard drugs, such as morphine and codeine were often prescribed for women's menstrual cramps, and they were often ingredients of other medicinal prescriptions. During this time more women became addicted than men—probably because they used these drugs more often. It was only after drugs were declared illegal, and dealing in them became a profitable business, that drug addiction became more men's illness. One recent account tells very graphically how plotting to obtain drugs can fill up an unemployed man's day with "important business." [12]

Some years ago an intensive study was made of one hundred men and one hundred women addicts in the USPH hospital at Lexington, Kentucky.[13] The men addicts were usually prisoners, with a serious antisocial record. The women addicts had usually entered the hospital voluntarily, in an effort to shake the drug habit. The men had begun taking drugs out of curiosity and because they had associated with other men already in the drug business. Women had begun taking drugs for relief of distressing physical symptoms. Women were generally on morphine only, unlike the men addicts who had sampled a wider variety of drugs. The men addicts were would-be exploiters who had got caught. The women addicts must have had hysterical symptoms which had been misdiagnosed and mishandled. The men had been active and aggressive in becoming addicts, the women had been passive. Both ended up the victims of an addictive illness, but by very different routes.

We come now to homosexuality. I am sure that many readers will have objected long before this point to my including homosexuality in a list of madness or perversions. They will point out that the American Psychiatric Association recently removed homosexuality as a blanket category from its list. Why then, do I include it? Especially since my own strong belief is that homosexuals ought not to be discriminated against in any way—legally or socially.

A digression and a bit of history are in order at this point to explain why I have included homosexuality in my list of deviations or perversions. During the nineteenth-century burgeoning of psychiatry, clinicians (for example, Krafft-Ebbing and Havelock Ellis) strove to avoid the prevailing condemnatory attitudes toward sexual perversions in order to be able to perceive the psychological function and meaning of unusual sexual behavior. Freud relied heavily on Ellis's and Krafft-Ebbing's descriptions, and he adopted their objective stance. Freud was able to discern that deviant sexual behavior was an outcome of deeply repressed emotional ties formed during infancy and childhood.[14] Freud showed that areas of the body not specifically designed for heterosexual copulation—principally the mouth and the anus—become involved in sex via oral and anal infantile sexual experiences. He pointed out that these areas of the body are normally involved in heterosexual intercourse as part of the "foreplay." Freud suggested, furthermore, that the choice of same-sex or opposite-sex adult partner is also linked to the vicissitudes of infantile experiences with parental figures.

Freud's dictum that "neurosis is the negative of the perversions" is still clinically sound: Neurotic symptoms can be understood as defenses against "forbidden" infantile modes of sexual gratification, involving the mouth and the anus in copulation.[15]

As Freud's insights spread, they helped to create a freer atmosphere for heterosexual intercourse, for homosexuality, and for sexual mores in general. The functional analysis of the reason for the involvement of areas of the body not specifically designed for heterosexual copulation helped to relieve the pejorative connotations of the term "perversion" because it helped to explain the "natural" basis for the existence of perversions. But it did not do away with the fact that there are perversions or deviations from species-determined, heterosexual "behavior of the sexes."

Frank Beach, a lifelong student of sexual behavior, makes an excellent and clarifying distinction in this connection.[16] He suggests that, for individual human beings, we ought to speak of "sexual behavior," reserving the term, "behavior of the sexes" for species-reproduction patterns. Individual sexual behavior, which is governed by a great variety of idiosyncratic, experiential factors cannot be regarded as biologically determined, since it is so profoundly influenced by learning—by life-history events. For each individual, his or her sexual behavior ought not to be labeled a perversion or deviation since it may represent the "optimum" outcome of interaction between biology and life experience. For each individual, his or her sexual choice may be the straightest line toward self-fulfillment. Against the framework, however, of a description of the species' behavior, perversions of the species-reproduction pattern occur among infrahuman as well as human beings. (As to whether one calls them "deviations" or "perversions," the choice is only between more or less pejorative terms.)

Thus, even though homosexual relationships can be as fulfilling and benign as heterosexual relationships, there is a scientific dilemma in viewing heterosexual and homosexual relationships as no different from each other. This is the same dilemma as is involved in using the term "crazy" or "mad," also pejorative terms. And something of the same dilemma is involved in considering genetic factors as determinants of human personality. It is the dilemma created when one turns away from exploring phenomena because they are politically charged. This is why I have chosen to use what may be pejorative terms rather than gloss over the injuries which society inflicts upon some of its members. "Crazy" is a more accurate description of what actually happens to people than is the assumption that mental illness exists only as a myth in the minds of insensitive observers. Similarly, homosexuality is a deviant form of "behavior of the sexes." As Beach put it, replying to Gide's famous appeal in *Corydon:* "We are at variance with him [Gide] in our belief that the strength of biological forces inclining most individuals toward heterosexual relations is greater than those that tend to produce homosexual alliances." [17]

"Perverted" and "crazy" are ugly terms, and they are incongruous when applied to homosexual preference. There is a healthy egalitarian impulse behind the wish to avoid all pejorative terms and an accepting spirit which refuses to shame the individual as well. But a view of human nature as intrinsically affectionate, and sexually differentiated requires us to acknowledge that people who find an affectionate, peaceful *heterosexual* relationship impossible have been injured in some way. This acknowledgement requires that we do not gloss over the deviant sexual experiences to which men more often fall victim than women.

According to Kinsey's countrywide surveys, about one-half to one-third as many women as men are primarily or exclusively homosexual, at all ages.[18, 19] As I indicated in an earlier chapter, these figures make sense in the light of the possibility that girls may have an easier time with their gender identity than boys. Statistics on admissions to a New York mental health clinic show that men apply more frequently for homosexual problems than women.[20] These figures, as well as Kinsey's, should be considered against the background fact that women, in general, are more willing than men to acknowledge psychological troubles. The fact that more men than women reported homosexuality to Kinsey's interviewers, and more men than women applied for psychiatric "help" with it, suggests that homosexuality is actually a more widespread phenomenon among men, and not, as one authority suggested, an artifact of women's ability to hide their homosexuality.[21]

In the case of other sexual deviations it is also well known that the deviants are predominantly men, because sex offenders often end up in jail. Among the sex offenders who end up in jail the women are prostitutes and the men are deviants.[22] The prostitutes caricature women's role of "service" to men, and characteristically, take the blame for both sexes. Men sex-offenders, in contrast, have fallen victim to the compulsion to perform strange sexual acts, some of which involve hurting other people. When one of them uses a lipstick to write "help" in a room where he knows he will shortly strangle a woman, we are all horrified, and some of us realize that the sex-offender is mentally ill. But there is such revulsion against these men and such a dread of their cruel impulses that we prefer to turn our heads away.

Very recently, a new method has been announced of treating male sex offenders, as well as sexual deviants who have not come afoul of the law.[23] This is by injecting them with anti-androgen drugs. Results have been reported, as might be expected, which indicate that sex offenders stop feeling sexy, thus they run less

chance of expressing their sexual compulsion. Androgens are hormonal substances that originally helped differentiate the male
embryo shortly after conception. So using anti-androgen drugs to
calm oversexed men makes a kind of primitive sense. This mode of
treatment reminds us, however, of the simple theory that women's
depression is hormonal. What this kind of easy reliance on hormones overlooks is that men patients have picked up and elaborated a culturally fostered confusion between aggression and
manhood. Their sexual symptoms reflect the dilemma in which
they have been caught and their attempts at a solution. Psychotherapy for sexual deviation involves a heavy investment in
time and energy, since the sexual deviations, like the drug addictions, are relatively hard to change. Even sharply focused attempts at symptom-removal by conditioning procedures
(behavior modification) find the sexual deviations very resistant for
the simple reason that such exquisite sexual pleasure has become
interwoven with aggression. Using anti-androgens is a pragmatic
measure which completely bypasses the culturally induced emotional conflicts involved in sexual deviations. It reduces a man's
masculinity in an effort to reduce his aggression. In so doing, it has
the potential for increasing society's oppression of the individual.

It is when we turn to actual clinical material that we can get a
sense of how sexual deviations represent an internalization of
society's contradictory demands on men. One clinical study
reviewed six cases of father-daughter incest performed by army
men. "These men," the study says, were "uncertain of their masculine identity and strongly motivated to maintain a façade of role
competence as family patriarch in the eyes of society." One man,
a thirty-two-year-old sergeant who had been in the army for
fifteen years, showed a terrible "sense of lack" whenever he was
required to act independently. He himself had had a sadistic
father and a withdrawn mother; he had been caught having sex
with his sister when *he* was six years old and had been severely
beaten for it. As an adult he impressed others as "well-groomed,
neat and sociable" and by no means particularly aggressive. His
rape of his eight-year-old daughter came as a complete surprise to
the people around him.[24]

The clinicians who studied these instances of incestuous rape
were struck by a generalization that could be made also about the
mothers and daughters in these families. The mothers and

daughters had had many demands to be nurturant thrust upon
them early in their own lives. They had been accustomed from a
very early age to catering to others. As both wives and daughters,
they were accustomed to being readily acquiescent. The incestuous acts had occurred after quarrels in the family and somehow
reduced "separation anxiety" for "all members of the family trio."
So it is visible to an observer how a man's act of rape can be a
"crazy" way of making life less aggressive.

We come now to the obsessional neurosis, about which there
are very few statistics about sex difference. Freud's observations had led him to remark that "hysteria has a strong affinity
with femininity, just as obsessional neurosis has with masculinity. . . ." [25] Obessional neurotics tend to be field-independent perceivers (who in turn tend more often to be men).[26]
The connection between field-independence and obsessional
neurosis emerged from a study which compared the perceptual
styles of hysterical and obsessional patients and found, as
predicted, that obsessionals were more field-independent than
hystericals.[27] Field-independent perceivers tend to use "isolation
of affect" as a principal defense. Their feelings disappear, leaving
behind lots of ideas. This is a different picture from alcoholics,
who drink in order to make their feelings of failure more bearable.
"Isolation of affect" is a hallmark of obsessional neurosis and of
schizophrenia as well.

There are, however, very few statistical studies of sex differences which include obsessional neurosis as a distinct category.
The statistics on obsessional neurosis as men's more frequent illness are therefore less well-documented than they should be.
There are a number of reasons for this. For one thing, obsessional
neurosis, sexual deviations or perversions, and schizophrenia
really form a continuum of compelling, "crazy" ideas. Some obsessional neurotics have not been included in the statistics of that
category because they are also sexual deviants; others because
they have gone over the border into schizophrenia.

Another reason why there are few studies of obsessional neurosis as a separate category is that the diagnosis has gone out of
fashion. This takes us on a brief but illuminating excursion into the
modern, post-Freudian history of psychiatry. With the general
spread of psychoanalytic thinking and its absorption into psychiatry, there came an awareness that "normal" people have

obsessional ideas, depressed moods, and hysterical symptoms. As a part of general psychological enlightenment there has been a tendency to avoid pejorative terms and to stress that all of us, even the healthiest, have hang-ups which result from our upbringing. As a consequence, psychiatry in modern times is undertaken especially among the middle class, in the spirit of enlarging the scope of inner awareness and increasing creative capacities. One by-product of these more generalized psychiatric goals is that symptoms tend to be ignored in favor of more general character-ological descriptions of patients. Diagnosing someone as obses-sional neurotic (or hysterical) has become less fashionable than diagnosing "character disorder." It has even been stated, without any evidence at all, that "classical" cases of obsessional neurosis and hysteria have disappeared in modern times.

A study done in Germany of several hundred psychoanalytic patients examined each case with the question in mind: Is there more tendency to hysterical symptoms or to obsessional symp-toms? It was found that men patients tended to have more obses-sional symptoms, while women patients had more hysterical symptoms.[28]

In a talk to the research seminar of a large outpatient psychi-atric facility in New York City, I reviewed the evidence I thought there was that men are more prone to obsessional neurosis than women. The research staff promptly went to work to review their records on this point.[29] In 2,566 cases recorded during twenty-five years of the clinic's operation, significantly more men patients had obsessional symptoms than women. There were also more cases of sexual deviation among men, and more cases of depression among women. But these latter statistics join a much larger body of evidence, all going in the same direction, while more statistics on obsessional neurosis in men are still needed.

Now that we have looked at the statistics, let's try to get a closer view of what a person's experience is like in obsessional neurosis. Obsessional neurosis, although bizarre enough, is still sufficiently like some ordinary experiences of superstitious thinking to make it possible to empathize with obsessions.

An obsession is an idea or set of ideas which the person recog-nizes as absurd or ridiculous, but nevertheless it will not go away. It bugs him. It will not go away because in some obscure way it seems to be generated by his conscience. It is as if his conscience had gone crazy and was telling him to think thoughts or to do things which he knows are the opposite of right.

Let us listen to the way a patient tells it.[30] He is alone in a hotel room, feeling a little guilty because he's taking a vacation without his wife (there isn't enough money for two to go) and he's tired. He's also jumpy and there's music playing outside; "some monotonous words—I mean one line was sung easily twenty-five times. So I got up to look out the window and all of a sudden I got the thought, 'Hey, I'd better get out of this room. If I don't I'm liable to jump out of the window.' Well, now, I never had anything like that happen to me in my life before."

T: "You were fed up with the monotony?"

P: "No, no, it's a funny thing. Uh, high places as a rule never bothered me. Now I remember in the last war, climbing around from ship to ship. But then it seemed to me an awfully small room. That's the way I felt actually. I could control myself I know, well, it was like a conscience, practically, like your conscience would say 'go ahead and jump,' and, of course, well, I'd know better."

The man's obsessive thought, which threatened for a moment to become an act of self-destruction, came with all the force of his conscience. I have chosen this particular example because the patient was able to verbalize his experience in a poetic, if not altogether grammatical simile, "like his conscience." Obsessions and compulsions are always as insistent as if they were the voice of an aroused conscience, although of course the voice of conscience does not always announce itself by name.

When our conscience is aroused, it is either to reproach us for some transgression or to prevent us from yielding to the temptation to commit one. In the case of obsessive-compulsive symptoms, both the transgression and the temptation are patently absurd. The patient is trapped in a dilemma of *having* to think or do something his judgment tells him is wrong. There is no solution to the dilemma, as in the instance just cited. If he jumps out the window he's dead. If he doesn't, he feels guilty for disobeying his conscience.

With the help of Freud's insights which unravelled the hidden meaning of obsessional symptoms, we can now guess that the patient's temptation to jump out of the window is a transformation and a disguise of some sexual feeling. It is an unconscious sexual temptation—unconscious because the patient would feel too guilty or too ashamed if he confronted it. Changing the temptation from something sexual into a temptation to jump disguises it; the transformation, however, still contains elements of the sexual feeling. Flying through the air is a symbolic way of expressing sexual experience. The patient's compulsive thought is simultaneously a punishment to him and a remnant of the experience of sexual excitement.

We can see that the lonely man in an empty hotel room is angry at being alone, even though he has chosen to be so. He is angry because he isn't enjoying himself as he expected himself—an "independent man"—to do. We can imagine that the patient might be feeling depressed. But no, the patient doesn't complain of depressed feelings, but of "crazy" thoughts, which *drive* him to *do* something. We guess that the only concession he might be making to his own lonely feeling is some sexual arousal. Maybe he has masturbated, or thought about doing so. In some mysterious way, however, sexual arousal has been converted into being "bugged" by a "crazy" conscience. It is scolding him, saying: "You wanted a vacation without her. Well, now you have it. Enjoy yourself, why don't you, you schmuck! Go jump out the window, why don't you!"

As we saw in Chapter 16, a woman's loneliness would be experienced directly as depression. Anger would be relatively absent. A man's longing is more often repressed and transformed into something he *ought* to be doing or thinking. Anger is more apparent, and in the form of being driven by an angry, guilty conscience.

In *The Iceman Cometh*,[31] Eugene O'Neill's character, Hickey, is speaking about how he came to shoot his wife, Evelyn:

> Christ, can you believe what a guilty skunk she made me feel! It kept piling up, inside her and inside me. God can you picture all I made her suffer, and how I hated myself! If only she hadn't been so damned good—if only she'd been the same kind of wife I was a husband. . . . It was written all over her face, sweetness and love and forgiveness. . . . It kept piling up like I said. I got so I thought of it all the time. I hated myself more and more, thinking of all the wrong I'd done to

the sweetest woman in the world who loves me so much. . . .
I began to be afraid I was going bughouse, because sometimes I couldn't forgive her for forgiving me. I even caught
myself hating her for making me hate myself so much.
There's a limit to the guilt you can feel and the forgiveness
and pity you can take! You have to begin blaming someone
else, too. I got so sometimes when she'd kiss me it was like
she did it on purpose to humiliate me, as if she'd spat in my
face! You'd never believe I could hate so much, a good-na-
tured, happy slob like me. . . . And then it came to me—the
only way out, for her sake. I remembered I'd given her a gun
for protection while I was away and it was in her bureau
drawer. She'd never feel any pain, never wake up from her
dreams. So I . . . I killed her.

A little later on in his soliloquy, Hickey says:

I felt as though a ton of guilt was lifted off my mind. I
remember I stood by the bed and suddenly I had to laugh.
I couldn't help it, and I knew Evelyn would forgive me. I
remember I heard myself speaking to her, it was always
something I wanted to say: "Well, you know what you can
do with your pipe dream now, you damned bitch.". . . Good
God, I couldn't have said that. If I had, I'd be insane. Why, I
loved Evelyn better than anything in life. . . ."

In order to express how much he loved her, Hickey shot Evelyn
to death. Let us look more closely at how this "crazy" form of
loving comes about by following the classic case of a man's obsessional neurosis which was first analyzed by Freud.[32] This is the
famous case of the Rat-Man, so nicknamed because rats played a
part in his terrible obsessive thoughts. The patient, a young, gifted
man, arrived at Freud's office after having been in an obsessive
dilemma which was so severe and had lasted for so many days that
the patient was almost delirious.
    The patient, Lieutenant H., the son of an army officer now
dead, was on army maneuvers when this bout of obsessional
symptoms developed. He had never been an enthusiastic soldier,
but on this stint of army duty he was keen to show that he was a
good officer. He felt ashamed of himself for not liking the army.

He thought of himself as a "coward." His father, in contrast to himself, had had gruff army ways which H. admired, even though he was also ashamed of his father for coarseness.

As a child, H. had been beaten by his father—but only once—and that occasion was family legend. H. didn't remember it himself, but he had been beaten for biting someone. He had made such a terrible fuss that his father vowed never to beat him again. The patient's brothers and sisters were beaten, however, and the patient regarded himself as a "coward" because he could not bear to be a witness to their punishments. Even as a child, then, Lieutenant H. was torn between revulsion against cruelty and his admiration for toughness.

This is a not uncommon dilemma for men. It reflects the contradiction between affectionateness and exploitativeness within our own culture. It is the contradiction internalized: H. expected himself to be tough as a man should be, but he found it hard to get rid of his own tender feelings. These he thought of as "cowardice."

Some weeks before the obsessional symptoms developed, H. had had a sharp altercation with a fellow-officer, a captain who was loudly recommending corporal punishment for privates. The conversation, which occurred during officers' mess, had been dropped. But during an interval when they were in the field, the captain had described to H. some special punishments that he had read about in the East. These involved putting rats in the anus of the victim. During this description, H. had lost his eyeglasses, a pince-nez. He had had to send to Vienna for another pair.

Some weeks later, the captain handed H. a package which had arrived at the post office, containing H.'s replacement glasses. Lieutenant H. thought he understood the captain to say that 3.80 crowns were owed to Lieutenant A., another officer, who had laid out the money for the postage. At the instant he heard Captain M. say: "You must pay back Lieutenant A.," a "sanction" formed itself in H.'s mind, which said: "You must *not* pay back the 3.80 crowns, or else *It* will happen to her (his fiancée) and to your father (long since dead)." In order to ward *It* off, H. made a *vow* that he must pay back A. His conscience had gone "crazy" and told him: "Captain says you must pay back A; you must *not* pay him or *It* will happen; you therefore *have* to pay him back or *It* will happen."

The trouble which developed was that H. was unable to pay

back A. because A. had *not* in fact laid out the money, and he therefore refused payment. H. then realized that he had misheard Captain M. So he developed plans in order to fulfill his *vow* and prevent *It* from happening. One plan was to beg A. to accept the money in order to relieve H.'s obsession. H. actually set out on a journey to find A. who had left town. But A. would scorn him for his cowardice in being unable to shake off the obsession, which H. himself knew was irrational. If, on the other hand, he really didn't fulfill his vow of paying A., *It* would happen. Even though H. knew that he was in the grip of irrational thoughts, he was powerless to stop the internal commands which were making him undertake contradictory journeys. And the dilemma was insoluble: If a plan to pay worked, he would be ashamed of himself for yielding to his irrational thoughts. If he were brave enough *not* to pay, then *It* would happen and he would be responsible—guilty for the suffering which *It* inflicts (in fantasy) on his loved ones.

Now what in the world is *It?* You've guessed—*It* is the special punishment which the cruel captain had described at the time H. lost his glasses. *It* is not only an unspeakable punishment, however, but the thought of it happening to someone is sexually arousing. *It* is accompanied by a sadistic feeling to which H. is drawn at the same moment that he is revolted.

Freud's account of how Lieutenant H. suffered when he had to tell Freud the details of his fantasy about the punishment is very vivid. H. was in agony of shame all the while he tried to speak the details of his fantasy.[33]

Here the patient broke off, got up from the sofa and begged me to spare him the recital of the details. I assured him that I myself had no taste for cruelty, and certainly no desire to torment him, but that naturally I could not grant him something that was beyond my power. He might just as well ask me to give him the moon. The overcoming of resistances was a law of the treatment and on no consideration could it be dispensed with . . . he expressed himself so indistinctly that I could not immediately guess in what position . . . "a pot was turned upside down on his (the criminal's) buttocks . . . some rats were put into it . . . and they,"—he had got up again and was showing every sign of horror and resistance—"bored their way into. . . ."—"Into his anus," I

helped him out. At all the more important moments while he
was telling his story, his face took on a very strange, composite expression. I could only interpret it as one of *horror at
pleasure of his own of which he himself was unaware.*
(Freud's italics)

Lieutenant H. had such a horror of his own sadistic fantasy that,
even though he was only thinking it, the protagonist within his
fantasy was not himself. Someone anonymous, not H., was in-
verting a pot full of rats on the anus of his fiancée and his father. H.
himself was only a spectator. Even so, his guilt at the fantasy was
enough to drive him into an obsessive fit about paying the postage
for a pair of eyeglasses he had lost on the occasion when the cruel
captain first described the rat-punishment.

Freud's unravelling of the hidden connections between the
obsessive dilemma and the sadistic fantasy was a marvel of insight.
Freud traced the way in which ideas work when we are under the
influence of strong but throttled feelings. The "primary-process"
transformation of ideas was worked out in the course of H.'s "free
associations." As Freud put it: "It was almost as though Fate,
when the captain told him his story, had been putting him (H.)
through an association test: she called out a 'complex-stimulus-
word,' and he had reacted to it with an obsessional idea."

The lost eyeglasses, for example, were actually a pince-nez.
This is significant only because the *word* reminded H. of an incident some years before in which he failed to meet a challenge to
a duel. This he considered a typical instance of his cowardice for
which the word "pince-nez" became a symbol.

Rats and money had become linked in H.'s mind by a series of
puns—"verbal bridges." H. remembered, for example, a story his
father had told him about losing army money at gambling. The
German word for gambler is *Spielratte*—a "play-rat." Father
would have been in considerable trouble if a comrade had not
offered to lay out the lost army money. Father had tried subsequently to repay the small debt but had never succeeded.
Hearing the captain say that H. was to pay back some money
reminded H. of his father's unpaid debt. It touched H.'s would-be
identification with his army father.

The puns were quite numerous, making not one but many
connections between the rat fantasy and paying money. For in-

stance, when Freud had told H. his hourly fee, H.'s internal response had been "so many florins—so many 'rats' (installments)." Even more important, rats bite. H. remembered that he had seen a rat coming out of his father's grave and had thought of it as having feasted on his father's corpse. But he himself was a "rat"—he had bitten someone and had been beaten for it by his father, in the family legend which led H. to feel what a coward he was for not being able to see his brothers or his sisters beaten.

Lieutenant H.'s horror (guilt) over his own sadistic fantasy had been with him since he was a child. Even as a child he could be in such a state of guilt as to be temporarily "out of it"—not able to remember, for example, whether he had said something out loud or only thought it. When he was six years old he suffered such thought-lapses over the fact that he had erections during which he had a "burning and tormenting wish to see certain girls naked." This burning wish to see certain girls naked implied triumphant power over the girls' wish *not* to be seen naked, over their modesty. ". . . At that time I used to have the morbid idea that my parents knew my thoughts; I explained this to myself by supposing that I had spoken them out loud, without having heard myself do it. . . . But . . . I had an uncanny feeling as though something must happen if I thought these things, *and as though I must do all sorts of things to prevent it*" (Freud's italics).[34] That something will happen if he thinks these things is the pattern of obsessive symptoms, which drive the person relentlessly. They are the transformed expressions of an aroused, guilty conscience.

A man is required by our society to be "tough." But he also has tender feelings which are violated by toughness. One way out of this conflict is to sexualize toughness which transforms it into sadism. The Marquis de Sade has described for us in great detail how the most tender, exquisite sexual pleasure can be fused with hurting people.[35] Sadism is itself, however, a reason for profound guilt feelings, even if sadism is expressed only in sexual fantasy, without really hurting anybody. Lieutenant H. was so horrified by his own sadism that he could not even bear to be the protagonist in his own fantasy. A description of sadism in reality threw him into an obsessive delirium.

The "solution" in sadism of the conflict between tenderness and toughness is no solution at all for many men. They become obsessional neurotics, or, as we shall shortly see, schizophrenics. For many other men, this sexualizing of toughness into sadism can become a way of life congruent with society's expectations that men should become exploiters who enjoy exploiting. These are the men who choose to lead the armies and give the orders for the destruction of life. They enjoy their triumph over others and their power to command others' obedient suffering. They are the male chauvinists who have accepted to the full the fusion between maleness and exploitativeness. But even among these men, it is not their maleness which is the issue, but their exploitativeness.

References

1. E. Zigler and L. Phillips, "Social Effectiveness and Symptomatic Behaviors," *Journal of Abnormal and Social Psychology,* 61 (1960), 231-238.

2. H. G. Cohn, J. Bamdad, A. Orhon and S. Furman, "Significant Sex Differences in Behavior and Ideational Symptoms as Reasons for Admission of Men and Women to a New York State Hospital," *Psychiatric Quarterly,* 36, (1962), pp. 79-82.

3. J. D. Cummings, "The Incidence of Emotional Symptoms in School Children," *British Journal of Educational Psychology* 14 (1944), 151-161.

4. Studies cited by Phyllis Chesler, *Women and Madness* (New York: Doubleday, 1972), appendix, n. 9, p. 337.

5. M. Keller, "Alcoholism: Nature and Extent of the Problem," *American Academy of Political and Social Science* 315 (1958), 1-11.

6. M. Maxwell, F. Lemiere and P. O'Halloran, "Changing Character-istics of Private Hospital Alcoholic Patients," *Quarterly Journal of Studies of Alcoholism* 19 (1958), 309-315.

7. Phyllis Chesler, op. cit.

8. Report in the American Psychological Association, *Monitor,* July, 1972.

9. H. A. Witkin, "Psychological Differentiation and Forms of Path-ology," *Journal of Abnormal Psychology* 1 (1965).

10. E. Brecher, ed., *Licit and Illicit Drugs* (Boston: Little Brown, 1962).

11. Ibid.

12. Ibid.

13. M. J. Pescor, "A Comparative Statistical Study of Male and Female Drug Addicts," *American Journal of Psychiatry* 100 (1944), 771-774.

14. S. Freud, *Three Essays on Sexuality*, Standard Edition, vol. 7.

15. Ibid.

16. Frank Beach, ed., *Sex and Behavior* (New York: Wiley 1965; reprinted New York: Krieger, 1974).

17. A. Gide, *Corydon* (New York: Farrar, Straus & Cudahy, 1950) p. 189. Comment by Frank Beach

18. A. C. Kinsey, W. B. Pomeroy and, C. E. Martin, *Sexual Behavior in the Human Male* (Philadelphia: W. B. Saunders, 1948).

19. A. C. Kinsey, W. B. Pomeroy, C. E. Martin and P. Gebhard, *Sexual Behavior in the Human Female* (Philadelphia: W. B. Saunders, 1953).

20. Personal communication from Jeanne Safer.

21. C. Socarides, "Homosexuality," ed. S. Arieti, *American Handbook of Psychiatry*, 2d ed. (New York: Basic Books, 1974).

22. P. Chesler, op. cit.

23. V. Laschet, "Anti-androgen Treatment of Sex Offenders," eds. J. Zubin and J. Money, *Contemporary Sexual Behavior: Critical Issues in the 1970's* (Baltimore, Md.: The Johns Hopkins University Press, 1971), 311-319.

24. N. Lustig, J. Dresser, S. Spellman and T. Murray, *Archives of General Psychiatry* 14 (1966), 31-40.

25. S. Freud, *Inhibitions, Symptoms and Anxiety*, Standard Edition, vol. 20.

26. H. A. Witkin, op. cit.

27. L. Zukmann, "Hysteric and Compulsive Factors in Perceptual Organization," doctoral dissertation (New York: The New School for Social Research, 1957).

28. Anna Marie Dührssen, "Zur Frage der Häufigkeit zwangsneurotischer und hysterischer Strukturen bei Männern und Frauen," *Zeitschrift für medizinische Psychologie* 1 (1951), 247-253.

29. Personal communication from Jeanne Safer.

30. F. Deutsch and W. Murphy, *The Clinical Interview*, vol. 2 (New York: International Universities Press, 1955).

31. Eugene O'Neill, *The Iceman Cometh.*

32. Case account is adapted from my review of Freud's cases, H. B. Lewis, *Shame and Guilt in Neurosis* (New York: International Universities Press, 1971), Chap. 12.

33. Ibid.

34. Ibid.

35. S. de Beauvoir, *Marquis de Sade. Selections from His Writings* (New York: Grove Press, 1953).

CHAPTER 19

Madness in Men: Schizophrenia

"Schizophrenia" is the technical term for out-and-out madness. Its special hallmarks are hallucinations, delusions, bizarre actions or thoughts, and "flattened affect," that is, an apparent absence of readily communicable feeling. Psychiatrists and psychologists often judge that they are dealing with a schizophrenic if there is an "absence of rapport." Although this is an admittedly subjective criterion, it is a valuable, if imprecise diagnostic indicator which is "handed down" to incoming students on hospital wards.

Sometimes schizophrenia is described as a "fragmenting of the self"—in fact, its name is derived from the Greek, meaning "splitting of the mind." Fragmenting is a phenomenon which occurs when thoughts have lost their usual connection to feelings. Schizophrenics sometimes speak in what is called a "word-salad"; they put words together in a concoction which is incomprehensible.

Although schizophrenia is the most serious mental illness, a most regressed state of being, some therapists who have treated schizophrenics have developed a profound respect for their patients' extreme actions and thoughts:

286

Schizophrenia represents the singularly human ability to substitute an internal world for external reality through alteration of thought and perception, and the creation of an idiosyncratic set of symbolic criteria through which to interpret experience. The attempt to identify and define the mechanisms of these distorting processes may ultimately shed light on the higher reaches of the mind, as well as on its disintegration.[1]

The same review of schizophrenia's symptomatology, quotes Jung, who wrote: "We healthy people, who stand with both feet in reality, see only the ruin of the patient in this world, but not the richness of the psyche that is turned away from us." [2] These observations about schizophrenia are not just a romanticizing of schizophrenic productions. They are an attempt to grasp the essence of a message of protest which is being conveyed. As we shall see later in this chapter, the case of paranoia analyzed by Freud conveys just such a message.

The statistics on sex differences in schizophrenia are, however, the hardest to pin down. There are a number of reasons for this. For one thing, schizophrenia is a not-too-trustworthy catchall category of diagnosis. Some schizophrenic patients are "silly," or inappropriately "happy." Others are totally mute, apathetic, and withdrawn; still others so negativistic they will not even move their limbs. Only some, the paranoids, are still willing or able to articulate their "crazy" ideas. The apathetic patients are sometimes diagnosed as depressed, while others, the silly ones, are called feeble-minded. But, on the whole, the criteria for placing people in one or another of the subcategories of schizophrenia are reasonably clear. If the person seems to show very little feeling, or if feelings are totally inappropriate to the ideas they go with, then the diagnosis is schizophrenia. It is a convenient shorthand formulation to say that schizophrenia is a "thought-disorder," in contrast to depression which is a "feeling-disorder."

Another difficulty in developing accurate statistics on sex differences in schizophrenia is that, as we saw in Chapter 16, the diagnosis of schizophrenia is more apt to be made if there is a greater distance in social class between the diagnostician and his patient. So statistics comparing men and women are useful only if they come from the same social class. Furthermore, as we noted in Chapter 18, flamboyant hysterical patients (mostly women) are more often diagnosed schizophrenic these days than they used to be. In fact, a trend toward the increased use of the diagnosis of schizophrenia and a decrease in the use of the category, manic-depressive, has been observed.[3] Women are more often depressed than men; and they more often enter mental hospitals after the age of thirty than before.[4] With more women entering mental hospitals after thirty, and an increased tendency to diagnose schizophrenia, the usually higher rate of schizophrenia for men might be expected to disappear in later years, or at least be attentuated after the age of thirty. This is, in fact, what does seem to occur.

Table 1 shows Malzberg's figures on statistics from 1910 on, in New York State hospitals prorated for sex ratio in the general population. These statistics show that men were more liable to schizophrenia than women from 1910 until 1944. After 1944, the difference between men and women in first admissions for schizophrenia disappeared, and, in fact, for 1946 and 1948 there were more women than men. A partial reason cited by Malzberg was that World War II had intervened, and that Veterans' Hospitals were established in which male patients were segregated, instead of entering state hospitals.

When Malzberg examined statistics from 1949 to 1951 by age groups, he found schizophrenia to be the much more frequent illness among men—particularly between the ages of fifteen to thirty.[5] These are the years during which there is the most pressure on men to achieve—to establish themselves in the working community. After the age of thirty, there are slightly more women than men admitted for schizophrenia, although the difference is small.

The following table shows these findings clearly.

Chesler has adduced evidence that more women than men are prone to schizophrenia; this is part of her general thesis that more women than men are "psychiatrically involved." [6] But when we examine the difference between men and women in state and county hospitals (the last resort of the poor), as shown in Chesler's own tables (p. 42), there is no difference between men and women in the category of schizophrenia. A graph showing first admission rates per 100,000 to outpatient psychiatric facilities for

Table 1
FIRST ADMISSIONS TO NEW YORK STATE HOSPITALS
1910-50 PER 100,000 POPULATION
FOR DEMENTIA PRAECOX (SCHIZOPHRENIA) °
(Adapted from B. Malzberg)

Year	Men	Women	Total
1910	10.8	10.0	10.4
1912	10.6	9.8	10.2
1914	12.6	11.6	12.1
1916	14.6	12.7	13.7
1918	18.4	16.2	17.3
1920	19.9	17.6	18.8
1922	19.2	16.3	17.8
1924	18.4	16.7	17.6
1926	19.4	16.7	18.1
1928	20.3	16.8	18.6
1930	20.0	17.0	18.5
1932	22.9	20.3	21.6
1934	24.4	22.4	23.4
1936	25.3	22.6	24.0
1938	26.0	23.2	24.6
1940	26.0	25.1	25.5
1942	26.1	24.4	25.2
1944	23.3	25.9	24.7
1946	23.7	29.1	26.4
1948	27.8	30.4	29.1
1950	31.5	31.0	31.2

° (Rates are based on the average number of first admissions during three years; that is, the rate for 1910 is the average for 1909–11 inclusive.)

schizophrenia (p. 325) actually shows more males than females, especially in the "career" years, between twenty-five and forty-four.

When we remember that schizophrenia occurs in the ecology of poverty and social disorganization and that the figures for male psychotics also follows the same pattern, it seems reasonable, on balance, to conclude that schizophrenia is more often the illness of young men. Chesler, in fact, acknowledges that schizophrenia is "crucially different from *female* symptoms such as depression and anxiety." [7]

It may also be that women are becoming more like men in their proneness to schizophrenia, especially since World War II. It seems likely that women's increasing rate of psychiatric hospitalization, as well as an increasing tendency to schizophrenia

Table 2
FIRST ADMISSIONS WITH DEMENTIA PRAECOX (SCHIZOPHRENIA)
IN NEW YORK STATE HOSPITALS, 1949-51, ACCORDING TO AGE°
° (Adapted from B. Malzberg, *Mental Hygiene*, 1955, p. 219.)

| Age | Average Annual Rate per 100,000 population | | |
	Males	Females	Total
15–19	60.57	49.31	54.83
20–24	115.00	68.58	90.46
25–29	98.73	80.42	89.12
30–34	70.74	77.06	74.07
35–39	57.14	69.40	63.59
40–44	43.41	49.78	46.67

might reflect the increasing economic burdens they have had to bear over the past decades. The constant increase in the number of women who are gainfully employed is a major contributor both to women's liberation, and, in an exploitative society, to an increase in their chances of being hospitalized for schizophrenia.

There is a childhood psychosis called "infantile autism," or "Kanner's syndrome," [8] after one of its first observers. Autism has been observed in relatively few children, but where it is observed, the ratio of boys to girls is 400 to 100.[9] Autistic children can best be described by saying that their emotional life has not developed properly. As their mothers put it, the infants never smiled at them! Here are Kanner's criteria for the diagnosis of infantile autism, as reported in a psychiatry handbook:

1. Aloneness, extreme in degree and evident in earliest infancy. The babies do not respond . . . as the adults reach to pick them up and do not adapt to the bodies of those who hold them. 2. Impaired communication. Speech and language are not used for purposes of communication. Often the children are entirely mute, or, if speech is present it . . . does not convey meaning. 3. Obsessive insistence on the maintenance of sameness . . . with repetitive ritualistic preoccupation. 4. Fascination for objects, in contrast to disinterest in people.[10]

(Autistic children, it should be noted, are not mentally retarded.)

Margaret Mahler, the child psychoanalyst who first developed a psychoanalytic theory of infantile autism, suggests that these infants are suffering from an underlying "symbiosis" with their mothers.[11] Mahler supposes that the normal emotional relationship which is usually well-established by the time of the three-month smile had failed (for reasons in both child and mother). Unable to differentiate a coping "self" out of the normal affectionate, symbiotic matrix, these children have retreated into withdrawal. Mahler's theory does not discount genetic factors in infantile autism but emphasizes a failure in the normally affectionate interaction between mother and infant.

A subcategory of overtly "symbiotic" infants has also been described.[12] These infants also do not develop an adequate emotional relationship with their mothers. But the trouble is that they are so inordinately clinging that they cannot let their mothers out of their sight. Symbiotic children do develop speech and are also not mentally retarded. Their emotional life, however, is so out of kilter that long after they should have outgrown it, they have an abnormally symbiotic relationship to their mothers: They behave, in other words, as if they were not separate individuals, capable of existing, even briefly, on their own. Their rage and terror on separation is massive. Although there are no formal statistics on the matter, since symbiotic children are extremely rare, there is general agreement that infantile symbiosis is a disorder of girl infants.[13]

The proneness of boy infants to autism and of girl infants to symbiosis seems a forerunner of the fact that adult men are more prone to schizophrenia, while women are more prone to depression. We are reminded of the fact that men and women inherit a different set of chromosomes. There are, in fact, many studies which are seeking a genetic factor in schizophrenia; and many studies are searching for it in depression. As yet, the evidence which definitively establishes the existence of genetic factors in either major psychosis has not been obtained. As a reviewer of the present status of the genetics of schizophrenia puts it: "Many researchers . . . are optimistic about a breakthrough in the 1970s. We can only wait and see." [14] Similarly, genetic factors in the affective disorders have not been definitely established.[15]

There may be some genetic factors which predispose men to have the defect of too little feeling, and a corresponding genetic factor which predisposes women to the defect of too much feeling. If such genetic factors exist, however, they are also operating within a noxious social climate which fosters too little feeling in men and too much in women.

In a very thoughtful paper on the sociology of depression and schizophrenia, Yehudi Cohen puts it this way: "In stratified societies in which men are responsible for 'providing,' it is they who become schizophrenic, telling us in their psychotic system that the world is too painful a place to be in; that it is 'standing in their way and crushing them.' " [16] Women, who are not directly involved in earning a livelihood, are expected, instead, to devote their lives to their husbands and children. Among women, then, it is just those who can afford to cultivate ideals of personal devotion to others most assiduously who are even more likely to fall ill of "undue emotional dependence on the people who hurt them." So the picture emerges of the depressed woman in suburbia's "empty nest," to which we can also add the depressed "Jewish mother," described by Bart.[17] And although Cohen does not say so, these depressed women evoke our scorn (and their own) for being "spoiled" and depressed "for no good reason." Schizophrenia, in contrast, evokes more respect for its often intellectualized, highly symbolic message of despair.

Perhaps the clearest picture—in miniature—of the way our exploitative society injures the sexes differently comes from an excellent study of young men and women who had suffered a schizophrenic breakdown requiring hospitalization in adolescence.[18] The investigator was looking for the ways in which the parents' personality might have been schizophrenia-producing. She was on the track of what has been called by the hideous name of the schizophrenogenic mother. She found no evidence to support such a concept—in fact, overall, the schizophrenic youngsters and their parents were no different from a control group of normal adolescents. But the investigator, Frances Cheek, did come upon an unexpected and "serendipitous" finding that the young *men* schizophrenics were very different indeed from the young *women* schizophrenics.

The most striking differences were in schizophrenic men's and women's relationships to their families. The men schizophrenics were much more emotionally withdrawn and inactive than normal men. The women schizophrenics were *more* interactive, with their parents particularly, than the normal women. In fact, all the women in the study, both schizophrenic and normal, were more interactive with the parents than the men. The picture thus emerges of schizophrenic men responding to the contradiction between the need for power and the need for love by becoming emotionally withdrawn and giving up on feelings. Schizophrenic women respond to the conflict between the need to be loving and the need for autonomy by becoming *more* emotionally involved than is "normal." Let's look more closely at the study.

The investigator's original search for the schizophrenogenic mother was begun during the late 1950s, when the tendency to blame parents for their children's mental illness was at its height. Such mothers were thought to be cold, rejecting, and dominating. When they were married to a passive and ineffectual man, the combination was thought to bring about madness. It will be noticed that implicit in this conception of the genesis of schizophrenia is the idea that the parents have reversed their "proper" sex roles: mother too dominating, father too passive. Also implicit in this conception of the origin of schizophrenia is the notion that the mothers were not loving enough to their infants. (The idea that this damages infants has some foundation in fact. This is why society ought to support mothers and fathers in their child rearing by more than exhortations to be loving.) What is missing from the conception that schizophrenia originates in the family is the whole background of exploitative influences which operate to poison the family atmosphere, for one thing by fostering the concept that domination is okay for fathers, while passivity is more becoming to mothers.

Frances Cheek went to considerable trouble to assemble a group of convalescent young schizophrenics of both sexes living at home after their discharge from hospital. She matched these young people with a comparable group of normal people also living at home. She then invited the young people and their parents to discuss problems of living together in a tape-recorded session. These tape recordings were then carefully scored according to a prearranged scheme which tried to measure "interactions"—positive and negative social-emotional exchanges, and such task behaviors as giving suggestions, giving opinions, asking for information, and so forth. Also measured were tension indicators during the discussion sessions. Interestingly enough, all the women, both schizophrenic and normal, showed more tension signs than the men. But the schizophrenic men were particularly low in indications of tension release. The schizophrenic men showed many fewer positive social and emotional interactions; they also showed fewer negative social interactions than normal men with their parents. In other words, schizophrenic men had given up on feelings. The schizophrenic women were much more active than the normal women, not so much in the social-emotional exchanges, either positive or negative, but in the task exchanges. They gave opinions much more often than the normal women, and "explained and clarified" things more than the normal women. The picture thus emerges of the schizophrenic women being much more active in these talk sessions—trying to get their ideas across and *not* letting go, *not* subsiding into passivity, as readily as the normal women. It is interesting to observe that Cheek interprets this female behavior as "hyperactive" and relates it to the general opinion current in psychiatric wards that women patients are "noisier" than men patients. In fact, one study of men and women newly admitted to a psychiatric hospital (roughly 80 percent of each sex with a diagnosis of schizophrenia) observed that there were similar symptoms in both sexes, except that the men were more retarded, while the women were more "excited." [19]

As Phyllis Chesler has pointed out, this "noisiness" or excitement is experienced as extremely inappropriate and often punished by the men who are mostly in charge of psychiatric wards.[20] Thus, society, acting through men as its unwitting agents, pressures schizophrenic women into submission on the hospital wards. Schizophrenic men have already retreated into emotional deadness.

Perhaps the clearest view of how men can go crazy from conflicting internal requirements that they be tough and tender comes from paranoid schizophrenia. In this form of schizophrenia, the patient is very articulate, and so we can have some insight into the beliefs which dominate his thinking. The patient no longer recognizes that his compelling ideas are bizarre, or if he does recognize it, is helpless to change the situation. Obsessional neurosis and schizophrenia thus form a kind of continuum of "crazy" ideas. As one would expect, paranoid schizophrenics are likely to be field-independent perceivers.[21]

An excellent illustration is the famous case of Dr. Daniel Paul Schreber, who wrote a memoir describing both his experiences when he was acutely ill and the religious beliefs with which he came out of the acute phase of his illness. This memoir was analyzed by Freud.[22]

Dr. Schreber was a judge of an Appeals Court in Dresden during the last part of the nineteenth century. He became acutely psychotic to the point of having to be hospitalized, and his delusion was that Dr. Flechsig, the psychiatrist who had treated him previously, was involved in a plot to emasculate him. During this acute phase of his illness, Schreber suffered from torturing ideas that his stomach, his intestines, his testicles, and his penis were all being cut away in order to make him into a woman—and an object of carnal abuse by Dr. Flechsig.

After a while the acute psychosis subsided. As this happened, he came to the realization that his transformation into a woman was a unique event in the world, ordered by God, not Flechsig, in order that God should be able to copulate with Schreber. As a result of this copulation with God, a new race of men were to be brought into existence who understood what God Himself had not previously understood—that the voluptuous pleasure of being a woman is the highest state of bliss.

When his condition had reached this point, Schreber applied for release from the asylum where he had been confined. Although his doctors disagreed, Schreber convinced the courts that he was indeed fit to resume his normal life. His religious convictions were, in his own view, of extreme importance to himself and to others. He convinced the court, further, that he would not harm anyone because of his religious convictions. After his release, he wrote a lengthy memoir describing both the acute phase of his illness and his new system of beliefs.

Schreber's own belief that he had had a mystical experience with God was unassailable. He acknowledged that some people might regard his ideas as delusional. If, for instance, they should even see him dressed in women's finery and looking at himself in the mirror (which he did only when alone), they might think that he was having the delusion that he was a woman. But they would be wrong! He had been transformed into a woman who copulates with God in order to bring to the world the realization that God's will is the cultivation of feminine voluptuousness.

Several ideas among the many Dr. Schreber believed are of particular interest to us here because they so clearly reflect the conflict between manly toughness and manly tenderness. Schreber had solved this conflict by adopting a set of ideas that he was a woman with a special mission. As a "woman" he taught God to understand the needs of *men*. God, since he lives in heaven, was accustomed to having intercourse only with the dead. He therefore did not understand the feelings of living men. Schreber's rage at God and ridicule of Him for his stupidity tell us how deadly Schreber must have found his life as a man. Let us listen to how he puts it: "The pen well-nigh shrinks from recording so monumental a piece of absurdity as that God, blinded by his ignorance of human nature, can positively go to such lengths as to suppose that there can exist a man too stupid to be able to do what every animal can do—too stupid to be able to shit." [23] This tirade against God was evoked because He failed to understand the voluptuous sensations of shitting. God therefore used to interfere with Schreber's exercise of these functions and the enjoyment of their attendant pleasures. This part of Schreber's description of his experiences is full of references to God's sadism—to the tortures which God visited upon Schreber's body and his mind because God did not understand living men.

Before he fell ill, Schreber himself clearly did not understand his own need either for sexuality or for tenderness any more than God did. "Few people," he wrote, "can have been brought up upon such strict moral principles as I was, and few people, all through their lives, can have exercised (especially in sexual matters) a self-restraint conforming to those principles as I may say of myself that I have done." [24]

For years, Schreber had been hoping that his wife would become pregnant, and they would have a child. Some weeks before he fell ill, he had a thought one night, as he was between sleeping and waking: "How nice it must be to be a female submitting to copulation." He then recoiled in horror from this thought. Immediately before he became ill his wife was away, and in her absence he had masturbated repetitively. He described the many emissions he had had on one night. These also he regarded with loathing.

But after Schreber's transformation into a woman he came to see that the cultivation of voluptuousness was incumbent on him as a duty—and he could only regret that he was not able to devote himself to it all day long. "I have inscribed upon my banner the cultivation of femaleness." It is pathetic if not tragic to see that a grown man should have needed to sacrifice his very reason in order to permit himself the "feminine" voluptuousness of his own body functions.

Judge Schreber's paranoid system is a myth which attempts to resolve men's dilemma in an exploitative society which casts them as the exploiters. An exploitative society violates men's affectionate natures by first forcing them to renounce loving and cultivate "manly" toughness, only to be confronted with ethical decisions about how tough they ought to be. Schreber's myth insists that only by emasculating himself can a man feel human.

References

1. J. Bemporad and H. Pinsker, "Schizophrenia: The Manifest Symptomatology" ed. S. Arieti, *American Handbook of Psychiatry*, 2d ed. (New York: Basic Books, 1974), pp. 524-551.

2. Ibid.

3. S. Arieti, "Affective Disorders" ed. S. Arieti, *American Handbook of Psychiatry*, 2d ed. (New York: Basic Books, 1974).

4. B. Malzberg, "Important Statistical Data About Mental Illness," ed. S. Arieti, *American Handbook of Psychiatry* (New York: Basic Books, 1959).

5. B. Malzberg, "Age and Sex in Relation to Mental Disease," *Mental Hygiene* 39 (1955), 196-206.

6. P. Chesler, *Women and Madness* (New York: Doubleday, 1972).

7. Ibid., p. 49.

8. L. Kanner, "Autistic Disturbances of Affective Contact," *Nervous Child* 2 (1942), 217-250.

9. D. C. Taylor and C. Ounsted, "The Nature of Gender Differences Explored Through Ontogenetic Analysis of Sex Ratios in Disease," C. Ounsted and D. C. Taylor, *Gender Differences: Their Significance and Ontogeny* (Baltimore, Md.: Williams and Wilkins, 1972).

10. W. Goldfarb, "Distinguishing and Classifying the Individual Schizophrenic Child," ed. S. Arieti, *American Handbook of Psychiatry*, 2d ed. (New York: Basic Books, 1974), p. 89.

11. M. Mahler, "On Human Symbiosis and the Vicissitudes of Individuation," vol. 1 *Infantile Psychosis* (New York: International Universities Press, 1968).

12. Ibid.

13. Remarks by Marjorie Leonard at the October 1974 joint meeting of the Boston and Western New England Psychoanalytic Societies.

14. D. Rosenthal, "The Genetics of Schizophrenia," ed. S. Arieti, *American Handbook of Psychiatry*, 2d ed. (New York: Basic Books, 1974), pp. 524-551, 598.

15. J. Mendels, "Biological Aspects of Mental Disease," ed. S. Arieti, *American Handbook of Psychiatry*, 2d ed. (New York: Basic Books, 1974), 491-524.

16. Yehudi Cohen, "The Sociological Relevance of Schizophrenia and Depression," ed. Y. Cohen, *Social Structure and Personality. A Casebook* (New York: Holt, Rinehart, and Winston, 1961), pp. 477-485.

17. P. Bart, "Depression in Middle-aged Women," eds. V. Gornick and B. Moran, *Woman in Sexist Society* (New York: New American Library, 1971).

18. F. Cheek, "A Serendipitous Finding: Sex Role and Schizophrenia," *Journal of Abnormal and Social Psychology* 69 (1964), 392-400.

19. M. Lorr and C. Klett, "Constancy of Psychotic Syndromes in Men and Women," *Journal of Consulting Psychology* 29 (1965), 309-313.

20. P. Chesler, op. cit.

21. H. A. Witkin, "Psychological Differentiation and Forms of Pathology," *Journal of Abnormal Psychology* (1) 1965.

22. S. Freud, *Psycho-Analytic Notes on an Autobiographical Account of Case of Paranoia (Dementia Paranoides)*, Standard Edition vol. 12.

23. Ibid.

24. Ibid.

CHAPTER 20

Sexism in Psychiatry

There are greater numbers of women than men who are seeking help for mental problems in our country today. Women are more likely than men to feel that there is something wrong with them psychologically.[1] In one study of seventeen psychotherapy groups, for example, women tended to devalue themselves, while men tended to overestimate themselves.[2] Women also have more interest in and respect for psychiatry than men have,[3] along with a greater interest in emotional intimacy.[4] The majority of people engaged in helping emotionally disturbed people, however, are men,[5] since men more often than women are expected to pursue a professional career. So the likelihood is that a woman patient seeking help for psychological problems will end up with a male therapist. In addition, women patients, asked to choose whether they preferred a man or woman therapist, chose to speak to a man as probably the better qualified. Men patients also prefer men therapists.[6] Both sexes thus demonstrate that they are caught up in the cultural stereotype of male superiority.

This combination of women's tendency to assume that they have psychological troubles and women's tendency to trust more in a male therapist's wisdom creates a treatment situation for which the only accurate label is sexist. This is not to blame the male therapists as sexist any more than the women patients are. Both are victims of their own unconscious assumptions about the superior qualities of the male sex, assumptions which reflect both sexes' absorption of a cultural stereotype. It is the psychiatric situation which is sexist, not the parties to it. And consequently, both patient and therapist are doomed to more frequent disappointments than might be the case if sexism in the psychiatric situation were better understood.

The stereotype of male superiority, which makes men less likely to admit to psychological problems than women and makes women patients prefer to trust themselves to a male therapist, reflects the prevailing power structure. This power structure is not just male supremacist, but exploitative. As is common in exploitative societies, men's aggression is valued, although guilt-inducing. Aggression cum guilt which is the more frequent conflict for men is, by implication, the dignified, intellectualized conflict which psychiatry recognizes. (Small wonder, since psychiatry was developed by men!) Gentleness, sympathy, empathy, and affectionateness are all devalued as agreeable weaknesses (if not phony virtues). Both patient and therapist try to exorcise aggression repressing tendencies; and women patients can become even more ashamed of these "weaknesses" than they were before therapy began.

There are a number of other ways in which the operation of sexism in psychiatry can be clearly seen. One of these is in the existence of a cultural standard of adult mental health which is modeled after virtues necessary in exploiters. This cultural standard operates silently to denigrate women. Because the standards of mental health are implicit rather than explicit, as well as being "male-exploiter" standards, clinicians often do not realize that their own attitudes are sexist.

Sexism in psychiatry is manifest also in how little attention is paid to differences between men and women in their ways of becoming mentally ill. The statistics on the greater frequency of depression and the hysterias in women stated in Chapters 16 and 17 are quite well known. But they are generally ignored in psychiatric theory. Similarly, the statistics on the greater frequency of addictions, perversion, obsessional neurosis, and schizophrenia in men, presented in Chapters 18 and 19 are by no means esoteric information. Yet the theoretical significance of this difference between the sexes is also neglected. This is not just a loss to abstract theory. It results in a diminished sharpness and accuracy of therapeutic technique which is always best when it is closely tailored to the individual's needs.

The assumption that the sexes are alike in their ways of falling mentally ill is part of an egalitarian attitude which focuses on the common humanity of the sexes. In this same spirit, as we saw in Chapter 13, intelligence tests were devised to cancel out differences between the sexes. These intellectual differences were recognized as the results of different cultural expectations for men and women and any test which did not allow for them was considered unfair. But the differences in intellectual functioning as well as in mental illness actually reflect the different ways in which our society injures both sexes. Ignoring these differences only appears to foster the equality of the sexes.

Still another instance of sexism in psychiatry is the difficulty which men therapists have in understanding their women patients' troubles because women are more prone to shame than men, as we saw in Chapter 15. Shame is itself a shameful experience compared to guilt, which is a more dignified mode of suffering. It is no accident that Freud was able to record the case of a guilt-ridden young man suffering from obsessional neurosis and report a full success in relieving the symptoms. However, when it came to understanding his young hysterical patient, Dora, Freud knew he was in trouble.[7] With our present-day insight, it is easy to see that Freud was missing Dora's monumental shame experience, although he caught it well enough to tell us that she was suffering from "mortification." We'll come back to Dora's case later on.

As I have listened to tape-recordings of therapy sessions by different therapists in the course of my research on shame and guilt experiences, I have been struck by the way even experienced male therapists miss their women patients' shame experiences. This happens mainly because shame experiences are ignored or avoided by the patients as well as by the therapists. Shame experiences, however, can cause patients much grief. But before turning to case accounts, let's look at cultural standards of mental health, as they are applied to men and women patients, respectively.

Stereotypes about what constitutes mental health for men and women operate even among experienced clinicians, reflecting the prevailing cultural standards of socially desirable traits. These stereotypes were recently exposed in a now widely quoted study by a research team including Drs. Inge and Donald Broverman.[8] A group of seventy-nine experienced psychiatrists, psychologists, and social workers of both sexes were divided into three sub-groups. One sub-group was asked to "think of a normal, healthy, mature, competent adult," a second sub-group was asked to "think of a normal, healthy, mature, competent man"; and a third sub-group was asked to "think of a normal, healthy, mature, competent woman." As the clinicians thought of their assigned images of a mentally healthy person, they judged the same series of 122 personality characteristics as "to which pole the socially competent man, woman or adult would be closer." The personality characteristics offered for judgment were actually sex-role stereotypes. Twelve of these turned out to be judged differently for "healthy" men and women.

All clinicians, of both sexes, strongly agreed with each other in their judgments. The characteristics of a "healthy adult" and a "healthy man" were thought to be the same. The image of a "healthy woman," however, was different in the clinicians' minds from the image of a "healthy adult." Although they would perhaps disown it in a direct confrontation, their image of a healthy woman allowed her to be different from men in being "more submissive, less independent, more easily influenced, less adventurous, less aggressive, less competitive, more excitable in minor crises, having their feelings more easily hurt, being more emotional, more conceited about their appearance, less objective and disliking math and science."

Following are the twelve sex-role stereotypes which experienced clinicians judged differently for healthy adult men and women. In tabular form, they have quite an impact.

As the researchers wryly remark about the healthy woman: "This constellation seems an unusual way of describing a healthy personality." They see an analogy with the way things might have been in pre-Civil War days, when a "healthy black" would fit the stereotype of a "docile, unambitious, childlike" person.

The trouble with the clinicians' judgment is not only that it reflects a *different* standard of mental health for men and women.

Table 1

CLINICIANS' STEREOTYPES OF MENTALLY HEALTHY MEN AND WOMEN°
° (Adapted from Broverman et al.)

Women	Men
1. Not at all aggressive	Very aggressive
2. Not at all independent	Very independent
3. Very emotional	Not at all emotional
4. Very subjective	Very objective
5. Very easily influenced	Not at all easily influenced
6. Very submissive	Very dominant
7. Dislikes math and science very much	Likes math and science very much
8. Very excitable in a minor crisis	Not at all excitable in a minor crisis
9. Not at all competitive	Very competitive
10. Feelings easily hurt	Feelings not easily hurt
11. Not at all adventurous	Very adventurous
12. Very conceited about appearance	Never conceited about appearance

In a better world, where no one suffered for the differences, a different standard might very well be necessary or desirable. The trouble is not even so much that the clinicians' standards are more lenient for women, although the insulting implication is that women can get away with fewer desirable qualities. It is rather that the standards for a healthy adult reflect so many of the qualities that are necessary for being an exploitative person: aggressiveness, independence of others, dominance, and competitiveness. That these qualities are automatically considered virtues is the major trouble. That they are expected in men makes one kind of trouble for them: aggression cum guilt. That they are less expected in women makes another kind of trouble for them: dependency cum shame. The solution for women in our society is not to try to achieve the aggressive "virtues" of men, but to educate both sexes to abolish an exploitative system which distorts the social nature of both sexes.

The difficulty Freud experienced in understanding his young woman patient, Dora, is a classic example of sexism in psychiatry.[9] As we read the case today, we can see that both Freud and Dora were constantly missing a powerful but elusive feeling in Dora, shame. Even when they named it, neither Freud nor Dora took it seriously—that is, they took it from an "objective" viewpoint. After all, shame is a "subjective" phenomenon. It is not like guilt, which is about *something,* so is objective. Shame is "only about the 'self,'" and from that viewpoint, can be considered to be a "trivial" experience even if it feels like death. Because they were both unable to deal with Dora's shame, her symptoms were not mastered. She left treatment abruptly in what Freud felt, quite accurately, was a burst of revenge. But he had no idea what he had done to deserve it. And she must have come away from the experience with the feeling that she could find vindication nowhere while being still ashamed of wanting it. Twenty-five years later, when a student of Freud's—Felix Deutsch—was called into psychiatric consultation for her, Dora was still struggling with feelings of mortification over being insufficiently appreciated and her symptoms were, if anything, worse.[10] Eventually she died of rectal cancer; the diagnosis had been made late because she had "cried wolf" so often. Dora was a case of "psychosomatic" illness, which, as we saw in Chapter 17, it is always tempting to consider a case of faking.

Let's look at the highlights of Dora's story. A young girl of eighteen, living in Vienna in a middle-class family, tells her father that Herr K., her father's friend, had made sexual advances to her. It is a terrible accusation. Dora's father doesn't believe her. Herr and Frau K. are Dora's parents' close friends; Dora had often visited the K.s, loved them both, and loved their children. Dora is so enraged by her father's refusal to believe her that she falls unconscious after they've had an argument about it, and the next day leaves a suicide note. Dora had been suffering from a variety of mysterious physical ailments for at least two years previously. She sometimes couldn't eat; sometimes she lost her voice; sometimes she had terrible headaches—in short, a case of conversion hysteria, having become now so depressed that she wanted to die. Her suicide threat pushed Dora's father into seeking Freud's help for his nervous daughter.

The actual situation Dora was in was this: Her father was having an affair with Frau K. Because of his affair with his friend's wife, it was convenient for Dora's father to look away from the sexual advances Herr K. was making to Dora. Herr K. denied Dora's story. Dora's father was only too eager not to stir up Herr K.'s anger since that might make him fuss about his wife. So, he sided against Dora, who suspected that she was being used by her father in the interest of his affair with Frau K.

Dora was in the midst of a dreadful game the adults around her were playing which might drive anyone crazy. For a Victorian girl to be disbelieved about a sexual incident by someone she trusted—her father—and to know that his disbelief was dishonest was a double personal betrayal. In addition, to compound the betrayal, Frau K., whom Dora loved, also sided against her. She told Dora's parents that Dora had too much interest in sex, as evidenced by the fact that Dora and Frau K. had read some sex books together. Frau K. also was willing to sacrifice Dora in the interest of protecting her own safety. Everyone was lying except Dora, who couldn't get her beloved father to believe her. Dora's father had told Freud the truth (at Freud's insistence), but he had not acknowledged it to his daughter.

Freud's focus in the case was on Dora's unconscious, which he saw as the source of her symptoms. And, in fact, in her early teens Dora had had a "crush" on Herr K. She had much enjoyed the lovely gifts he gave her, and her own position as a person Herr K. praised. She was also deeply attached to her father's "intimate friend," Frau K., and loved being a "little mother" to the K.s' children. Dora told Freud that two years before the present incident Herr K. had suddenly made a sexual advance to her—had tried to kiss and fondle her. She had been "disgusted" by his advances and had fought him off, but had said nothing. Freud was able to interpret her earlier hysterical symptoms as the by-products of this guilty secret which Dora had been keeping. As might be expected from a guilt-prone male therapist, Freud's attention was called to Dora's unconscious sense of guilt as the source of her suffering.

Dora left treatment suddenly, immediately after what Freud regarded as two very "fruitful" sessions. In these sessions Freud had analyzed her dreams and brought forward very "convincing" evidence that Dora was still unconsciously in love with Herr K. Freud wondered, as he speculated on the reasons for her wanting revenge on him, whether he had been "kind" enough to Dora. He concluded that he had been, but that she was reliving with him, in the "transference," the guilt she had unconsciously felt for forbidden sexual wishes toward her father and forbidden sexual wishes toward Herr K!

It did not occur either to Freud or to Dora to take really seriously her feelings of mortification at the personal betrayals she suffered at the hands of Frau K. and her father and, for that matter, Herr K. As Freud saw it, and Dora also, she was "exaggerating" to feel so embittered. Freud puts it this way:

> When she was feeling embittered she used to be overcome by the idea that she had been handed over to Herr K. as the price of his tolerating the relations between her father and his wife; and her rage at her father for making such use of her was visible behind her affection for him. At other times she was quite well aware that she had been guilty of exaggeration in talking like this. The two men had, of course, *never made a formal agreement in which she was the object of barter;* her father in particular would have been horrified at any such suggestion. But he was one of those men who knew how to evade a dilemma by falsifying their judgement. . . . °

Dora's understandable mortification at being betrayed since it was only a subjective reaction, was not to be taken as seriously as if there had been a breach of "formal" contract! Even Freud, with his enormous sensitivity to the emotional basis of human neurotic suffering was not free of "marketplace" thinking at this moment. Dora also felt that she was exaggerating to be so enraged at being personally betrayed and was ashamed of her humiliated fury. After all, "mortification" or shame is only about one's self and always brings the shame of caring so much about being unloved.

When Felix Deutsch, a pupil of Freud's, visited Dora twenty-five years later, he found her occupied with the same theme which had made her so distraught in adolescence: the theme of personal betrayal. But now the betrayal was by her husband whose faithfulness she doubted. She also complained that her son did not love her enough. When Deutsch observed how much Dora "play-acted," how proud she was of having been one of Freud's first patients, he was quite scornful of her "other-directed" behavior. He quotes an informant as calling Dora "a repulsive hysteric." It is clear that she irritated him, just as Dora's shame-based behavior mystified Freud.

Freud had not grasped that his clever interpretation of Dora's

---

° Italics mine.

unconscious love for Herr K. was calculated to evoke enormous shame in her, all the more so if it were true. So he did not grasp what made her so furious at him that she abruptly left treatment. Dora's father, Herr K., Frau K., and even Freud really wanted Dora to continue to be loving toward Herr K. Dora *couldn't* be; she was being used by him as a sex object instead of as a favorite daughter as she had been accustomed to expect. She was also being used by her father, and by an older, beloved mother-figure. Dora was unable to be as loving as everyone expected her to be, including herself. Her fury at Herr K. must, of course, have been fired in part by her own guilt, as Freud suspected and showed her. But what drove her to the desperate state she was in when she wanted to die was the utter helplessness, the shame of the failure of her courageous attempt to extricate herself from complicity in the lie that everyone around her was living. Freud was able to help her some, because he did believe her. But he tried too fast to show her that she could have sexual wishes, too. He did not appreciate all the horrors which an unanalyzed state of shame can inflict on the self.

Let's look more closely at how difficult it still can be today for a woman patient to convey her conflicts to a male therapist. In order to illustrate the point sharply, I have chosen an excerpt from the transcript of a depressed woman patient in treatment with an experienced, sympathetic male therapist.[11] This is the depressed patient from Chapter 16, who told us that "a sickness comes over her" after she fights with her mother, from whom she used to be inseparable. The therapist's (male) superiority is so taken for granted by them both that when she challenges him as being wrong about something, he reacts to her challenge only as an irrational provocation. Since her challenge to him had its origin in her own unconscious need to turn the tables on him and humiliate him because she is coping with the shame of being a patient (and a woman), his reaction has an understandable basis. But both are caught in the workings of her unanalyzed shame because both take for granted not only her doctor's greater wisdom as a therapist, but his superiority as a male.

We come upon the therapy sessions at a point where the patient is telling the therapist about how easily her mother can make her feel guilty and how "silly" she knows it is for her to feel this way, but she can't help it.

As an example, the patient had offered the therapist the prediction that her mother would make her feel guilty over having Thanksgiving dinner with her boyfriend away from home. The therapist, responding in the spirit of minimizing mother's power, had suggested that the patient was "worrying too much in advance." The patient's opening comments in the next session, although phrased as a trivial point, which the therapist probably wouldn't even remember, were to the effect that the therapist was "wrong." The patient was "right": her mother *did* again make her feel guilty. The therapist caught that he was being disputed; the content of the patient's point was indeed trivial—he wasn't disputing that her mother made her feel guilty but only that maybe it wouldn't happen next time. But the feeling of shame which was pushing her to dispute him was important to acknowledge without his "putting her down." The patient had signaled him by obviously embarrassed laughter as she told him how he was wrong, but the message went by him. In the next moment, the patient was having some tics. And she was terribly disconcerted by the therapist's calling them to her attention. (She usually knew when she had them.) She actually thought he might be out to trick her, but benignly, for therapeutic reasons! She lost her train of thought, and within moments she was off on a depressed feeling about her many failings: lapses of memory, inability to keep things organized, and excessive anxiety. In other words, under the influence of undischarged, unanalyzed shame vis-à-vis the trusted male therapist, she experienced a temporary increase in her neurotic symptoms.

Here is the excerpt from the transcript of this therapy session, with some headings of mine interspersed to point up the events taking place:

T: [*pause*] What's on your mind?
[1. *The patient's prediction was accurate.*]
P: I just wanted to tell you that. . . . well, the last time when we were talking about—uh—I said my mother would have a certain reaction. Uhm, and you sort of thought—well—at least you sounded like you, you thought that I didn't have much basis for, you know, thinking that. But sure enough I got the reaction I expected. I mean, frankly, I would have been surprised if—uh— maybe even disappointed, if I didn't get it. And I got it.

T: You were right.

P: Yeah. When I told her that—uh—you have probably forgotten that this thing about eating over my boyfriend's house Thanksgiving and—uh—I was afraid to tell her because I knew there was gonna be a big uproar, and—uh—at first just like last year the same pattern. . . . [*A description follows of the quarrel with her mother.*] I mean, I knew . . . she was going to get me upset, and that she would—uhm—you know, make me feel bad, or try to make me feel bad, and—uh—and I was right. And so there you are [*slight laugh*] I wasn't, you know, just making it up. I do have grounds for it because it happens so often.

T: And?

P: And I just wanted to tell you, you know, that was the outcome. It did happen.

T: You wanted to tell me you were right.

[2. *As soon as she is challenged, the patient is uncertain of her recollection.*]

P: Hm? Because I—you seem to think I was showing some sort of pattern there about—I, I forgot what it was now, but—uhm—you didn't seem to think that . . . you, you thought it was sort of silly of me to—uh—say that because . . . you know, to predict something like that because it might not come true at all. Or something like that. I can't remember exactly. But it did. I didn't wanna show you what a rat my mother is [*laugh*].

T: But it looks like you want to show me how wrong I was too.

[3. *She was only trying to be helpful.*]

P: [*pause*] Mm. Yeah, well, I thought maybe . . . uhm uh. . . . you know, it would be helpful if I told you that. It did . . . you know, it might give you some insight into something [*slight laugh*]. I don't know what, but—uh—I just wanna tell you that—uh—you know, show you that these things do go on and—uh—you know, I, I just wasn't sort of making, sort of making something up or imagining . . . imagining it. You know? I guess that's it.

The patient's apologetic attitude for thinking the therapist was wrong is pathetically clear in her tentative, halting exposition of this point. It is also clear that the therapist, with the patient's concurrence, is ready to make some point *against* the patient out of her thinking him wrong. She calls it "some pattern" or some "insight." He has said nothing concrete but has repeated three

times with what must have been ominous meaning that she
wanted to show him to be wrong. In the next moment, the therapist told the patient that she was having some tics (a chronic
symptom of the patient's).

T: I got the impression that just there for a moment you were
doing some of this nervous twitching.
P: No. [*pause*] I . . .
T: No?
P: Not now. Right before you . . .
T: [*pause*] No?
P: If I was then . . . [*slight laugh*] mm, don't say that!
T: Maybe it's what?
[4. *The patient is incredulous and disputes the therapist's
perception.*]
P: If I was, and I don't realize it, that's bad [*slight laugh*]. Well,
if I was [*inaudible*], then I certainly wasn't aware of it, and I've
never had anyone tell me that I was doing, doing it, when I wasn't
aware of it before. But I really didn't—uh [*inaudible*]—not at that,
that instant.
T: So I must be wrong.
P: Hm?
T: I must be wrong.
P: [*laugh*] No [*laugh*]. What is it a mistaken perception or
something like that?
T: I'm seeing things.
P: Yeah [*laugh*]. You're not wrong, you're just seeing things
[*pause*]. Well, you could, you know, just—I, I, I don't think you can
say right or wrong in this situation. . . .
[5. *The patient doubts her senses; she then thinks that the
therapist may be trying to trick her to "see her reaction," that is, for
a therapeutic purpose.*]
P: Did you? Did you just say that?
T: What do you mean?
P: [*laugh*] Are you trying to trick me? No, I mean did you say—I
mean that, that you saw, you know, that, you know, did you do
something and I'd say, "No" and then you'd say, "O well, that
means I'm wrong." I mean is it—did you really, you know, think
that you saw something?
T: [*laugh*] You have the feeling that I'm sitting here trying very
hard to think up ways of—uh—trapping you.

As we read the transcript we can see what both the therapist and the patient are missing: the patient's shame before the superior person. He must be sensing it subliminally because he speaks of himself "sitting up here." But he does not analyze the shame component of her feelings. Instead of acknowledging that her feeling "silly" is evidence of her good judgment, he ignores her shame experience. He therefore does not acknowledge her need to turn the tables on him. Instead of acknowledging that she is fundamentally right in telling him how often her mother makes her feel guilty, the therapist focuses on the irrational content of her shame-anger at him. And the likelihood is that he *is* nettled by her insistence that she was right.

This entire exchange between patient and therapist reminds us that Dora was also struggling with the frustration of being disbelieved. Hysterical and depressed patients live so much in their thoughts about what other people are thinking about them that they sometimes don't know whether to believe themselves. The patient's thought that the therapist was trying to play some kind of benign trick on her reflects the way depressed and hysterical patients image themselves in the eyes of others, and, vice versa, that others function for their sakes. It is a measure of how close the self is to the self of the "other." It is easy to misunderstand and to ridicule the operation of the "self-in-the-eyes-of-the-other." And this mechanism is very irritating because it often *does* involve the patient in consciously playing tricks or manipulating the other person. The patient is, however, unable to do otherwise at some moments than live in the eyes of the important other person. In just the same way, as we saw in Chapter 8, a patient caught in an obsessive or compulsive command is unable to do otherwise than obey it.

A few moments later on in the session we find the patient talking at length about her many failings.

P: Another thing that, you know, I find—like when I have a lot of things to do not even in school but in gen—well, I should say, not tests, but you know but making appointments to see people and —um—but to see more than one person, and doing little things, buying little things that—unless I make a long list of things that I have to do, I'm constantly rehashing it in my mind. I, I go crazy. I just . . . I get so nervous, and I do it over, and over, and over again, and I leave out one, and then I have to go back and do it all over again. And I say I know there is supposed to be ten things, but I really only count nine. You know, I really can't take it. I really get very—uh—upset when I have a lot of things to think about. I just can't handle it [pause]. . . .

So, in the aftermath of an unsuccessful encounter with the therapist, which ended with a put-down for her, the patient is feeling how "crazy," disorganized, and anxious she is. She is in a familiar state of shame of her own failings and shortcomings. Her symptoms: tics, anxiety, and depression are all upon her in a temporary upsurge of feeling worse.

All patients, not only women, suffer from the shame of having to be in psychiatric treatment. In fact, it may be said that there is an undercurrent of humiliated feeling in the ignominy and helplessness of any kind of illness, physical as well as mental. But when a male patient is in treatment with a male psychotherapist, both are dealing with each other as members of the superior sex. When a woman is in treatment with a male therapist, she is not only the sick one, but a member of the inferior sex as well.

Suffering over being unloved and unappreciated, over mortifications of the self is the fate of all human beings, since we are all socialized with love as well as by threats. It is particularly to be expected in people who grow up in an exploitative society since their earliest and most profound affectionate experiences are doomed to disappointment. Freud's idea that people become neurotic because they are "striving to be too perfect" captured these dynamics. Freud's concept of an irrational, unconscious sense of guilt and shame (the superego) as a source of neurosis has been a boon to many patients of both sexes. Women patients suffer a special penalty for their exclusion from and admiration of the aggressive arena. It is particularly the fate of women in our society to be reared into the expectation that they will live in an arena of gentleness to others and then to be shamed and shame themselves for these very qualities. And many women patients are still caught in the failure of a male-dominated psychiatric profession to pay attention to implicit male-exploiter values.

The solution to sexism in psychiatry is certainly not in any simple avoidance of opposite-sex, patient-therapist pairs. There are as many women as men who have absorbed the doctrine of male superiority, as we saw in Chapter 14. There are also as many women clinicians as men who do not question the values of an exploitative society. I think a fundamental solution to the problem of sexism in psychiatry will not come until the helping professions have shed their exploitation-dominated notions of individual development, and their implicit acceptance of aggressive values.

References

1. J. Garai, "Sex Differences in Mental Health," *Genetic Psychology Monographs* 81 (1970), 123-142.

2. G. A. Talland, "Sex Differences in Self-Assessment," *Journal of Social Psychology* 48 (1958), 25-35.

3.E. H. Fischer and J. L. Turner, "Factors in Attitudes toward Seeking Professional Help," *Proceedings of the 77th Annual Convention of the American Psychological Association* 4 (1969), 487-488.

4. M. Lowenthal and C. Haven, "Interaction and Adaptation: Intimacy As a Critical Variable," *American Sociological Review* 33 (1968), 20-30.

5. Phyllis Chesler, *Women and Madness* (New York: Doubleday, 1972).

6. Ibid.

7. H. B. Lewis, *Shame and Guilt in Neurosis* (New York: International Universities Press, 1971).

8. I. Broverman, D. Broverman, F. Clarkson, P. Rosenkrantz and S. Vogel, "Sex-role Stereotypes and Clinical Judgments in Mental Health," *Journal of Consulting Psychology* 34 (1970), 1-7.

9. H. B. Lewis, op. cit.

10. H. B. Lewis, op. cit.

11. H. B. Lewis, op. cit.

Index